THE CHICANO HERITAGE

This is a volume in the Arno Press collection

THE CHICANO HERITAGE

Advisory Editor
Carlos E. Cortés

Editorial Board
Rodolfo Acuña
Juan Gómez-Quiñones
George F. Rivera, Jr.

See last pages of this volume for a complete list of titles.

THREE YEARS

IN

CALIFORNIA

WALTER COLTON

ARNO PRESS
A New York Times Company
New York — 1976

LEARNING RESOURCES CENTER
COLLEGE

Editorial Supervision: LESLIE PARR

Reprint Edition 1976 by Arno Press Inc.

Reprinted from a copy in
The University of Illinois Library

THE CHICANO HERITAGE
ISBN for complete set: 0-405-09480-9
See last pages of this volume for titles.

Manufactured in the United States of America

Library of Congress Cataloging in Publication Data

Colton, Walter, 1797-1851.
   Three years in California.

   (The Chicano heritage)
   Reprint of the 1850 ed. published by A. S. Barnes,
New York.
   1. California--History--1846-1850--Sources.
2. California--Description and travel--1848-1869.
3. Colton, Walter, 1797-1851. I. Title. II. Series.
F865.C7 1976   979.4'03   76-1221
ISBN 0-405-09496-5

THREE YEARS

IN

CALIFORNIA

THREE YEARS

IN

CALIFORNIA.

BY

REV. WALTER COLTON, U. S. N.

LATE ALCALDE OF MONTEREY; AUTHOR OF "DECK AND PORT,"
ETC., ETC.

WITH ILLUSTRATIONS.

NEW YORK:
PUBLISHED BY A. S. BARNES & CO.
NO. 51 JOHN-STREET.
CINCINNATI:—H. W. DERBY & CO.
1850.

Entered according to Act of Congress, in the year Eighteen Hundred and fifty,

By A. S. BARNES & COMPANY,

In the Clerk's Office of the District Court of the United States for the Southern District of New York.

Stereotyped by
RICHARD C. VALENTINE,
New York.

F. C. GUTIERREZ, Printer,
No. 51 John-street, corner of Dutch.

TO

GEN. MARIANO GUADALUPE VALLEJO,

ONE OF CALIFORNIA'S DISTINGUISHED SONS,

IN WHOM

THE INTERESTS OF FREEDOM, HUMANITY, AND EDUCATION

HAVE FOUND AN ABLE ADVOCATE AND MUNIFICENT BENEFACTOR,

This Volume

IS MOST RESPECTFULLY DEDICATED

BY HIS FRIEND

THE AUTHOR.

PREFACE.

MANY events of moment occurred in California during my residence of three years in that country, and which were sketched in a journal kept by me at the time. They are interspersed with anecdotes and incidents of a less general concern, but which may not be without some interest with the reader, as affording a clue to the leading features of society, and traits of individual character. The circle of engaging objects in a community, just emerging into the refinements of civilization, is never broad; but every phase in the great change going on possesses an intense individuality, and leaves its ineffaceable impression, like a ship sweeping a solitary sea, or a bird scaling a sunset cloud. California will be no more what she has been: the events of a few years have carried her through the progressive changes of a century. She has sprung at once from the shackles of colonial servitude to all the advantages and dignities of a sovereign state.

Her emigrants are rushing from every continent and isle; they crest every mountain, they cover every sea; they sweep in like a cloud from the Pacific, they roll down like a torrent from the slopes of the Sierra Nevada. They crowd to her bosom to gather gold; their hammers and drills, their mattocks and spades divert the deep stream, and are echoed from a thousand caverned hills; the level plain, the soaring cliff and wombed mountain, give up their glowing treasures. But the gifts of nature here are not confined to her sparkling sands and veined rocks, they extend to the productive forces of her soil; they lie along her water-courses, through her verdant valleys, and wave in her golden grain; they reel in her vintage, they blush in her fruits, while her soft zephyrs, as they float the landscape, scatter perfume from their odorous wings.

But with all these gifts disease is here with its pale victims, and sorrow with its willow-wove shrine. There is no land less relieved by the smiles and soothing cares of woman. If Eden with its ambrosial fruits and guiltless joys was still sad till the voice of woman mingled with its melodies, California, with all her treasured hills and streams, must be cheerless till she feels the presence of the same enchantress. It is woman alone that can make a home for the human heart, and evoke from the recesses of nature the bright and beautiful : where her footsteps light, the freshest flowers spring; where her voice swells, the softest echoes wake : her smiles garland the domestic hearth; her sympathy melts through the deepest folds of grief; her love clothes the earth with light. When night invests the heaven, when the soft pleiads in their storm-rocked cradle sleep, and the sentinel stars on their watch-towers wane dim, her vigil flame still pours its faithful beam, still struggles with the encroaching darkness till the day-spring and the shadows flee away. Of all these sources of solace and hope multitudes in California are now bereft; but the ties of kindred, the quick-winged ship, and the steed of flame, on his iron-paved track, will soon secure them these priceless gifts. The miner, returning from his toil, will yet half forget the labors of the day in the greetings of his home:

> " At length his lonely cot appears in view,
>   Beneath the shelter of an aged tree ;
> Th' expectant *wee things*, toddlin', stacher thro'
>   To meet their dad, wi' flichterin noise an' glee.
> His wee bit ingle, blinkin' bonnily,
>   His clean hearth-stane, his thriftie *wifie's* smile,
> The lisping infant prattling on his knee,
>   Does a' his weary carking cares beguile,
> An' makes him quite forget his labor an' his toil."

PHILADELPHIA, July, 1850.   W. C.

CONTENTS.

Page

CHAPTER I.—The flag.—Meeting of citizens.—Disposition of forces.—Col. Fremont's band.—Alcalde of Monterey.—Indian mother.—Military leaders.— A California farm.. 13

CHAPTER II.—Fecundity of the Californians.—First intelligence of the war.— Wild Indians on board ship.—The chief.—First newspaper published in California.—Raising the materials.—The rival suitors.—Flight of Gen. Castro.— A Californian on horseback 27

CHAPTER III.—A thief obeying orders.—Game.—No penitentiary system.— The California cart on a gala-day.—The runaway daughter.—Faith of the Indians.—Return from the war.—First trial by jury.—Indian and his squaw on the hunt.—Whales in the bay.—The two gamblers.—Ladies on horseback.— Merriment in death.—The Englishman and his mistress........................ 39

CHAPTER IV.—Funeral ceremonies.—Elected alcalde.—Flight of Gen. Castro.—Los Angeles taken.—Oven-bath.—Grog in a chimney.—The flea.—First rain.—Rising of the Californians.—Measures of Com. Stockton.—Mormons . 54

CHAPTER V.—Fire on the mountains.—Emigrants.—Pistols and pillows.— Leaders of the insurrection.—California plough.—Defeat at San Pedro.—Col. Fremont's band.—The Malek Adhel.—Monterey threatened.—Soldier outwitted.—Raising men.—Bridegroom.—Culprits....................................... 72

CHAPTER VI.—Santa Barbara taken.—Lieut. Talbot and his ten.—Gambling in prison.—Recruits.—A funny culprit.—Movements of Com. Stockton.— Beauty and the grave.—Battle on the Salinas.—The captain's daughter.— Stolen pistols.—Indian behind a tree.—Nuptials in California 89

CHAPTER VII.—San José garrisoned.—A California rain.—Escape of convicts. —Shooting Edwards.—Two washerwomen.—Death of Mr. Sargent.—Indian hens.—Hunting curlew.—The California horse.—An old emigrant.—The grizzly bear 106

CHAPTER VIII.—Little Adelaida.—Col. Fremont's battalion.—Santiago in love. —Sentiments of an old Californian.—The prize Julia.—Fandango.—Winter climate.—Patron Saint of California.—Habits of the natives.—Insurrection in the north.—Drama in a church.—Position of Com. Stockton 121

CONTENTS.

CHAPTER IX.—Day of the Santos Innocentes.—Letting off a lake.—Arrival of the Dale with home letters.—The dead year.—Newly-arrived emigrants.—Egg-breaking festivities.—Concealment of Chaves.—Plot to capture the alcalde 134

CHAPTER X.—Destruction of dogs.—The wash-tub mail.—The surrender in the north.—Robbing the Californians.—Death-scene in a shanty.—The men who took up arms.—Arrival of the Independence.—Destitution of our troops.—Capture of los Angeles 149

CHAPTER XI.—Arrival of the Lexington.—The march to los Angeles, and battle of San Gabriel.—The capitulation.—Military characteristics of the Californians.—Barricades down 163

CHAPTER XII.—Return of T. O. Larkin.—The tall partner in the Californian.—Mexican officers.—The Cyane.—War mementoes.—Drama of Adam and Eve.—Carnival.—Birth-day of Washington.—A California captain.—Application for a divorce.—Arrival of the Columbus 173

CHAPTER XIII.—The people of Monterey.—The guitar and runaway wife.—Mother ordered to flog her son.—Work of the prisoners.—Catching sailors.—Court of Admiralty.—Gamblers caught and fined.—Lifting land boundaries 189

CHAPTER XIV.—A convict who would not work.—Lawyers at Monterey.—Who conquered California.—Ride to a rancho.—Leopaldo.—Party of Californians.—A dash into the forests.—Chasing a deer.—Killing a bear.—Ladies with firearms.—A mother and volunteer 199

CHAPTER XV.—A California pic-nic.—Seventy and seventeen in the dance.—Children in the grove.—A California bear-hunt.—The bear and bull bated.—The Russian's cabbage head 210

CHAPTER XVI.—A Californian jealous of his wife.—Hospitality of the natives.—Honors to Guadalupe.—Application from a Lothario for a divorce.—Capture of Mazatlan.—Larceny of Canton shawls.—An emigrant's wife claiming to have taken the country.—A wild bullock in Main-street 220

CHAPTER XVII.—Rains in California.—Functions of the alcalde of Monterey.—Orphans in California.—Slip of the gallows rope.—Making a father whip his boy.—A convict as prison cook.—The knacka.—Thom. Cole.—A man robbing himself.—A blacksmith outwitted 230

CHAPTER XVIII.—First discovery of gold.—Prison guard.—Incredulity about the gold.—Santiago getting married.—Another lump of gold.—Effects of the gold fever.—The court of an alcalde.—Mosquitoes as constables.—Bob and his bag of gold.—Return of citizens from the mines.—A man with the gold cholic.—The mines on individual credit. 242

CHAPTER XIX.—Tour to the gold-mines.—Loss of horses.—First night in the woods.—Arrival at San Juan.—Under way.—Camping out.—Bark of the

CONTENTS. 9

wolves.—Watch-fires.—San José.—A fresh start.—Camping on the slope of a hill.—Wild features of the country.—Valley of the San Joaquin.—Band of wild horses 257

CHAPTER XX.—The grave of a gold-hunter.—Mountain spurs.—A company of Sonoranians.—A night alarm.—First view of the mines.—Character of the deposits.—A woman and her pan.—Removal to other mines.—Wild Indians and their weapons.—Cost of provisions.—A plunge into a gold river.—Machines used by the gold-diggers 269

CHAPTER XXI.—Lump of gold lost.—Indians at their game of arrows.—Camp of the gold-hunters.—A Sonoranian gold-digger.—Sabbath in the mines.—The giant Welchman.—Nature of gold deposits.—Average per man.—New discoveries 282

CHAPTER XXII.—Visit to the Sonoranian camp.—Festivities and gambling.—The doctor and teamster.—An alcalde turned cook.—The miner's tattoo.—The little Dutchman.—New deposits discovered.—A woman keeping a monté table.—Up to the knee and nine-pence.—The volcanoes and gold.—Arrival of a barrel of rum 295

CHAPTER XXIII.—Natural amphitheatre.—No scientific clue to the deposits of gold.—Soil of the mines.—Life among the gold-diggers.—Loss of our caballada.—The old man and rock.—Departure from the mines.—Travelling among gorges and pinnacles.—Instincts of the mule.—A mountain cabin 309

CHAPTER XXIV.—A lady in the mountains.—Town of Stockton.—Crossing the valley of the San Joaquin.—The robbed father and boy.—Ride to San José.—Rum in California.—Highwayman.—Woodland life.—Rachel at the well.—Farewell to my camping-tree 324

CHAPTER XXV.—Cause of sickness in the mines.—The quicksilver mines.—Heat and cold in the mines.—Traits in the Spanish character.—Health of California ladies.—A word to mothers.—The pingrass and blackbird.—The Redwood-tree.—Battle of the eggs. 339

CHAPTER XXVI.—The public domain.—Scenery around Monterey.—Vineyards of los Angeles.—Beauty of San Diego.—The culprit hall.—The rush for gold.—Land titles.—The Indian doctress.—Tufted partridge.—Death of Com. Biddle 351

CHAPTER XXVII.—The gold region.—Its locality, nature, and extent.—Foreigners in the mines.—The Indians' discovery of gold.—Agricultural capabilities of California.—Services of United States officers.—First decisive movement for the organization of a civil government.—Intelligence of the death of Gen. Kearny 365

CHAPTER XXVIII.—Ride of Col. Fremont from los Angeles to Monterey and back.—Character of the country.—The rincon.—Skeletons of dead horses.—A stampede.—Gray bears.—The return.—The two horses rode by Col. Fremont.—An experiment.—The result.—Characteristics of the California horse.

—Fossil remains.—The two classes of emigrants.—Life in California.—Heads against tails 377

CHAPTER XXIX.—The tragedy at San Miguel.—Court and culprits.—Age and circumstances of those who should come to California.—Condition of the professions.—The wrongs of California.—Claims on the Christian community.—Journalists 391

CHAPTER XXX.—The gold-bearing quartz.—Their locality.—Richness and extent.—The suitable machinery to be used in the mountains.—The court of admiralty at Monterey.—Its organization and jurisdiction.—The cases determined.—Sale of the prizes.—Convention and Constitution of California.—Difficulties and compromises.—Spirit of the instrument..................... 403

CHAPTER XXXI.—Glances at towns sprung and springing.—San Francisco.—Benicia.—Sacramento City.—Sutter.—Vernon.—Boston.—Stockton.—New York.—Alvezo.—Stanislaus.—Sonora.—Crescent City.—Trinidad............ 414

CHAPTER XXXII.—Brief notices of persons, whose portraits embellish this volume, and who are prominently connected with California affairs 425

CHAPTER XXXIII.—The mission establishments in California.—Their origin, objects, localities, lands, revenues, overthrow.—California Railroad......... 439

LIST OF PORTRAITS.

Captain John A. Sutter.
Thomas O. Larkin, Esq.
Hon. J. C. Fremont.
Hon. Wm. M. Gwin.
Hon. G. W. Wright.
Jacob R. Snyder, Esq.

A LIST

OF THE DELEGATES IN CONVENTION

ASSEMBLED AT MONTEREY, UPPER CALIFORNIA, SEPTEMBER AND OCTOBER, A. D. 1849.

NAMES.	WHERE BORN.	RESIDENCE.	AGE.
Robert Semple.	Kentucky.	Benicia.	Forty-two.
John A. Sutter.	Switzerland.	New Helvetia.	Forty-seven.
Thomas O. Larkin.	Massachusetts.	Monterey.	Forty-seven.
M. G. Vallejo.	California.	Sonoma.	Forty-two.
Wm. M. Gwin.	Tennessee.	San Francisco.	Forty-four.
H. W. Halleck.	New York.	Monterey.	Thirty-two.
Wm. M. Steuart.	Maryland.	San Francisco.	Forty-nine.
Joseph Hobson.	Do.	Do.	Thirty-nine
Thos. L. Vermeule.	New Jersey.	Loetown.	Thirty-five.
O. M. Wozencraft.	Ohio.	San Joaquin.	Thirty-four.
B. F. Moore.	Florida.	Do.	Twenty-nine.
Wm. E. Shannon.	New York.	Sacramento.	Twenty-seven.
Winfield S. Sherwood.	Do.	Do.	Thirty-two.
Elam Brown.	Do.	San José.	Fifty-two.
Joseph Aram.	Do.	Do.	Thirty-nine.
J. D. Hoppe.	Maryland.	Do.	Thirty-five.
Jno. McDougal.	Ohio.	Sutter.	Thirty-two.
Elisha O. Crosby.	Tompkins Co., N. Y.	Vernon.	Thirty-four.
K. H. Dimmick.	New York.	Pueblo San José.	Thirty-four.
Julian Hanks.	Connecticut.	Do.	Thirty-seven.
M. M. McCarver.	Kentucky.	Sacramento City.	Forty-two.
Francis J. Lippitt.	Rhode Island.	San Francisco.	Thirty-seven.
Rodman M. Price.	New York.	Do.	Thirty.
Lewis Dent.	Missouri.	Monterey.	Twenty-six.
Henry Hill.	Virginia.	Do.	Thirty-three.
Ch. T. Botts.	Do.	Do.	Forty.
Myron Norton.	Vermont.	San Francisco.	Twenty-seven.
J. M. Jones.	Kentucky.	San Joaquin.	Twenty-five.
P. Sainsevain.	Bordeaux.	San José.	Trente ans.
José M. Covarrubias.	France.	Santa Barbara.	Forty-one.
Antonio Ma. Pico.	California.	San José.	Forty.
Jacinto Rodriguez.	Do.	Monterey.	Thirty-six.
Stephen C. Foster.	Maine.	Los Angeles.	Twenty-eight.
Henry A. Tefft.	New York.	San Luis Obispo.	Twenty-six.
J. M. H. Hollingsworth.	Maryland.	San Joaquin	Twenty-five.
Abel Stearns.	Massachusetts.	Los Angeles.	Fifty-one.
Hugh Reid.	Scotland.	San Gabriel.	Thirty-eight.
Benj. S. Lippincott.	New York.	San Joaquin.	Thirty-four.
Joel P. Walker.	Virginia.	Sonoma.	Fifty-two.
Jacob R. Snyder.	Pennsylvania.	Sacramento City.	Thirty-four.
L. W. Hastings.	Mt. Vernon, Ohio.	Sacramento.	Thirty.
Pablo de la Guerra.	California.	Santa Barbara.	Thirty.
José Anto. Carrillo.	Do.	Angeles.	Fifty-three.
Manl Dominguez.	Do.	Do.	Forty-six.
P. Ord.	Maryland.	Monterey.	Thirty-three.
Edw. Gilbert.	New York.	San Francisco.	Twenty-seven
Miguel de Pedrorena.	Spain.	San Diego.	Forty-one.
A. J. Ellis.	New York.	San Francisco.	Thirty-three.

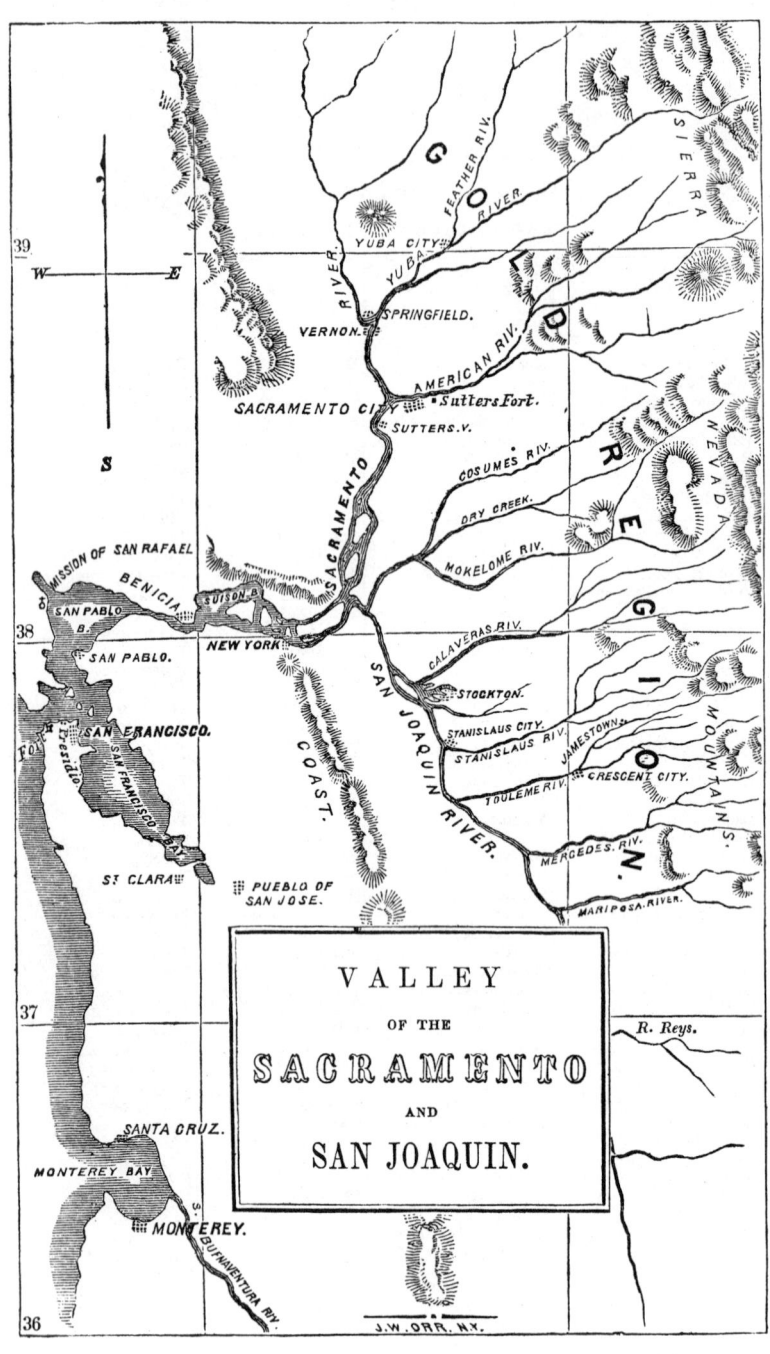

THREE YEARS IN CALIFORNIA.

CHAPTER I.

THE FLAG.—MEETING OF CITIZENS.—DISPOSITION OF FORCES.—COL. FREMONT'S BAND.—ALCALDE OF MONTEREY.—INDIAN MOTHER.—MILITARY LEADERS.—A CALIFORNIA FARM.

A few words will place within the clear comprehension of the reader, the posture of public affairs in California at the time my journal opens. The U. S. flag was raised at Monterey and San Francisco on the 10th of July, 1846. This event was wholly unexpected by the Californians, and struck the public heart with the deepest surprise; other causes of alarm and apprehension faded into shadow in the presence of this decisive measure; they were the admonitory vibrations, but here was the earthquake itself. The people were more astounded than indignant, and quite as intent over problems of preservation as measures of resistance.

At a public meeting held at Monterey, in which the patriotism, talents, and sagacity of the country were largely represented, the question of throwing the territory under the protection of England, through the naval forces commanded by Admiral Seymour, who was on the coast at the time, was excitingly discussed. But this proposition received its quietus under the successful railery of Don Raphael, of Monterey. "Our object," said this witty counsellor, "is to preserve our country; but she is gone,—California is lost to us: and this proposal to invoke the protection of England, is only to seek another *owner*. The redress is worthy of the market-woman: a dog had robbed her hamper of a leg of mutton, and she sent another dog more powerful after him to get it away; when asked what good that would do her, she replied, it would be some satisfaction to see the *first* dog deprived of the stolen leg. And so it is with us; the mutton is gone, and a choice of the dog only remains: others may prefer the bull-dog, but I prefer the regular hound; he has outstripped the other in the chase, and so let him have the game." The convention broke up without adopting any decisive measures; leaving each one to act as his impulses or convictions of duty suggested.

The military forces of the country were at this time under the command of Gen. José Castro, an officer of high pretensions, but utterly deficient in strength and steadiness of purpose, and that capacity which can work out important results with slender and inapposite means. His followers had gathered to him with as little discipline, sobriety, and order, as would characterize a bear-hunt. Their prime impulse lay in the excitement which the camp presented. It was the same thing to them whether their weapon was a rifle or a guitar,—whether they were going to a skirmish or a fandango. With six or eight hundred of these waltzing warriors Gen. Castro was now on his march into the southern department, with the evident purpose of taking up his position near the Pueblo de los Angeles.

Such was the posture of affairs when Com. Stockton resolved to rest in no half-way measures. The wave had been set in motion and must roll on, or its returning force might sweep him and his temporary garrisons into the Pacific. And yet aggressive measures in the present condition of the squadron seemed to border on rashness. The Portsmouth, under Commander Montgomery, must be left at San Francisco to garrison the posts occupied by the flag; the Savannah, commanded by Capt. Mervin, must remain here to hold Monterey; the Warren, under Commander Hull, was at Mazatlan; only the Congress, Lieut. Livingston commanding, and the Cyane, under Commander Du Pont, remained. With the crews of these, and a hundred and sixty men under Col. Fremont, California was to be conquered and held, and this too in the presence or defeat of a military force that had the entire resources of the country at their command. But a gallant purpose will often achieve what a questioning prudence would relinquish. The mountain torrent, with its impetuosity, sweeps away the barrier which effectually obstructs the level stream.

Monday, July 27. The bustle of preparation is active in the squadron. Commander Du Pont received orders last evening to have the Cyane ready for sea in twenty-four hours. She has tripped this afternoon, and is off for San Diego, though it has been given out on shore that she is bound elsewhere, but this is a war stratagem. She has on board Col. Fremont and a hundred and fifty of his riflemen. The wind is fresh, and they are by this time cleverly sea-sick, and lying about the deck in a spirit of resignation that would satisfy the non-resistant principles of a Quaker. Two or three resolute old women might tumble the whole of them into the sea. But they will rally before they reach their port, and see that their rifles spring true to their trust.

The colonel is a man of small stature, of slender but wiry formation, and with a countenance indicative of decision and firmness. This is the fifth time he has crossed the continent in connection with his scientific purposes. His enterprises are full of hardship, peril, and the wildest romance. To sleep under the open heaven, and depend on one's rifle for food, is coming about as near the primitive state of the hunter as a civilized man can well get; and yet this life, in his case, is adorned with the triumphs of science. The colonel and his band are to land at San Diego, secure horses, and advance upon the position of Gen. Castro, at los Angeles.

" War's great events lie so in Fortune's scale,
That oft a feather's weight may kick the beam."

TUESDAY, JULY 28. Com. Stockton informed me to-day that I had been appointed Alcalde of Monterey and its jurisdiction. I had dreamed in the course of my life, as most people have, of the thousand things I might become, but it never entered my visions that I should succeed to the dignity of a Spanish alcalde. I much preferred my berth on board the Congress, and that the judicial functions in question should continue to be discharged by the two intelligent gentlemen, Purser R. M. Price and Dr. Edward Gilchrist, upon whom they had been devolved. But the services of these officers were deemed indispensable to the efficiency of the ships to which they were attached. This left me no alternative; my trunks were packed, my books boxed, and in an hour I was on shore, a guest in the house of our consul, T. O. Larkin, Esq., whose munificent hospitalities reach every officer of the squadron, and every functionary in the interest of the flag. This is the more appreciated from the fact that there is not a public table or hotel in all California. High and low, rich and poor, are thrown together on the private liberality of the citizens. Though a quasi war exists, all the amenities and courtesies of life are preserved; your person, life, and liberty, are as sacred at the hearth of the Californian as they would be at your own fireside. He will never betray you; the rights of hospitality, in his generous judgment, require him to peril his own life in defence of yours. He may fight you on the field, but in his family, you may dance with his daughters, and he will himself wake the waltzing string.

WEDNESDAY, JULY 29. The sloop-of-war Levant, under Commander Page, sailed to-day, with Com. Sloat on board, for the United States. We gave the commodore a parting salute. He has rendered the squadron under his command efficient, and preserved harmony among the officers. The expediency of his measures in California will be canvassed elsewhere. He acted on the light and intelligence within his reach. If war has been declared, the laurel awaits him.

The Levant takes home in her my friend, Lieut. T——: he has resigned his commission in the navy, and takes orders in the church. He is a pretty good classical scholar, and has made himself familiar with the principles of biblical exegesis. All this has been accomplished during those few leisure hours which the duties of a watch-officer leave one at sea. It is seemingly reversing the order of things for the navy to supply the church with spiritual teachers. But few, however, have left the deck for the pulpit; a much larger number have reached it from the diagrams and drills of West Point. Among them are some of our most eloquent and impressive preachers. Of this class is the present Bishop of Ohio.

We have all been busy in writing letters home, and shall make up a pretty large mail, filled with tender recollections, and overflowing with the California news. How the intelligence of our proceedings here will strike our friends and the country at large, is mere matter of conjecture. We are acting, however, not only in view of the alleged collision between the American and Mexican forces on the Rio Grande, but in reference to the anarchy and confusion into which this country has been thrown by a revolution which did not originate with us.

THURSDAY, JULY 30. To-day I entered on the duties of my office as alcalde of Monterey: my jurisdiction extends over an immense extent of territory, and over a most heterogeneous population. Almost every nation has, in some emigrant, a representative here— a representative of its peculiar habits, virtues, and vices. Here is the reckless Californian, the half-wild Indian, the roving trapper of the West, the lawless Mexican, the licentious Spaniard, the scolding Englishman, the absconding Frenchman, the luckless Irishman, the plodding German, the adventurous Russian, and the discontented Mormon. All have come here with the expectation of finding but little work and less law. Through this discordant mass I am to maintain order, punish crime, and redress injuries.

FRIDAY, JULY 31. Nearly all the houses in Monterey are of one story, with a corridor. The walls are built of adobes, or sun-baked brick, with tiled roofs. The centre is occupied by a large hall, to which the dining-room and sleeping apartments seem mere appurtenances. Every thing is in subordination to the hall, and this is designed and used for dancing. It has a wood floor, and springs nightly to the step of those who are often greeted in the whirl of their amusements, by the risen sun. The dance and a dashing horse are the two objects which overpower all others in interest with the Californians. The fiddle has been silent since our flag went up, from the fact that many of the gentlemen have left to join Gen. Castro. But if they return, though covered with disaster, the fiddle will be called upon to resume its fantastic functions. You might as well attempt to extinguish a love of air in a life-preserver as the dancing propensity in this people.

SATURDAY, AUG. 1. The Congress has sailed to-day, with all her marines and full complement of men, for San Pedro. Com. Stockton intends to land there with a force of some three hundred, march to the Pueblo de los Angeles, capture that important place, and fall upon Gen. Castro, who, it is now understood, has posted himself, with some eight hundred soldiers, in a pass a few miles below. The general will find his southern retreat cut off by Col. Fremont's riflemen and the sailors of the Cyane, his western route obstructed by the Colorado, while the forces of the Congress will bear down upon him from the north. He has seemingly no escape, and must fight or capitulate. But his sagacity, his thorough knowledge of the country, and his fleet horses, may extricate him. We shall know in a few days; the interest felt here in the result is most intense. Many mothers have sons and many wives husbands involved in the issue.

SUNDAY, AUG. 2. I officiated to-day on board the Savannah. It is much to the credit of the officers of this ship that though without a chaplain, they have had, during a three years' cruise, their religious services regularly on the Sabbath. Four of their number, two lieutenants, the surgeon, and master, are professors of religion, and exert a deep influence through their consistent piety. Their Sabbath exercise has consisted in reading prayers, selections from the Scriptures, and a brief, pertinent sermon. They have had, also, their Sabbath-school. Such facts as these will win for the navy a larger share of public confidence than the capture of forty barbaric fortresses. The American people love valor, but they love religion also. They will confer their highest honors only on him who combines them both.

MONDAY, AUG. 3. An Indian woman of good appearance came to our office to-day, stating that she had been for two years past a domestic in a Mexican family near Monterey; that she had, during this time, lost her husband, and now wished to marry again; but wished, before she did this, to recover her child, which was forcibly detained in the family in which she had served. It appeared that the father of this family had baptized her child, and claimed, according to custom here, a sort of guardianship over it, as well as a right to a portion of its services.

I asked her if her child would be kindly treated where it now was: she said she thought so; but added, she was a mother, and wanted it with hei We told her as she was going to marry again, she had better perhaps leave the child for the present; and if she found her husband to be a good, industrious man, and disposed to furnish her with a comfortable home, she might call again at our office, and we would get her child. She went away with that mild look of contentment which is as near a smile as any expression which lights an Indian's face.

TUESDAY, AUG. 4. The military chieftains, who have successively usurped the government of California, have arbitrarily imposed such duties on foreign imports as their avarice or exigency suggested. A few examples will be sufficient to show the spirit and character of these imposts. Unbleached cottons, which cost in the United States six cents the yard, cost here fifty, and shirtings cost seventy-five. Plain knives and forks cost ten dollars the dozen; coarse cowhide shoes three dollars the pair; the cheapest tea three dollars the pound; and a pair of common truck-wheels seventy-five dollars. The duty alone on the coarsest hat, even if made of straw, is three dollars.

The revenues derived from these enormous imposts have passed into the pockets of a few individuals, who have placed themselves, by violence or fraud, at the head of the government, and have never reached the public in any beneficial form. These exactions, enforced by an irresponsible tyranny, have kept California poor, have crushed all enterprise, and have rolled back the tide of emigration from her soil as the resisting rock the rushing stream. But the barriers are now broken, and broken forever. California is free,—free of Mexican rule and all domestic usurpers.

WEDNESDAY, AUG. 5. We have in one apartment of our prison two Californians, confined for having robbed a United States courier, on his way from Monterey to San Francisco, with public dispatches. They have not yet been tried. Yesterday they applied to me for permission to have their guitars. They stated that their situation was very lonely, and they wanted something to cheer it. Their request was complied with; and last evening, when the streets were still, and the soft moonlight melted through the grates of their prison, their music streamed out upon the quiet air with wonderful sweetness and power. Their voices were in rich harmony with their instruments, and their melodies had a wild and melancholy tone. They were singing, for aught they knew, their own requiem.

THURSDAY, AUG. 6. It sounds strange to an American, and much more so to an Englishman, to hear Californians talk of farms. They never speak of acres, or even miles; they deal only in leagues. A farm of four or five leagues is considered quite small. It is not so large, in the conception of this people, as was the one-acre farm of Horace in the estimation of the Romans. Capt. Sutter's farm, in the valley of the Sacramento, is sixty miles long. The Californians speak in the same way of the stock on their farms. Two thousand horses, fifteen thousand head of cattle, and twenty thousand sheep, are only what a thrifty farmer should have before he thinks of killing or selling. They are to be his productive stock, on which he should not encroach, except in an emergency. Only fancy a farm covering sixty miles in length! Why, a man would want a railroad through it for his own private use. Get out of the way, ye landlords of England and patroons of Amsterdam, with your boroughs and dykes, and give place to the Californian with his sixty mile sweep!

Friday, Aug. 7. The Mormon ship Brooklyn, which we left at Honolulu, has arrived at San Francisco, and her passengers have debarked on the shores of that magnificent bay. They have not yet selected their lands. The natives hold them in great horror. They seem to think cannibalism among the least of their enormities. They consider the term Mormon the most branding epithet that can be applied to a man. A mother complained to me, a few days since, that a gentleman in Monterey had struck her son and called him a Mormon. She dwelt with great earnestness on the opprobrious character of the epithet, and appeared to consider its application to her son a higher crime than that of his fist. I told her what sort of people these Mormons were; but it was to her as if I had represented Satan as an angel of light. I lectured the wrong-doer.

SATURDAY, AUG. 8. Capt. Fauntleroy, of the Savannah, and Maj. Snyder, with fifty mounted men under their command, occupy San Juan, which lies inland about thirty miles from Monterey. A report reached them a few days since, that a hundred wild Indians had descended upon the town of San José and driven off over two hundred horses. They started immediately with twenty men, well mounted, got upon their trail, and came up with them at a distance of sixty miles. The Indians finding themselves hotly pressed, left their horses and took to the bush, throwing back upon their pursuers the most wild and frantic imprecations. Three or four of their number only were killed. The denseness of the forest and the approach of night rendered further pursuit impracticable.

The horses were all recaptured and brought back to their owners, who received them with acclamations of surprise and gratitude. This was the first time, they said, that their property had been rescued from savages by the government, and they run up the

American flag. This prompt interference of Capt. Fauntleroy and Maj. Snyder will do more to win the confidence of the Californians than forty orations delivered in the most liquid Spanish that ever rolled from a Castilian tongue. There is something in action which the most simple can appreciate, and which the most crafty cannot gainsay.

SUNDAY, AUG. 9. I officiated to-day on board the Savannah. The weather was pleasant, and several gentlemen from the shore attended. There was no service in the Roman Catholic Church, owing to the absence of one of the priests and the infirmities of the other. But when there is service, only a few of the people attend. It is sometimes, however, forced upon them in the shape of penance. When a friend of mine here was married, it was necessary that he should confess. The penance imposed on him for his previous negligences and transgressions was, that he should attend church seven Sabbaths.

CHAPTER II.

FECUNDITY OF THE CALIFORNIANS.—FIRST INTELLIGENCE OF THE WAR.—WILD INDIANS ON BOARD SHIP.—THE CHIEF.—FIRST NEWSPAPER PUBLISHED IN CALIFORNIA.—RAISING THE MATERIALS.—THE RIVAL SUITORS.—FLIGHT OF GEN. CASTRO.—A CALIFORNIAN ON HORSEBACK.

MONDAY, AUG. 10. The fecundity of the Californians is remarkable, and must be attributed in no small degree to the effects of the climate. It is no uncommon sight to find from fourteen to eighteen children at the same table, with their mother at their head. There is a lady of some note in Monterey, who is the mother of twenty-two living children. The youngest is at the breast, and must soon, it is said, relinquish his place to a new-comer, who will, in all probability, be allowed only the same brevity of bliss.

There is a lady in the department below who has twenty-eight children, all living, in fine health, and who may share the "envied kiss" with others yet to come. What a family—what a wife—what a mother! I have more respect for the shadow of that woman than for the living presence of the mincing being who raises a whole village if she has one child, and then puts it to death with sugar-plums. A woman with one child is like a hen with one chicken; there is an eternal scratch about nothing.

TUESDAY, AUG. 11. A deserter from Gen. Castro's camp presented himself at my office to-day and gave himself up to the American authorities. He represents the general as in rather a forlorn condition. His troops, it appears, are daily deserting him. His present force is estimated at less than six hundred. He is anxious to fly into Mexico, but is unable to raise a sufficient number of volunteers. The expectation here is, that he will surrender to Com. Stockton.

The British brig-of-war Spy anchored in the harbor of Monterey this evening. She is from San Blas, with dispatches for Admiral Seymour. Her officers are perfectly silent as to news from the United States and Mexico. She leaves in a few hours for the Collingwood at the Sandwich Islands. She has, undoubtedly, news of moment, but will not reveal it.

WEDNESDAY, AUG. 12. The U. S. ship Warren, under Commander Hull, arrived this afternoon in thirty days from Mazatlan, bringing the eventful intelligence that war had been declared between the United States and Mexico. The mysterious silence of the officers of the Spy is now explained. But their secrecy has availed them for only twenty-four hours.

The war news produced a profound sensation here. The whole population were instantly thrown into groups in the corridors and at the corners of the streets. The hum of voices continued late into the night. It was an extinguisher on the hopes of those who had looked to Mexico for aid, or who had clung to the expectation that the American government would repudiate our possession of California, and order the squadron withdrawn. They now relinquish all idea of a return to their old political connection, and appear resigned to their fate, which seems inevitable. These disappointed families compose but a part of the population; another portion has become thoroughly wearied with revolutions, and are prepared to countenance almost any government that promises stability.

THURSDAY, AUG. 13. The Warren sailed this morning for San Pedro, to convey the war intelligence to Com. Stockton. It will throw a new aspect upon his operations in California. Expediency gives place to moral necessity. We have now a double motive for exertion—national honor, which looks at home, and an enlarged philanthropy, which looks here. It is of but little moment what the ultimate action of our government may be in reference to California. It cannot change her destiny. She is severed forever from Mexico. Should our government attempt to throw her back on that country, she will not stay thrown back. The rebound will carry her further off than ever. She is on a wave which will not ebb till this generation have mouldered in their graves.

FRIDAY, AUG. 14. Sixty of a tribe of wild Indians, who live in the mountains, about two hundred miles distant, made a descent a few days since upon a farm within thirty miles of Monterey, and carried off a hundred horses. Twenty of the tribe, with the chief, remained behind to secure further booty. Intelligence of this having reached Capt. Mervin, he dispatched a mounted force, apprehended them in their ambush, and brought them to Monterey, and delivered them over to our court for trial.

They were as wild a looking set of fellows as ever entered a civil tribunal. The chief was over seven feet high, with an enormous blanket wrapped round him and thrown over the shoulder like a Spanish cloak, which set forth his towering form to the best advantage. His long black hair streamed in darkness down to his waist. His features strikingly resembled those of Gen. Jackson. His forehead was high, his eye full of fire, and his mouth betrayed great decision. His step was firm; his age must have been about fifty. He entered the court with a civil but undaunted air. When asked why he permitted the men of his tribe to steal horses, he replied that the men who took the horses were not properly members of his tribe, that they had recently attached themselves to him, and now, that he had found them horse-thieves, he should cut them. I could get at no satisfactory evidence that he, or the twenty with him, had actively assisted those who took off the horses. I delivered them over to Capt. Mervin, who commanded the military occupation of the town.

The United States troops were formed into a hollow

square, and they were marched into the centre where they expected to be shot, and still not a muscle shook, and the features of each were as set as if chiselled from marble. What must have been their unbetrayed surprise, when Capt. Mervin told them they were acquitted by the tribunal! He then told the chief he should recognize him as king of the tribe—that he must not permit any of his men to commit the slightest depredations on the citizens, that he should hold him responsible for the conduct of his tribe, and that he must come and report himself and the condition of his tribe every two moons. To all this the chief fully assented.

They were then taken on board the frigate, where the crew had been mustered for the occasion. Here they were told how many ships, men, and guns we had at our command; so much to inspire them with awe: and now for their good will. The whole party were rigged out with fresh blankets, and red handkerchiefs for each, which they use as a turban. The chief was attired in a uniform of one of our tallest and stoutest officers: navy buttons, epauletts, sword, cap with a gold band, boots, and spurs; and a silver chain was put about his neck, to which a medal was attached, recognizing him as the high chief of the tribe. He looked every inch a chief. The band struck up Hail Columbia, and they departed, vowing eternal allegiance to the Americans. The sailors were delighted with these savages, and half envied them their wild life.

SATURDAY, AUG. 15. To-day the first newspaper ever published in California made its appearance. The honor, if such it be, of writing its Prospectus, fell to me. It is to be issued on every Saturday, and s published by Semple and Colton. Little did I hink when relinquishing the editorship of the North American in Philadelphia, that my next feat in this line would be off here in California. My partner is an emigrant from Kentucky, who stands six feet eight in his stockings. He is in a buckskin dress, a fox-skin cap; is true with his rifle, ready with his pen, and quick at the type-case.

He created the materials of our office out of the chaos of a small concern, which had been used by a Roman Catholic monk in printing a few sectarian tracts. The press was old enough to be preserved as a curiosity; the mice had burrowed in the balls; there were no rules, no leads, and the types were rusty and all in pi. It was only by scouring that the letters could be made to show their faces. A sheet or two of tin were procured, and these, with a jack-knife, were cut into rules and leads. Luckily we found, with the press, the greater part of a keg of ink; and now came the main scratch for paper. None could be found, except what is used to envelop the tobacco of the cigar smoked here by the natives. A coaster had a small supply of this on board, which we procured. It is in sheets a little larger than the common-sized foolscap. And this is the size of our first paper, which we have christened the Californian.

Though small in dimensions, our first number is as full of news as a black-walnut is of meat. We have received by couriers, during the week, intelligence from all the important military posts through the territory. Very little of this has transpired; it reaches the public for the first time through our sheet. We have, also, the declaration of war between the United States and Mexico, with an abstract of the debate in the senate. A crowd was waiting when the first sheet was thrown from the press. It produced quite a little sensation. Never was a bank run upon harder; not, however, by people with paper to get specie, but exactly the reverse. One-half of the paper is in English, the other in Spanish. The subscription for a year is five dollars; the price of a single sheet is twelve and a half cents; and is considered cheap at that.

SUNDAY, AUG. 16. A brilliant day, and no sounds to disturb its tranquillity save the moan of the pine-grove as the wind sighs through it, and the thunder of the breaking waves on the beach. We had divine service on board the Savannah,—a much more grateful occupation to me than the investigation of crimes in the Alcaldean court.

Till the Americans took possession of Monterey, tne Sabbath was devoted to amusement. The Indians gave themselves up to liquor, the Mexicans and Californians to dancing. Whether the bottle or the fiddle had the most votaries it would be difficult to say.

But both had so many, that very few were left for the church. Some, however, attended mass before they dressed for the ball-room. But their worship and their waltz came so close together, that a serious thought had only time to dodge out of the way.

MONDAY, AUG. 17. A complaint was lodged in my court this morning, involving the perplexities of a love-matter. The complainant is a Californian mother, who has a daughter rather remarkable for her personal attractions. She has two rival suitors, both anxious to marry her, and each, of course, extremely jealous of the attentions of the other, and anxious to outdo him in the fervency and force of his own assiduities. The family are consequently annoyed, and desire the court to interfere in some way for their repose. I issued an order that neither of the rival suitors should enter the house of the complainant, unless invited by her, till the girl had made up her mind which she would marry; for it appeared she was very much perplexed, being equally pleased with both: and now, I suppose, roses and all the other silent tokens of affection will pass plenty as protestations before.

"The course of true love never did run smooth."

TUESDAY, AUG. 18. The ado made to reach the hand of the undecided girl shows how very rare such specimens of beauty are in these parts. She has nothing to recommend her as a sober, industrious, frugal housekeeper. She knows how to dance, to play on the guitar and sing, and that is all. She would be as much lost in the kitchen as a dolphin on dry land. She would do to dress flowers in the balcony of a millionaire, but as the wife of a Californian, her children would go without a stocking, and her husband without a shirt. Her two suitors own, probably, the apparel which they have on and the gay horses which they ride, but neither of them has a real in his pocket. Yet they are quite ready to be married : just as if the honey-moon had a horn of plenty instead of a little urn of soft light, which gushes for a few brief nights, and then leaves its devotee like one of the foolish virgins, whose lamp had gone out!

WEDNESDAY, AUG. 19. Several of Gen. Castro's officers have just arrived in town, delivered themselves up, and been put upon parole. They state that the general's camp, near the Pueblo de los Angeles, broke up a few days since in the night; that the general and Gov. Pico had started for Sonora with fifty men and two hundred horses; that their flight was hastened by the approach of Com. Stockton, with the forces of the Congress, on the north, and Maj. Fremont, with his riflemen, on the south. The commodore had reached, it appears, within a few hours' march of his camp. The general had taken the precaution to send forward in advance a portion of his horses, to serve as fresh relays on his arrival. He expects to leave Col. Fremont on the right, and will be obliged to cross an immense sandy plain, lying between the Pueblo and Red River, where his horses will be for two days without water or food. He is to cross Red River, a broad and rapid stream, on a raft, the construction of which will detain him a day; his horses will swim, for California horses are trained to rush over mountain-torrents. The only hope of his capture lies in his detention at the river, unless Col. Fremont, anticipating his flight, has thrown a force south to intercept him. Once across the river he is safe; nothing but a tornado, or a far-striking thunderbolt, can overtake a Californian on horseback.

THURSDAY, AUG. 20. An Indian was brought before me to-day, charged with having stolen a horse. He was on his way, it appears, to Monterey, and when within thirty miles, his own horse having given out, he turned him adrift, and lassoed one belonging to another man, which he rode in, and then set him at liberty as he had his own. The owner arrived soon after, recovered his horse, and had the Indian arrested, who confessed the whole affair, and only plead in excuse that his own horse had become too tired to go further. I sentenced the Indian to three months' labor on the public works. He seemed at first very much surprised at what he considered the severity of the sentence; but said he should work his time out faithfully, and give me no further trouble. As he was half-naked, I ordered him comfortable apparel, and then delivered him over to Capt. Mervin, to be employed in excavating a trench around the newly-erected fort.

FRIDAY, AUG. 21. A Californian is most at home in his saddle; there he has some claims to originality, if not in character then in costume. His hat, with its conical crown and broad rim, throws back the sun's rays from its dark, glazed surface. It is fastened on by a band which passes under his chin, and rests on a red handkerchief, which turbans his head, from beneath which his black locks flow out upon the wind.

The collar of his linen rolls over that of his blue spencer, which is open under the chin, is fitted closely to his waist, and often ornamented with double rows of buttons and silk braid. His trowsers, which are fastened around his loins by a red sash, are open to the knee, to which his buckskin leggins ascend over his white cotton drawers. His buckskin shoes are armed with heavy spurs, which have a shaft some ten inches long, at the end of which is a roller, which bristles out into six points, three inches long, against which steel plates rattle with a quick, sharp sound.

His feet rest in stirrups of wood, carved from the solid oak, and which are extremely strong and heavy. His saddle rises high fore and aft, and is broadly skirted with leather, which is stamped into figures, through the interstices of which red and green silk flash out with gay effect. The reins of his bridle are thick and narrow, and the headstall is profusely ornamented with silver plate. His horse, with his long flowing mane, arching neck, broad chest, full flanks, and slender legs, is full of fire. He seldom trots, and will gallop all day without seeming to be weary. On his back is the Californian's home. Leave him this home, and you may have the rest of the world.

SATURDAY, AUG. 22. Our little paper, the Californian, made its appearance again to-day. Many subscribers have sent in their names since our last, and all have paid in advance. It is not larger than a sheet of foolscap; but this foolscap parallel stops, I hope, with the shape. Be this as it may, its appearance is looked for with as much interest as was the arrival of the mail by the New Yorkers and Bostonians in those days when a moon waxed and waned over its transit.

SUNDAY, AUG. 23. Officiated to-day on board the Savannah. There is no Protestant church here. Emigrants have generally become Roman Catholics. Policy, rather than persuasion or conviction, suggested it. Men who make no pretensions to religion, have nothing to give up in the shape of creeds or conscientious scruples. They are like driftwood, which runs into the eddy which is the strongest; or like migratory birds, which light where they can find the best picking and the softest repose. The woodpecker never taps an undecayed tree; and a worldling seldom embraces a thoroughly sound faith.

CHAPTER III.

A THIEF OBEYING ORDERS.—GAME.—NO PENITENTIARY SYSTEM.—THE CALIFORNIA CART ON A GALA-DAY.—THE RUNAWAY DAUGHTER.—FAITH OF THE INDIANS.—RETURN FROM THE WAR.—FIRST TRIAL BY JURY.—INDIAN AND HIS SQUAW ON THE HUNT.—WHALES IN THE BAY.—THE TWO GAMBLERS.—LADIES ON HORSEBACK.—MERRIMENT IN DEATH.—THE ENGLISHMAN AND HIS MISTRESS.

MONDAY, AUG. 24. One of our officers, bound with dispatches to San Juan, fell in with an Indian to-day, on a horse, without saddle or bridle, save a lasso; and knowing from this circumstance that he had stolen the animal, ordered him to come to Monterey and deliver himself up to the alcalde, and then passed on. So on the Indian came with the horse, and presented himself at our office.

I asked him what he wanted; he told me the order he had received; but I could not at first comprehend its import, and inquired of him if he knew why the order had been given him. He replied, that it was in consequence of his having taken the horse of another man. I asked him if he had stolen the animal; he said yes, he had taken him, but had brought him in here and given himself up as ordered; that he could not escape, as the Americans were all over California. I told him stealing a horse was a crime, and sentenced him to three months' labor on the public works. He was half naked. I ordered him comfortable clothes, and gave him a plug of tobacco, and in an hour he was at his task, chewing and cheerful. He is not wanting in intelligence; and if he only had as much respect for the rights of property as he has for military orders, he might be a useful member of the community.

Oats in California grow wild. The last crop plants the next, without the aid of man. The yield is sufficient to repay the labors of the husbandman, but is gratuitously thrown at his feet. But the fecundity of nature here is not confined to the vegetable kingdom, it is characteristic of the animals that sport in wild life over these hills and valleys. A sheep has two lambs a year; and if twins, four: and one litter of pigs follows another so fast that the squeelers and grunters are often confounded.

Wednesday, Aug. 26. The Californians breakfast at eight, dine at twelve, take tea at four, supper at eight, and then go to bed—unless there is a fandango. The supper is the most substantial meal of the three, and would visit anybody but a Californian with the nightmare. But their constant exercise in the open air and on horseback, gives them the digestion of the ostrich.

The only meat consumed here to any extent is beef. It is beef for breakfast, beef for dinner, and beef for supper. A pig is quite a rarity; and as for chickens, they are reserved for the sick. The woods are full of partridges and hare; the streams and lagoons are covered with ducks and wild geese; and the harbor abounds with the most delicious fish. But no Californian will angle or hunt, while he has a horse or saddle left. And as for the Indians, but very few of them have any hunting gear beyond the bow and arrow; with these they can kill the deer and elk, but a partridge and hare are too shy and too quick. They spear a large salmon which frequents Carmel river, three miles distant, and bring it in to market. This fish is often three feet long, extremely fat, and of a flavor that takes from Lent half the merit of its abstinence. Spearing them is high sport for the Indian, and is another feature in California life.

THURSDAY, AUG. 27. Nothing puzzles me so much as the absence of a penitentiary system. There are no work-houses here; no buildings adapted to the purpose; no tools, and no trades. The custom has been to fine Spaniards, and whip Indians. The discrimination is unjust, and the punishments ill suited to the ends proposed. I have substituted labor; and have now eight Indians, three Californians, and one Englishman at work making adobes. They have all been sentenced for stealing horses or bullocks. I have given them their task: each is to make fifty adobes a day, and for all over this they are paid. They make seventy-five, and for the additional twenty-five each gets as many cents. This is paid to them every Saturday night, and they are allowed to get with it any thing but rum. They are comfortably lodged and fed by the government. I have appointed one of their number captain. They work in the field; require no other guard; not one of them has attempted to run away.

FRIDAY, AUG. 28. The ox-cart of the Californian is quite unique and primitive. The wheels are cut transversely from the butt-end of a tree, and have holes through the centre for a huge wood axle. The tongue is a long, heavy beam, and the yoke resting on the necks of the oxen, is lashed to their horns, close down to the root; from these they draw, instead of the chest, as with us; and they draw enormous loads, but the animals are large and powerful.

But to return to the cart. On gala days it is swept out, and covered with mats; a deep body is put on, which is arched with hoop-poles, and over these a pair of sheets are extended for a covering. Into this the ladies are tumbled, when three or four yoke of oxen, with as many Indian drivers, and ten times as many dogs, start ahead. The hallooing of the drivers, the barking of the dogs, and the loud laughter of the girls make a common chorus. The quail takes to the covert as the roaring establishment comes on, and even the owl suspends his melancholy note. What has his sad tone to do amid such noise and mirth? It is like the piping cry of an infant amid the revelry and tumult of the carnival.

SATURDAY, AUG. 29. Four Californians—a girl, her

father, mother, and lover, all well clad and good-looking—presented themselves before me to-day. The old man said he had come to reclaim his daughter, who had run away with the young Mexican,—that he had no objection to his marrying her, but this running away with her didn't look decent. The rash lover stated in his defence that he was ready to marry her, had run away with her for that purpose, had placed her immediately with his sister, and that she was still as chaste and pure as the driven snow. To all this the father and mother assented.

I now expected we should have a wedding at once, and that I might be called upon to officiate. But to my utter surprise, on asking the girl if she insisted on marrying her lover, she declined. She said her escape with him was a wild freak; she had now got over it, and wished to return with her father. This fell like a death-knell on the ears of her lover, who again protested his affection and her purity. Having been once myself a disappointed suitor, I had a fellow feeling for him, and advised the girl to marry him; but she said no, that she had changed her mind: so I delivered her to her father, and told my brother in misfortune he must wait; that a woman who had changed her mind once on such a subject, would change it again.

SUNDAY, AUG. 30. Several gentlemen and ladies of Monterey were present to-day at our service on board the Savannah. I have it in contemplation to establish a service on shore. There are plenty of halls, which are now used for dancing, and I should have as little scruple in converting one of them into a church, as Father Whitfield had in appropriating to his use the popular airs of the day, when he said he had no notion of letting the devil run away with all the fine tunes. Blessings on the memory of that devoted missionary! He has embalmed in his church melodies that will live when the profane lyres from which they flowed have long since been silent.

The wild Indians here have a vague belief in the soul's immortality. They say, "as the moon dieth and cometh to life again, so man, though he die, will again live." But their future state is material; the wicked are to be bitten by serpents, scorched by lightning, and plunged down cataracts; while the good are to hunt their game with bows that never lose their vigor, with arrows that never miss their aim, and in forests where the crystal streams roll over golden sands. Immortal youth is to be the portion of each; and age, and pain, and death, are to be known no more.

Monday, Aug. 31. I am at last forced into a systematic arrangement of my time; without it, I could never get through with my duties. I rise with the sun, read till eight o'clock, and then breakfast; at nine, enter on my duties as alcalde, which confine me till three, p. m., then dine; and at four take my gun and plunge into the woods for exercise and partridges; return at sunset, take tea, and in the evening write up my journal, and an editorial for the Californian.

When the Sabbath comes, I preach; my sermons are composed in the woods, in the court-room, or in bed, just where I can snatch a half-hour. I often plan them while some plaintiff is spinning a long yarn about things and matters in general, or some defendant is losing himself in a labyrinth of apologetic circumstances. By this forbearance both are greatly relieved; one disburdens himself of his grievances, the other lightens his guilt, and, in the mean time, my sermon develops itself into a more tangible arrangement. My text might often be— "And he fell among thieves."

TUESDAY, SEPT. 1. It is singular how the Californians reckon distances. They will speak of a place as only a short gallop off, when it is fifty or a hundred miles distant. They think nothing of riding a hundred and forty miles in a day, and breaking down three or four horses in doing it, and following this up by the week. They subsist almost exclusively on meat, and when travelling, sleep under the open sky. They drive their ox-carts, loaded with lumber or provisions, two hundred miles to market. Their conceptions seem to annihilate space.

WEDNESDAY, SEPT. 2. The officers of Gen. Castro

have been permitted to return to their homes, after having taken an oath that they will not, on pain of death, be found in arms against the United States during the existence of the present war. A few, perhaps from national pride, refused at first the oath, but were compelled to take it, or be treated as prisoners of war. They of course preferred the former. The ladies don't seem to care much about these nice points in military etiquette: they want their husbands at home; and their return, though on parole, is the signal for getting up a ball. A Californian would hardly pause in a dance for an earthquake, and would be pretty sure to renew it, even before its vibrations had ceased. At a wedding they dance for three days and nights, during which time the new-married couple are kept on their feet. No compassion is shown them, as they have so much bliss in reserve.

THURSDAY, SEPT. 3. Dispatches were received this morning, by courier, from Com. Stockton, dated at the Pueblo de los Angeles. They contain his second address to the people of California, which defines the new attitude in which the country is placed by the declaration of war between the United States and Mexico. The address is humane in its tone, expansive and vigorous in its spirit. It has had the salutary effect to set the community at rest, by establishing in the minds of the wavering the full conviction that California is henceforth a part of the

United States. Ex-Gov. Pio Pico, it seems, did not escape with Gen. Castro, but has surrendered to the commodore. He is one of the few who commanded the confidence and respect of the public.

FRIDAY, SEPT. 4. I empannelled to-day the first jury ever summoned in California. The plaintiff and defendant are among the principal citizens of the country. The case was one involving property on the one side, and integrity of character on the other. Its merits had been pretty widely discussed, and had called forth an unusual interest. One-third of the jury were Mexicans, one-third Californians, and the other third Americans. This mixture may have the better answered the ends of justice, but I was apprehensive at one time it would embarrass the proceedings; for the plaintiff spoke in English, the defendant in French, the jury, save the Americans, Spanish, and the witnesses all the languages known to California. But through the silent attention which prevailed, the tact of Mr. Hartnell, who acted as interpreter, and the absence of young lawyers, we got along very well.

The examination of the witnesses lasted five or six hours; I then gave the case to the jury, stating the questions of fact upon which they were to render their verdict. They retired for an hour, and then returned, when the foreman handed in their verdict, which was clear and explicit, though the case itself was rather complicated. To this verdict, both parties bowed without a word of dissent. The inhabitants who witnessed the trial, said it was what they liked— that there could be no bribery in it—that the opinion of twelve honest men should set the case forever at rest. And so it did, though neither party completely triumphed in the issue. One recovered his property, which had been taken from him by mistake, the other his character, which had been slandered by design. If there is any thing on earth besides religion for which I would die, it is the right of trial by jury.

Saturday, Sept. 5. I encountered on my hunting excursion to-day a wild Indian, with a squaw and papoose. They were on horses, he carrying his bow, with a large quiver of arrows hung at his side, and she with the child in the bunt of her blanket, at the back. They were dashing ahead in the wake of their dogs, which were in hot chase of a deer. The squaw stuck to her fleet animal as firmly as the saddle in which she sat, and took but little heed of the bogs and gullies over which she bounded. His glance was directed to a ridge of rocks, over which he seemed to expect the deer to fly from the field of wild oats through which the chase lay. I watched them till they disappeared in their whirlwind speed over the ridge. Whether the deer fell into their hands or escaped, I know not; but certainly I would not hazard my neck as they did theirs for all the game even in the California forests. But this, to them, is life; they seek no repose between the cradle and the grave.

SUNDAY, SEPT. 6. The bell of the Roman Catholic church, which has been silent some weeks, rung out loud and clear this morning. I directed the prisoners, sentenced to the public works, to be taken to the service. I had given them soap, and sufficient time to clean their clothes, on Saturday; though having but one suit, they had only their blankets for covering while these were washing and drying. With a marine at their head, armed and equipped, they made quite a respectable appearance. Their conduct, during service, was reported to me as very becoming. They may yet reform, and shape their lives after the precepts of morality and religion. My own service was on board the Savannah, where we had the officers of the Erie.

MONDAY, SEPT. 7. We have been looking for a whale-ship, or spouter, as she is called by our sailors, to come in here, and take care of the whales which are blowing around us. One belonging to the genuine old Nantucket line, came to anchor last evening. She had been on the northwest coast in pursuit of the black whale; but found them so wild, owing to the havoc that has been made among them, that she captured but very few.

This morning her boats were lowered, and their crews put off in pursuit of one of these monsters.

The fellow plunged as they approached, and was out of sight for some minutes, when he hove up at a distance. "There she blows!" was the cry, and off they darted again; but by the time they had gained the spot another plunge was heard, and only a deep foaming eddy remained. The next time she lifted they were more successful, and lodged one of their harpoons. The reel was soon out, and away the boat flew, like a little car attached to a locomotive. But the harpoon at last slipped its hold, and the whale escaped. The loss seemed proportionate to the bulk of the monster.

TUESDAY, SEPT. 8. We have had for the last five days hardly an hour of sunshine, owing to the dense fogs which prevail here at this season. These murky vapors fill the whole atmosphere; you seem to walk in them alone, like one threading a mighty forest. A transcendentalist might easily conceive himself a ghost, wandering among the cypresses of a dead world. But, being no ghost or transcendentalist, I had a fire kindled, and found refuge from the fog in its cheerful light and warmth.

WEDNESDAY, SEPT. 9. A Californian came into my court in great haste last evening, and complained that another Californian was running away with his oxen. Suspecting the affair had some connection with a gambling transaction, I immediately handed him a warrant for the arrest of the fugitive, when off he started at the top of his speed to execute it. In less than an hour he returned with his prisoner.

I then asked the plaintiff if the oxen were his; he said they were. I asked him of whom he obtained them; he said of the man who attempted to run away with them. I asked him what he gave for them; this was a puzzler, but after hemming and hawing for a minute, he said he had played for them, and won them. I asked him what else he had won of the man; he replied, the poncho, and a thin jacket, both of which he had on. I then ordered them both into the calaboose for the night. The winner, who had apprehended the other, and who, no doubt, expected to get the oxen at once, looked quite confounded.

This morning I had the two gamblers before me: neither of them looked as if he had relished much his prison-couch. I made the winner return all his ill-gotten gains, oxen, poncho, and jacket, and then fined them each five dollars. The one who had served the warrant shrugged his shoulders, as if he had made a great mistake. There was no escape from the judgment, so they paid their fine and departed. The next time they gamble, they will probably settle matters between themselves, without a resort to the alcalde.

THURSDAY, SEPT. 10. My alcalde duties required me to-day to preside at the executive sale of two dwelling-houses and a store. I was about as *au fait* at the business as Dr. Johnson at the auction of widow Thrales' brewery, when he informed the bidders, in his towering language, that he offered them, not a few idle vats and worms, but the "potentiality of becoming rich." The property sold well, forty per cent. higher than it would under the Mexican flag. All real estate has risen since our occupation of the territory. This tells what the community expects, in terms which none can mistake. A Californian told me to-day that he considered his lands worth forty thousand dollars more than they were before our flag was hoisted. The old office-holders may, perhaps, grumble at the change, but they whose interest lies in the soil silently exult. They desire no ebb in the present tide of political affairs.

FRIDAY, SEPT. 11. An express came in to-day, bringing the intelligence that a thousand Wallawalla Indians had reached the Sacramento from Oregon. They have come, as the express states, to avenge the death of a young chief, who was wantonly and wickedly killed about a year since, by an American emigrant. They belong to a tribe remarkable for their intelligence, hardihood, and valor. Their occupation is that of trappers, and they are thoroughly used to fire-arms. Capt. Mervin has sent a force from the Savannah, and Capt. Montgomery another from the Portsmouth, to arrest their progress. Capt. Ford, with his company of California rangers, who understand the bush-fight, will also be on the spot.

SATURDAY, SEPT. 12. My partner in the "Californian" has been absent several weeks. All the work of the office has devolved upon a sailor, who has set the type for the whole paper, with fingers stiff as the ropes around which they have coiled themselves into seeming fixtures. Yet the "Californian" is out, and makes a good appearance. Who would think, except in these uttermost ends of the earth, of issuing a weekly journal, with only an old tar to set the type, and without a solitary exchange paper! By good fortune, a hunter brought along a copy of the "Oregon Spectator;" it was quite a windfall, though the only intelligence it contained from the United States, was that brought its editor by some overland emigrant. The "Spectator" speaks of the institutions of the "City of Oregon" with as much reverence as if they had the antiquity of the Egyptian Pyramids; when there is scarce a crow's nest which does not date further back. But age is no certain evidence of merit, since folly runs to seed as fast as wisdom.

CHAPTER IV.

FUNERAL CEREMONIES.—ELECTED ALCALDE.—FLIGHT OF GEN. CASTRO.—LOS ANGELES TAKEN.—OVEN-BATH.—GROG IN A CHIMNEY.—THE FLEA.—FIRST RAIN.—RISING OF THE CALIFORNIANS.—MEASURES OF COM. STOCKTON.—MORMONS.

SUNDAY, SEPT. 13. Officiated to-day on board the Savannah, and called on my way to see a sick child, whose mother seems at a loss whether to grieve or rejoice in prospect of its death. If it dies, she says it will at once become a little angel: if it lives, it will be subject to sorrow and sin. She desires, for her sake, that it may live; but, for its own, that it may die. This balancing between life and death, is common here among mothers. Their full persuasion of an infant's future bliss, forbids that they should mourn its loss. They therefore put on no weeds, and utter no lamentations. The child, when its pure spirit has fled, is dressed in white, and stainless roses are strewn upon its little shroud. It is borne to the grave as if it were to be laid at the open portal of heaven, and few are the tears which fall on that threshold of immortal bliss.

MONDAY, SEPT. 14. A letter from the Sacramento, received to-day, informs me of the arrival of two thousand emigrants from the United States. They are under the guidance of experienced men, and have been but a little over four months on the way. The Mormons are selecting the site of their city, which they intend shall be the paradise of the west.

TUESDAY, SEPT. 15. The citizens of Monterey elected me to-day alcalde, or chief magistrate of this jurisdiction—a situation which I have been filling for two months past, under a military commission. It has now been restored to its civil character and functions. Their election is undoubtedly the highest compliment which they can confer ; but this token of confidence brings with it a great deal of labor and responsibility. It devolves upon me duties similar to those of mayor of one of our cities, without any of those judicial aids which he enjoys. It involves every breach of the peace, every case of crime, every business obligation, and every disputed land-title within a space of three hundred miles. From every other alcalde's court in this jurisdiction there is an appeal to this, and none from this to any higher tribunal. Such an absolute disposal of questions affecting property and personal liberty, never ought to be confided to one man. There is not a judge on any bench in England or the United States, whose power is so absolute as that of the alcalde of Monterey.

WEDNESDAY, SEPT. 16. The Congress, bearing the broad pennant of Com. Stockton, returned last evening from her trip to the south. She has captured, during her absence, Santa Barbara, San Pedro, and the Pueblo de los Angeles. Over these the American flag is now flying.

Gen. Castro had taken up his position just outside the Pueblo, on an elevation which commands the town and adjacent country. He was well supplied with field-pieces, and had a force of seven hundred men. Com. Stockton landed at San Pedro with three hundred seamen and marines from the Congress, and marched against him. His route, which extended some thirty miles, lay through several narrow passes, which Gen. Castro might easily have defended against a much superior force. But the general kept in his entrenched camp; and informed the commodore by a courier, that if he marched upon the town he would find it the grave of his men. "Then," said the commodore, "tell the general to have the bells ready to toll in the morning at eight o'clock, as I shall be there at that time." He was there; but Castro, in the mean time, had broken up his camp, mounted with an armed band, and fled towards Sonora, in Mexico. The town was taken, the American flag hoisted and cheered.

THURSDAY, SEPT. 17. The U. S. ship Cyane, under Commander Du Pont, proceeded from this port to San Diego, took that important place, and landed Col. Fremont, with his riflemen, who hastened to cut off the retreat of Castro. He would have done it could he have anticipated his route; but to overtake him was impossible, as the general had taken the precaution to send on in advance relays of fresh horses, sufficient to take him and his band beyond the reach of any pursuit.

FRIDAY, SEPT. 18. A bearer of dispatches from Commodore Stockton to our government is to leave to-morrow morning in the Erie, and we are all busy in writing letters home by him. The Erie is to take the dispatch-bearer to Panama, and then proceed to the Sandwich Islands. We have not received any letters from home since we sailed from Callao; the year has rolled from the buds of spring into the sear leaf of autumn since any intelligence has reached us from those we love. Death may have stricken them into the grave, but the sad tidings is yet a melancholy secret. We ought to have a regular mail between the United States and California. We seem remarkably eager to possess ourselves of foreign territory, and then leave the wild geese to convey all intelligence. If the land is only ours, and those at home can hear from it once in fifty or a hundred years, that will do; a more frequent communication would be quite superfluous. Had we possessed Egypt in the days of Cheops, all information would still be considered seasonable which should come when his pyramid had crumbled.

SATURDAY, SEPT. 19. I encountered to-day a company of Californians on horseback, bound to a picnic, each with his lady love on the saddle before him.

He, as in duty bound, rides behind, throws his feet forward into the stirrups, his left hand holds the reins, his right encircles and sustains her, and there she rides safe as a robin in its nest; sprigs of evergreen, with wild flowers, wave in her little hat, and larger clusters in his; both are gayly attired, and smiles of light and love kindle in their dark expressive eyes. Away they gallop over hill and valley, waking the wild echoes of the wood. One of my hunting dogs glanced at them for a while, and seemed so tickled, he had to plunge into the bushes to get rid of his mirth.

SUNDAY, SEPT. 20. At the invitation of Captain Richardson, I preached this afternoon on board the Brooklyn. The crew assembled in the cabin, which the captain had converted for the occasion into a chapel. None attended by compulsion, but all were present of their free will. The good order and respectful attention which prevailed showed the spirit which pervaded the ship, and conveyed a testimony of the wise and Christian conduct of the captain which none could mistake. I have never met with a ship where a greater degree of harmony and alacrity in duty were observable; all this, too, without any resort to physical force; such is the result of moral influence when brought into full play. Give us more of this in the navy.

MONDAY, SEPT. 21. A Californian mother came to me to-day to plead her son out of prison. He had driven off a herd of cattle which had another owner, and sold them, and I had sentenced him to the public works for a year. She felt as a good mother must feel for her son, and plead for his liberation with a pathos that half shook my resolution. Nothing but an iron sense of duty kept me firm. There is something in a mother's tears which is almost irresistible; she wept and trembled, and would have kneeled, but I would not let her. I lifted her to her feet, and told her I once had a mother, and knew what her sorrows were. I told her I would liberate her son if I could, but it was impossible; law and justice were against it. But if he behaved well, I would take off a few months from the close of the year; and in the mean time she might see him as often as she desired. She thanked me, lingered as if she would plead again, and departed. What depths there are in a mother's soul!

TUESDAY, SEPT. 22. The frigate Savannah sailed this morning for San Francisco. She left her berth, where she has lain since our flag was raised here, and with her royals set, glided gracefully out of the bay. The Congress gave her three cheers as she passed,— still she goes with a heavy heart. The time of her crew is out; they are almost half the circuit of the globe from their home, and have now, seemingly, as little prospect of reaching it as they had a year since. Com. Stockton went on board a few days since and addressed them, but even with his happy tact in inspiring enthusiasm, it was difficult to arouse their despondency, and make them cheerful in a resignation to their lot. The war being against a power unarmed at sea, is with them a mere bubble. To chase or capture a privateer is a game not worth the candle. Were an English or French squadron in this ocean, n declared hostility, they would not murmur while a tattered sail could be set, or a shot be found in the locker.

WEDNESDAY, SEPT. 23. I was waked this morning by sounds of merriment in the street. Day had only begun to glimmer, and its beam was contending with the glare of rockets, flashing over the lingering shadows of night. The child which I had visited a few evenings since had died, and this was its attendant ceremony to the grave. It had become, in the apprehension of those who formed the procession, a little angel—and they were expressing their joy over the transformation. The disruption of ties which bound it here—its untimely blight—and the darkness of the grave—were all forgotten. Its little coffin was draped in white, and garlanded with flowers; and voices of gladness, ringing out from childhood and youth, heralded its flight to a better world.

THURSDAY, SEPT. 24. An Englishman called at the court to-day, and desired me to issue a warrant for the apprehension of his mistress, who he said had run away and carried off a rich shawl and diamond breastpin which did not belong to her. I told him, when he entered into a criminal compact of that kind with a person, he might expect just such results as he had experienced,—and as for a warrant, I should issue none, and would not if she had carried off every thing in his house, and him too; for I should consider the community quit of two persons who could in no way benefit its morals. He looked not a little surprised at this decision, shrugged his shoulders, and departed. The first thing a foreigner does here is to provide himself with a horse; the second, with a mistress; the third, with a pack of cards. These, with a bottle of aguardiente, are his capital for this world and the next. This is true of many, but not all; there are some high and honorable exceptions.

FRIDAY, SEPT. 25. The Congress left her moorings last evening, and held her course majestically out of the bay for San Francisco. Com. Stockton proposes, while there, to construct batteries which can command the entrance to the harbor, and afford protection to our merchantmen in the absence of our squadron. The new city will probably be located before his return. It is the point towards which all eyes are now turned. The tide of emigration is setting there with as much steadiness and strength as the rivers which roll into its capacious bosom. The day is coming when the spires of a great city will be mirrored in its waters.

SATURDAY, SEPT. 26. The Indians here are practical Thomsonians or Hydropathists; they sweat for every kind of disease. Their bath is a large ground-oven, to which you descend by a flight of narrow steps, and which has a small aperture at the top for the escape of the smoke. In the centre of this they build a fire, close the entrance, and shut themselves in till the temperature reaches an elevation which throws them into a profuse perspiration. They then rush out and plunge themselves into a stream of cold water. This is repeated every day till the disease leaves or death comes.

But many, without any ailment, resort to this bath as a luxury. They will stay in the oven till they are hardly able to crawl out and reach the stream. It is great fun for the more sturdy ones to lift out the exhausted and dash them in the flood. You hardly expect to see them rise again, but up they come, and regain the earth full of life and vigor. The reaction is instantaneous, and the effect, I have no doubt, in many cases beneficial. It, at least, gives them a good washing, which they would hardly get without, and which they too often need. The Indian also takes to the water to quench the flames of rum. His poor mortal tenement is often wrapped in such a conflagration. It would be a good thing if all the rum-drinkers could be marched once a week under the falls of Niagara.

SUNDAY, SEPT. 27. There is no day in the week in which my feelings run homeward so strongly as on the Sabbath. That day makes me feel indeed as an exile. A vast moral desolation spreads around me: only here and there a speck of verdure sprinkles the mighty waste. All else is bleak and barren. You turn your eyes to the hills where you were born, the church where you were baptized, and would rush back to them on the steep wave of time.

MONDAY, SEPT. 28. When Monterey was taken by our squadron, an order was issued by the commander-in-chief that all the grog-shops should be closed. The object of this was to prevent disorder among the populace and among the sailors, whose duties as a patrol confined them to the shore. It was with great difficulty that this order could be enforced. All moderate fines failed to secure its observance. The price of aguardiente rose to four and five dollars the bottle, more than ten times its original cost: for such a premium the shopkeeper would run the hazard of the penalty.

We searched for it as for hid treasures, but only in one instance found its hiding-place. This was in a chimney, hanging about midway from the top. When discovered, the shopkeeper laughed as loudly as they who made the search. He was fined, not for having grog in his chimney, for that is a very good place for it, but for retailing it at his counter. An offer of four or five dollars from a customer never failed to bring down a bottle. He paid his fine of twenty-five dollars, but begged hard for the liquor. I took it into my custody, and told him to call for it when the last American man-of-war had left port.

TUESDAY, SEPT. 29. A brother and sister of a Mexican family applied to me to-day for permission to leave their mother. On inquiring the cause of this singular request, they stated that their father was dead, and that their mother by her immoralities had brought sore discredit on their house. I ascertained from other sources the truth of their statement, and then gave them permission to rent another dwelling. They were both modest and genteel in their appearance, but jealousy of a sister's fair reputation had prevailed with the brother over filial affection. And yet when he spoke of his mother his eyes filled with tears.

WEDNESDAY, SEPT. 30. An express arrived last night from the Pueblo below, bringing the startling intelligence that the populace had risen upon the small American force left there under command of Capt. Gillespie—that the insurgents had entire possession of the town—that the Americans were closely besieged in their quarters, and it was doubtful if they would be able to hold out much longer. The express stated that he left the town under a volley of musketry, which he narrowly escaped, but whch took such deadly effect on his horse, that he dropped under him about two leagues out.

He had a permit from the American alcalde to press horses wherever found. He rode the whole distance—four hundred and sixty miles—in fifty-two hours, during which time he had not slept. His intelligence was for Com. Stockton, and in the nature of the case was not committed to paper, except a few words over the signature of the alcalde, rolled in a cigar, which was fastened in his hair. But the commodore had sailed for San Francisco, and it was necessary he should go on a hundred and forty miles further. He was quite exhausted; I ordered him a bowl of strong coffee, which revived him, and a hearty supper, which he eagerly devoured. He was allowed to sleep three hours: in the mean time I procured fresh horses, and penned a permit for him to press others when these should begin to flag. Before the day glimmered he was up and away.

THURSDAY, OCT. 1. Com. Stockton, before the departure of the Congress, appointed T. H. Green, Esq., collector of customs at this port. Mr. G. is a native of Pennsylvania, has resided in this country several years, and enjoys a wide reputation for business habits, and sterling integrity of character. Mr. Hartwell, an Englishman by birth, has been appointed inspector and translator. He is familiar with all the languages spoken in California, and filled the same office under the Mexican government to which he has been appointed under this. But we are gratified with his appointment for another reason. He has some twenty children of his own, and in addition to these, five adopted orphans.

FRIDAY, OCT. 2. A Spaniard of some note and noise here, and consul of her Christian Majesty, attempted in court to-day to flourish down the claim of an humble Californian to whom he was indebted some eight hundred dollars. He said this creditor was once his servant, that he could neither read nor write, and that he felt quite indignant that he should have the assurance to bring him into court. I told him the first question was, whether he really owed the man the amount claimed : this being settled, we could very easily dispose of the belles-lettres part of the matter. He at first recollected nothing, except that the man had once been his servant, but on being shown the account, reluctantly admitted that it might be correct. I told him, if correct, and he had the means, he must pay it, though the creditor were fresh from Congo. Finding that we had in our court only a horizontal justice, holding its level line alike over kings and slaves, he signed an obligation for the payment in six months, and gave the security required. So much for attempting to liquidate a debt by an hidalgo flourish. Law which fails to protect the humble, disgraces the name which it bears.

SATURDAY, OCT. 3. A heavy mist hung over the landscape this morning till the sun was high in the heavens, and many began to predict rain, a phenomenon which I have not yet witnessed in California. But towards noon the mist departed like a shadow dissolved in light. The scorched hills lifted their naked summits, and the deep ravines revealed their irregular lines of lingering verdure. In these the cattle still graze, though the streams which once poured their waters through them exist now only in little motionless pools, hardly sufficient to drift a duck. A stranger looking at these hills might be excused if he inquired the distance to Sodom. It would never enter his most vagrant dreams that he had reached that land towards which the tide of emigration was rolling over the cliffs of the Rocky Mountains.

SUNDAY, OCT. 4. The presiding priest of this jurisdiction applied to me a few days since to protect the property of the San Antonio Mission. A Spaniard, it seems, who owns a neighboring rancho, had, under color of some authority of the late administration, extended his claims over the grounds and buildings, and was appropriating the whole to his private purposes. I summoned the Spaniard before me, and asked for the evidence of his right and title to the establishment. He had no document to exhibit. His sole claim evidently rested in some vague permission, in which the lines of moral justice were wholly omitted, or too faintly drawn to be seen.

I therefore ordered that the mission buildings and grounds should be delivered back to the presiding priest, and that the fixtures, which had been removed, should at once be restored. The order was forthwith carried into effect. This decision is of some moment, as it will serve as a precedent in reference to other missions. These sacred domains are the patrimonial inheritance of the Indian, and they once embraced the wealth of California. But they have fallen a prey to state exigencies and private rapacity. They ought at once to be restored to their primitive objects, or converted into a school-fund.

Monday, Oct. 5. A courier arrived to-day from San Francisco, bringing the intelligence that the Savannah had sailed for San Pedro. They will there land a large force, which will march at once to the Pueblo de los Angeles, and, if possible, bring the insurgents to an engagement. But the probability is, that they will instantly disband and fly to the forests. If they declined battle, with Gen. Castro and his regular troops at their head, they will undoubtedly do it when left to themselves, unless frantic passion has entirely overcome inherent fickleness.

Tuesday, Oct. 6. The usual rate of interest for money loaned here on good security, is twenty-four per cent. This is sufficient evidence of its scarcity, and yet it is almost valueless when you come to the question of labor. A foreigner may be induced to work for money, but not a Californian, so long as he has a pound of beef or a pint of beans left. Nor is it much better with the Indian: take from him the inducements to labor which rum and gambling present, and he will refuse to work for you. The blanket, which he wore last year, will answer for this; his shirt and pants can easily be repaired; his food is in every field and forest, and he seems to have as little scruple in taking it from the one as the other.

Hunger is unknown here; the man who has not a foot of land seems about as independent as he who has his ten-league farm, and has vastly less trouble and vexation. It is true he will now and then kill a bullock that is not his, but the fact that there are vast herds roaming about which never had an owner, seems, in his estimation, greatly to diminish the private trespass which he commits. It is with him only as if he had taken a pickerel from a pond instead of the ocean.

WEDNESDAY, OCT. 7. The great Mormon company, who came out in the Brooklyn, have had a split. The volcano, it seems, has been rumbling for some time, and has at last broke forth in flame. The explosion will undoubtedly throw them into different parts of California, and defeat any attempts at a distinct political community. The difficulty lay in the assumptions of the leader. He has all the ambition of their lost prophet, without any of his affected meekness. He attempted the iron rod, without first having persuaded those who were to feel its force that it had been put in his hands by a higher power.'

THURSDAY, OCT. 8. One of the rooms in the house which I have rented, has been occupied by some of the goods and chattels of the previous tenant. To-day they were called for, and I observed among them a large basket filled with egg-shells. They had been perforated at both ends, and their contents blown out. But to what use could any one put these empty shells? They had been prepared, it seems, for the festivities of the carnival. On this occasion they are to be filled with scented water or tinsel, the apertures closed with wax, and then broken, in merriment, over the heads of guests. This liberty with caps and wigs is warranted only where some intimacy exists between the parties. Where this is found, the eggs fall thick as hail. The young and old float in lavender and cologne. This expensive frolic is often indulged in by those who, perhaps, have hardly money enough left to purchase one of the forty hens that laid the eggs.

FRIDAY, OCT. 9. The trouble of young and old here is the flea. The native who is thoroughly inured to his habits may little heed him, but he keeps the stranger in a constant nettle. One would suppose, from his indiscriminate and unmitigated hostility, he considered himself the proprietor of all California. Indeed, he does seem to be the genuine owner of the soil, instead of a tenant at will. It is true he may construct no dwellings, but he will plant himself in every nook and corner of the one which you may construct. He jumps into your cradle, jumps with you all along through life, and well would it be for those who remain if he jumped with you out of it.

But no, he remains still; and grief for your loss will half forget its bereavement in parrying his assaults.

SATURDAY, OCT. 10. We are waiting with some anxiety for news from the Pueblo de los Angeles. A rumor reached here yesterday, that the small American force there would not be able to hold out much longer against the overwhelming odds of the insurgents. But the Savannah must by this time have reached San Pedro, and her crew be on their march to the scene of action. They are a body of brave, unflinching men, and are commanded by officers of great firmness and force. A sailor on land never thinks of running more than he would at sea. He is trained to stand to his post, and will do so on the field as well as the deck. The last man who left the ground in that disreputable retreat from Bladensburg was a sailor. When the rest were far out of sight he remained at his gun, and was wadding home to give the enemy another shot. In the fight of the Essex many threw themselves out of the ports, determined to drown sooner than surrender.

SUNDAY, OCT. 11. Another bright and beautiful Sabbath has dawned; but there is little here to remind one of its sacredness. A few of the larger stores are closed, but the smaller shops are all open. More liquors are retailed on this day than any other three. I have the power to close these shops, and shall do it.

CHAPTER V.

FIRE ON THE MOUNTAINS.—EMIGRANTS.—PISTOLS AND PILLOWS.—LEADERS OF THE INSURRECTION.—CALIFORNIA PLOUGH.—DEFEAT AT SAN PEDRO.—COL. FREMONT'S BAND.—THE MALEK ADHEL.—MONTEREY THREATENED.—SOLDIER OUTWITTED.—RAISING MEN.—BRIDEGROOM.—CULPRITS.

MONDAY, OCT. 12. A wide conflagration is sweeping over the hills which encircle the bay of Monterey. The forests, and the grass with which they are feathered, are as dry as tinder, and the flame rolls on with its line of fire clearly and fearfully defined. This has become still more grand and awful since the night set in. The clouds seem to float in an atmosphere of fire ; and the billows, as they roll to the rock-bound shore, are crested with flame. The birds are flying from their crackling covert, and the wolves go howling over the hills. It is a type of that final conflagration in which the great frame of nature will at last sink.

TUESDAY, OCT. 13. Emigrants from the United States are still pouring into the rich valley of the Sacramento. A letter from one of them says :—" It may not be uninteresting to you to know that the emigrants by land the present season far exceed the expectation of the most sanguine. No less than two thousand are now in the interior, and within a hundred miles of the settlements. They bring with them a large amount of intelligence, wealth, and industry, all of which are greatly needed in their new home. The Mormons alone have a train of more than three hundred wagons."

These emigrants will change the face of California. We shall soon have not only the fruits of nature, but of human industry. We shall soon be able to get a ball of butter without churning it on the back of a wild colt; and a potatoe without weighing it as if it were a doubloon. Were it possible for a man to live without the trouble of drawing his breath, I should look for this pleasing phenomenon in California

WEDNESDAY, OCT. 14. The success of the insurgents at the south has emboldened the reckless here. Bands have been gathering in the vicinity to make a night assault on Monterey. Their plan is to capture or drive out the small American force here, and plunder the town. Those engaged in it are men of desperate fortunes. The streets to-day have been barricaded, and the true and trusty among the citizens have been formed into a night patrol. I sleep with my rifle at my bedside, and with two pistols under my pillow. My servant, who is a brave little fellow, is also armed to the teeth. He ought to be brave, for he was born in St. Helena, close to the tomb of Napoleon, and must have caught some fire from the hero's ashes. My house has grated windows, and an entrance that is easily defended against odds, so that we shall probably make a pretty good fight of it.

One thing is certain, neither of us go out alive. I will not be taken, tortured, and hacked to pieces, as two of our countrymen were a few months since.

THURSDAY, OCT. 15. No assault yet; but a company of horsemen have been seen to-day crossing the southern plain, and winding off behind the hills at the west. They have, as a messenger informs us, joined another party much larger than their own, and are now encamped in the woods. The citizens here who have been true to our flag, feel deeply alarmed; and in truth they have some occasion, for if the town is sacked they will be among the first sufferers. I have sent an express to Com. Stockton, who is at San Francisco, where he has been engaged in raising and dispatching a heavy force for San Pedro. He will be here with the Congress as fast as the winds and waves can bring him.

FRIDAY, OCT. 16. Our relief has come. The Congress arrived to-day, and the commodore immediately landed, under Capt. Maddox, U. S. marine corps, a sufficient force to repel any attack that may be made. Our friends now breathe more freely. They may go outside the town without the fear of having their retreat cut off by a flying horseman, and sleep at night without the apprehension of awaking under a flaming roof. The noble tars of the Congress, when they saw our flag still flying on the fort, hailed it with three stout cheers, which were heard over all Monterey.

They feared, and not without reason, that it had been captured; and when they saw it still streaming on the wind, their enthusiasm and joy broke forth.

SATURDAY, OCT. 17. As soon as the intelligence of the insurrection below reached Com. Stockton, he dispatched the Savannah to San Pedro; and sent fast in her wake a quick coaster, with Col. Fremont and two hundred riflemen on board, who are to land in the night at Santa Barbara, and take the place by surprise. This was managed with so much celerity and secrecy, that the disaffected here are still ignorant of the fact.

What will be the surprise of the insurgents at los Angeles, if defeated by the forces of the Savannah, to find their retreat cut off by the riflemen of Col. Fremont! Between these two fires there will be little chance of escape. Not a few of them have given their parol of honor that they will not, on pain of death, take up arms against the United States. They are now in the field, and their treachery may cost them their lives. It is painful, but may be necessary to make examples of them. California will never have any repose while they are in it. They have headed every revolution that has taken place for years, and they have now headed their last.

SUNDAY, OCT. 18. I issued, a few days since, an ordinance against gambling—a vice which shows itself here more on the Sabbath than any other day of the week. The effect of it has been to drive the gamblers from the town into the bushes. I have been informed this evening, that in a ravine, at a short distance, some thirty individuals have been engaged through the day in this desperate play. They selected a spot deeply embowered in shade, and escaped the eye of my constables. But there is an eye from the glance of which the gloom of the forest and even the recesses of night afford no refuge.

Monday, Oct. 19. Some twenty men left the precincts of Monterey, last night, to join the insurgents at the south. They are all men of desperate fortunes, and may find that they have started too late. They who have been duped may perhaps be spared, but the ringleaders are doomed. There is only one resting-place for them in California. He who breaks his solemnly plighted faith, can claim no mercy for the past and no confidence for the future.

Were this frantic insurrection sustained by the slightest probability of success, it would relieve, perhaps, its madness and atrocity. But they who instigated it knew it must end in disaster and blood. They knew its only trophies must be a little plunder, cursed by the crimes through which it had been procured. They threw themselves down this cataract, and will never again reascend its steep wave.

Tuesday, Oct. 20. The mode of cultivating land in California is eminently primitive. In December or

A United States deserter, from the fort at Monterey, on his way to the mines, upon the back of a mule which the Vulture claims.

January they take a piece of wood in the shape of a ship's knee, dress it down a little with a dull axe, and spike a piece of iron to the lower point. A pole, by which the oxen draw, runs from the inner bend of the knee to the yoke. This pole has a mortise, about eight inches long, made slanting, and about a foot from the after end; a piece of wood, about two inches by six, runs up through the plough and pole, and is so wedged into the mortise of the pole, as to make the plough run shallow or deep as required. But if the ground happens to be hard the plough will not enter an inch, and if there are roots in the ground it must be lifted over, or it will be invariably broken. Such is a California plough; such a fair specimen of the arts here.

WEDNESDAY, OCT. 21. If late in the season, the Californian rarely prepares the ground by any furrowing attempts. He scatters the seed about the field, and then scratches it in with the thing which he calls a plough. Should this scratching fail of yielding him sixty bushels to the acre, he grumbles. In reaping he cuts so high, to save a little trouble in threshing, which is done here by horses, that he loses one-eighth of his crop; but this eighth serves for seed the next season; and what to him is better still, saves the trouble of sowing. So that his second crop plants itself from the first, and is often nearly as large as its predecessor. Even the third self-planted crop is quite respectable, and would satisfy a New England farmer for his laborious toil; but here it generally goes to the blackbirds.

THURSDAY, OCT. 22. A mother came to me, to-day, with a request that I would summon before me another woman, who had slandered her daughter. I tried to dissuade her from it—told her that persevering virtue would outlive all scandal. But she said she was a poor widow, and the reputation of her family was all she had to depend on. So I summoned the woman, who confessed her injurious words, but said they had been uttered in passion, and that she now deeply regretted them. On her assurance that she would repair as far as in her power any injury she had done, I dismissed the parties.

FRIDAY, OCT. 23. The merchant ship Vandalia is just in from San Pedro, with intelligence from the seat of war. Capt. Gillespie, it seems, had been obliged to capitulate; but the terms were that he should leave the Pueblo with all the honors of war. He marched out of the town with his flag flying; and, on arriving at San Pedro, embarked on board the Vandalia.

The frigate Savannah soon hove in sight. Her forces under Capt. Mervin, and those from the Vandalia under Capt. Gillespie, started at once for the Pueblo. After a march of fifteen miles, they encamped for the night. But their slumbers were soon disturbed by a shot, which thundered its way into their midst. They seized their arms, but in the darkness of the night nothing could be seen, and nothing heard save the distant tramp of horses. At break of day they renewed their march, but had not proceeded far before they were attacked by a Californian force on horseback, drawing a four-pounder. Their enemy kept out of the range of their muskets, fled as fast as they charged, and, having gained a safe distance, wheeled and played upon them with their four-pounder, charged with grape. Capt. Mervin, finding himself unable to bring the enemy to a general engagement, and having five of his men killed, and a greater number wounded, ordered a retreat, and returned without further molestation on board the Savannah. His defeat lay in the fact that his men were all on foot, and without any artillery to protect them against the longer range of the piece which the enemy had brought into the field.

SATURDAY, OCT. 24. Col. Fremont having fallen in with the Vandalia, and ascertained from her that no horses could be procured for his men at Santa Barbara, decided on returning in the Sterling to this port. His arrival has been delayed by a succession of light head winds, and dead calms. When within fifty miles of the port, a boat was dispatched, which is just in. Several of his men came in her, who are to start in advance in quest of horses. They will probably have to go as far as the Sacramento, for all the horses in this immediate vicinity have been driven south by the insurgents. I have lost both of mine; but what are two to the hundred and fifty which were driven from the farm of one man. If misery loves company, I have a plenty of that sort of consolation. But the extent of a misfortune depends not so much on what is taken, as what is left. The last surviving child in a family is invested with the affections which encircled the whole.

SUNDAY, OCT. 25. With us the sound of the church-going bell has been exchanged for the roll of the drum. One of the moral miseries of war is the profanation of the Sabbath which it involves. There is something in military movements which seems to cut the conscience adrift from its moorings on this subject.

MONDAY, OCT. 26. We shall soon see what the genius of Com. Stockton is equal to in a great emergency. He will arrive at San Pedro without horses, or any means of procuring them. They are all driven off, or under men who seem as if born on the saddle. He will encounter on his march to los Angeles the same flying artillery which foiled the forces under Capt. Mervin. But he will have several well-mounted pieces; they must be drawn, however, by oxen over a deep sandy road. If the enemy comes within range, he will open and give them a volley of grape. In this way he will reach, recapture the place, and unfurl the stars and stripes. But how he will maintain himself—how he will procure provisions with the country around in the hands of a mounted enemy, remains to be seen. Military genius, however, asserts its fullest force in the greatest emergency. It is like the eagle exulting in peril, and throwing its strong pinions on the mountain storm.

TUESDAY, OCT. 27. The prize brig Malek Adhel, commanded by Lieut. W. B. Renshaw, arrived in port this afternoon in thirty days from Mazatlan. She brings the first intelligence of her own capture. The U. S. ship Warren, under Commander Hull, anchored off Mazatlan on the sixth ult., and found there the Malek Adhel, moored within a hundred and fifty yards of the mole, with sails unbent, and running rigging unrove. The next day her rudder was to have been unshipped, and she was to have been hauled up the creek for safe keeping. Commander Hull determined immediately to cut her out; hauled his ship in close to the bar, and sent sixty men in the launch and the three cutters, under charge of Lieuts. Radford and Renshaw, with orders to bring her out, or finding that impracticable, to burn her. On their approach, the officer in charge escaped to the shore: they boarded her without opposition, unmoored and warped her outside the bar. While doing this, about two hundred and fifty Mexican soldiers mustered on the mole; another party dragged a field-piece up the hill abreast of the brig, commanding her and the channel to the bar; but upon a second thought the governor determined to offer no resistance, alleging that the

Warren's guns would do more damage to the town than the brig was worth. The Malek Adhel, however, is a valuable prize, being a fine sailer and a good sea-boat; she was gallantly captured.

WEDNESDAY, OCT. 28. The Sterling is just in with Col. Fremont and his riflemen. They are in a half-starved condition, having been for several days on the very shortest commons. I never met with a more famished crew. The call for meat and bread roused up all the butchers and bakers in Monterey. What an energy there is in downright hunger!

THURSDAY, OCT. 29. Our Indian scouts, who came in yesterday, reported the discovery of a large band of Californians in the cover of the hills within the vicinity of Monterey. They probably purposed an attack on the town last night, as the garrison had been weakened by the absence of thirty men, who had left, under the command of Capt. Maddox, for San Juan. But the unexpected arrival of Col. Fremont frustrated their plans. We might have a battle with them were there horses here; but to attempt it on foot, would be like a man with a wooden leg chasing a hare.

Monterey has at present much the aspect of a military garrison. The streets are barricaded; a patrol is kept up night and day; no one is permitted to leave without a written passport, and no one allowed to enter without reporting himself to the police.

No one can be in the streets after nine without the countersign. Every thing, of course, in the shape of amusement is at an end; even ordinary business is in a great measure suspended. You hear only the roll of the drum at muster, and the toll of the bell over some one going to his last rest.

FRIDAY, OCT. 30. One of the guard in charge of Col. Fremont's horses, in the vicinity of the town, was approached, this afternoon, by two Californians on horseback, who inquired if he had seen a buck break from the woods near by. Having by this natural question laid suspicion, they entered into conversation on other topics, watched their opportunity, seized his rifle, shot him, and dashed off at full speed. The nefarious act produced a profound sensation in the camp. The shot, however, proves not mortal, so that the wounded man may yet have an opportunity of facing his foe in the field.

SATURDAY, OCT. 31. Enlistments are going on actively among the emigrants recently arrived on the banks of the Sacramento. The women and children are placed in the missions; the men take the rifle and start for the battle-field: such is their welcome to California. The Israelites entered the land of promise by arms, and established themselves by the force of their military prowess. But this is not quite the land of promise, nor are these Israelites who stream over the Rocky Mountains. But they are a sturdy band, whose enterprise will cover these fertile hills with golden harvests. They have pitched their tents by the water-courses, and those tents they will never strike.

They are enlisted into the service mainly through the activity of Capt. Montgomery, who commands the Portsmouth, and is military commandant of the northern department of California. His measures have been judicious, his action prompt, and he has rendered substantial service in supplying from the emigrations the sinews of war. Every American in California shows his entire stature; no one is lost in the crowd; no voice is drowned by a general clamor; every action tells. It is a blow which thunders by itself on the great anvil of time. It is another rock rolled into the foundations of a mighty empire.

SUNDAY, Nov. 1. An Indian was taken up by one of our scouts yesterday, who confessed that he was the bearer of a message from a Roman Catholic priest to a party that were arming themselves to join the insurrection. The message conveyed intelligence of the approach of our forces. The Indian was sent back to his master with the intelligence that if he attempted any further correspondence with the enemy, it would be at the peril of his life.

MONDAY, Nov. 2d. Our bay is full of the finest fish, and yet it is rare to meet one on the table. There is not a boat here in which one can safely trust himself a cable's length from land. And if there were, there would be no Californians to row it. Could they go to sea on their horses, and fish from their saddles, they would often be seen dashing through the surf; but to sit quietly in a boat and bob a line, is entirely too tame a business. Put a fish on land, and give him the speed of the buck, and he would have a dozen Californians and forty hounds on his trail.

TUESDAY, Nov. 3. A Californian in my employ asked me to-day to pay him a small sum in advance of his services, stating that he was on the eve of being married, and wanted this advance to enable him to put silver mountings on his saddle and bridle. Had he asked me for money with which to pay the priest, I should have understood the propriety of the request; but the connection between a silver star on the head-stall of his bridle and a marriage celebration, surpassed my dim comprehension. However, as there was a lady in the case, I let him have the money. But it seems it is the custom here, for the bridegroom to appear on his wedding-day upon a splendid horse, elegantly caparisoned. It is then the silver star shines out. The noble steed and glittering trappings divide with the bride the admiration of the crowd.

WEDNESDAY, Nov. 4. The Californians now in arms number twelve or fourteen hundred. They are from every section of the country. Their rallying point is los Angeles They have made a clean sweep of all the horses along the coast. Natives as well as fore'gners are left to get along on foot. This is not an easy task in a country where furlongs stretch into leagues. Of these twelve hundred in arms, probably not a hundred have a foot of land. They drift about like Arabs, stealing the horses on which they ride, and the cattle on which they subsist. They are ready to join any revolution, be its leaders whom they may. If the tide of fortune turns against them, they disband and scatter to the four winds. They never become martyrs in any cause. They are too numerous to be brought to punishment. No government has been strong enough to set them at defiance, or dispense with their venal aid. They have now, however, to deal with a power too sagacious to be cajoled, and too strong to be overawed. They will not be permitted to spring a revolution, and leave its consequences to others. The results will follow them into every forest and fastness. They have but one escape, and that leads into Mexico. Men of substance will regret their loss about as much as the Egyptians the disappearance of the locusts.

THURSDAY, Nov. 5. The second rain of the season fell last night. It came down copiously for several hours: multitudes forgot their dreams in listening to its grateful patter on the roof. The effects of the first shower, which fell a few days since, are visible in the landscape.

From the moist meadow to the withered hill,
Led by the breeze, the vivid verdure runs,
And swells and deepens to the cherished eye.

FRIDAY, Nov. 6. Two Californians were arrested to-day by one of my constables, charged with having broken open a shop and robbed it of many valuable articles. The burglary was committed several nights since, but no clue to the perpetrators could be obtained. By keeping silent on the subject, one of them had at last the imprudence to offer for sale one of the stolen articles, which was immediately identified, and led to the detection of both. Most of the property was found in their possession, and restored to its owners. The evidence of their guilt being conclusive, and there being no young lawyer here to pick a flaw in the indictment, or help them to an *alibi*, they were sentenced each to the public works for one year. The way of transgressors is hard.

SATURDAY, Nov. 7. In Monterey, as in all other towns that I have ever seen, crimes are perpetrated mostly at night. The Indian, however, steals when the temptation presents itself, and trusts luck for the consequences. And in truth if any being has a right to steal, it is the civilized Indian of California. All the mission lands, with their delicious orchards, waving grain, flocks and herds, were once his, and were stolen from him by the white man. He has only one mode of retaliating these wrongs. But Californians and foreigners, more wary, steal at night. It is as true here as elsewhere—

> "That when the searching eye of heaven is hid
> Behind the globe, and lights the lower world,
> Then thieves and robbers range abroad unseen,
> In murders, and in outrage, bloody here;
> But when, from under this terrestrial ball,
> He fires the proud tops of the eastern pines,
> And darts his light through every guilty hole,
> Then murders, treasons, and detested sins,
> The cloak of night being plucked from off their backs,
> Stand bare and naked, trembling at themselves."

SUNDAY, Nov. 8. There is not, except myself, a Protestant clergyman in California. If the tide of emigration continues, there will be thousands here without a spiritual teacher. Years must elapse before any can be trained here for the sacred office. The supply must come from abroad. The American churches must wake up to their duty on this subject. These emigrants are their children, and they should extend to them their most jealous care.

Thomas O. Larkin

CHAPTER VI.

SANTA BARBARA TAKEN.—LIEUT. TALBOT AND HIS TEN.—GAMBLING IN PRISON.—RECRUITS.—A FUNNY CULPRIT.—MOVEMENTS OF COM. STOCKTON.—BEAUTY AND THE GRAVE.—BATTLE ON THE SALINAS.—THE CAPTAIN'S DAUGHTER.—STOLEN PISTOLS.—INDIAN BEHIND A TREE.—NUPTIALS IN CALIFORNIA.

MONDAY, Nov. 9. The guard of ten, commanded by Lieut. T. Talbot, and posted at Santa Barbara to maintain the American flag, arrived here last evening. When the insurrection broke out at the south, they were summoned by some two hundred Californians to surrender. They contrived, however, under cover of night, to effect their escape. Their first halt was in a thicket, to which they were pursued by some fifty of the enemy on horseback. They waited, like lions in their lair, till the foe was within good rifle shot, and then discharged their pieces with terrific effect. The surviving assailants left their dead, and rushed back for reinforcements: but in the mean time, the hardy ten had pushed their way several leagues to the east, and gained a new ambush. An Indian might perhaps have trailed them; but their pursuers had not this wild sagacity. They rode here and there, penetrating every thicket, but the right one, and to prevent their escape at night, set fire to the woods. But one ravine, overhung with green pines, covered them with its mantling shadows; through this they made their noiseless escape.

To avoid the Californians, who were coming down in great numbers from the north to join their comrades in the south, the party of ten held their course to the east. They spent several days in attempting to find the pass which leads through the first range of the Californian mountains to the valley of the San Joaquin; but being unacquainted with the topography of the country, their utmost efforts were baffled. During this time they suffered greatly from hunger and thirst: the rugged steeps, among which they were straying, yielded neither streams nor game. At last, they fell in with a Cholo, the Arab of California, who kindly offered to conduct them to the mountain pass, and surrendered the use of his horse to carry their knapsacks and blankets. The pass was gained; but their hospitable guide still continued with them till they reached a tribe of Indians on the opposite side. Here he took leave of them, declining all compensation for his pains, and started back for his wild mountain home.

The Indians received them kindly, gave them their best acorns to eat, and their purest water to drink. These are the Indians who were brought before me a few months since, charged with an attempt to steal a drove of horses from Carmel. There being no positive proof of guilt, they were kindly treated, and instead of being threatened with dungeons and death, were dismissed with many beautiful presents. These presents they still preserved, and exhibited them with evident gratification and pride to their new guests.

Lieut. Talbot and party, guided by these faithful Indians, now held their course through the valley of the San Joaquin. Their progress was delayed by the sickness of one of their companions, whom they were obliged to carry on a litter. They subsisted entirely on the wild game which they killed. They were all on foot; and after travelling nearly five hundred miles in this manner, reached Monterey, where they were welcomed to the camp of Col. Fremont with three hearty cheers.

TUESDAY, Nov. 10. The merchant ship Euphemia arrived to-day from the Sandwich Islands, bringing the intelligence that the Columbus, bearing the broad pennant of Com. Biddle, had sailed from Honolulu for Valparaiso. We shall not then see that noble ship on this coast; she is bound homeward round the Cape. Her eight hundred men, with Com. Biddle at their head, would have been a great accession to our strength. It is not, however, a naval force of which we stand in greatest need. The war in California can never be decided from the deck. We want some five hundred horsemen, thoroughly accustomed to the saddle and the rifle, and a few pieces of flying-artillery. Without these we shall have constant attempts at revolution. They will invariably end in the defeat of those who get them up, but will involve private property and the public tranquillity.

WEDNESDAY, Nov. 11. I found one of our prisoners at work to-day without a shirt, and supposed at first that he was indulging in some whim; but ascertained, upon further inquiry, that he had gambled it away to a fellow-prisoner. They had no cards or dice, but had managed to substitute a bone, which they whirled into the air, and which decided the game by falling with this or that end into the ground. I made the winner give back the shirt, which he did with evident reluctance, as he had played his own against it, and would have been, had he lost, as naked as his neighbor. An Indian, and Californian too, will gamble to the skin of their teeth, and even part with their grinders were they articles of value to others. But a tooth is much like the principle of life, which avails no one save its owner.

THURSDAY, Nov. 12. Capt. Grigsby arrived to-day from Sonoma with thirty mounted riflemen and sixty horses, and joined Col. Fremont's encampment. Capt. Hastings is expected in every day from San José with sixty men, well mounted, and twice that number of horses. Every rider here, destined on an arduous expedition, must have one or two spare horses, especially at this season of the year, when no feed can be procured except the slender grass which has sprung up in the recent showers, and which contains very little sustenance. It is easier to procure provender for a thousand horses on a march in the United States than ten here. And yet the table-lands here are covered through the summer with wild oats,

But where are the reapers ? On horseback, galloping about and carousing at this rancho and that. Their sickles are the rein, their sheaves a pack of cards, their flails a guitar.

> "No cocks do them to rustic labor call,
> From village on to village sounding clear;
> To tardy swain no shrill-voiced matron's squall,
> Nor hammer's thump disturbs the vacant ear."

FRIDAY, Nov. 13. Two fellows of Mexican origin were brought before me to-day, charged with breaking open the money-chest of the eating-house where they had transiently stopped, and taking from it about five hundred dollars. The owner having immediate occasion to go to his chest, dicovered his loss, and suspected at once the persons concerned in it. They were apprehended, and soon after the money was found in the back yard, where it had been hastily buried after having been tied up in a handkerchief, which was identified as the neck-cloth of one of the accused. One discovery led to another, till the evidences of guilt, involving both, were fully established.

One of them then said there was no use in trying to get rid of the business any longer, and he would now tell the whole story straight as an arrow. He said that he and Antonio had talked over the matter the night before, and that he then attempted to reach the chest, but that the person in whose room it lay, and who had been asleep, suddenly stopped snoring, and getting alarmed he ran down stairs. But this morning, while Antonio was entertaining the rest, and treating them to cocktails, he slipped up to the chamber, broke the lock, and filled his pockets with the coin. He had no time, he said, to pick out the gold, which would have been a great convenience, but scraped up silver and gold as they came, leaving in the chest about as much as he took. It was very vexatious, he said, to leave so much, but his pockets would hold no more: he was really afraid they would fetch away with what they had got. But he buoyed them up with his hands, reached the back yard, where he delivered the money over to Antonio, who received it in his handkerchief and buried it; but buried it in exactly the wrong spot, for he went off into a corner instead of sinking it where everybody must step over it.

He told this story with a countenance which played between a tragic and comic expression. Antonio, who had been both diverted and alarmed by the narrative of his accomplice, when it came his turn to speak, said his companion was the funniest fellow alive; he believed he would joke on the scaffold, if he could shake a kink out of the rope, and get breathing time for it. They were both a strange compound of wit and villany. They were sentenced to the public works for three years.

SATURDAY, Nov. 14. The Savannah arrived here to-day from the leeward, and reports the Congress on her way to San Diego, where she had gone to reenforce the garrison. This important post had been recaptured by the Americans, under the command of Capt. Merrit, an emigrant officer of undaunted courage. He had been obliged to evacuate it a few weeks before, and was fortunate in being able to get his men on board a whale ship lying in the offing at the time. But a portion of the force opposed to him having been withdrawn to support the Mexican flag at los Angeles, he landed again in the night, and took the garrison by surprise. This being the most southern post in California, Com. Stockton deemed it of the first importance to make its possession secure. To effect this object, he was obliged to postpone his purpose of recapturing at once the capital of the province. The best way to fight the Californians is to hem them in. They never turn upon you as lions at bay. The possibility of an escape is an element in their courage. They never borrow resolution from despair. They are so accustomed to range at freedom, to make their homes wherever adventure or caprice may carry them, that the idea of being cooped up to one place has almost as much privation and misery in it as the slave-ship inflicts upon its captives.

> They still might deem their scope too pent,
> Though each had leave to pitch his tent
> Where'er his wildest wish might urge,
> Within creation's utmost verge.

SUNDAY, Nov. 15. One of the most beautiful ladies in Monterey has this day been consigned to the silent grave. She was in the bloom of life, and visions of happiness threw their enchantments along the vista of her future years. She had all that wealth and beauty can bestow. Her personal charms were rivalled only by those of her mind. Her heart trembled through every fibre of her frame.

> " Whene'er with soft serenity she smiled,
>   Or caught the orient blush of quick surprise,
> How sweetly mutable, how brightly wild,
>   The liquid lustre darted from her eyes!
> Each look, each motion, waked a new-born grace,
>   That o'er her form a transient glory cast:
> Some lovelier wonder soon usurped the place,
>   Chased by a charm still lovelier than the last."

But she is gone! she has left us like the bird which carolled in the morn, and departed upon its slanting ray. But her virtues survive in a brighter sphere; her beauty is stamped with immortality; her hand strikes a harp that will pour its melodies when the groves and streams of earth are silent.

Monday, Nov. 16. A Delaware Indian, quite out of breath, entered Col. Fremont's camp this morning with the intelligence that an irregular engagement took place last evening between a party of forty Americans, and a hundred and fifty Californians, on the Salinas river, about fifteen miles from Monterey. The Americans were coming down from San Juan, and had with them three hundred fresh horses which they had brought from the Sacramento. The intelligence of their approach had reached the Californians, who had mustered all their force in this quarter, more for the purpose of capturing the horses than their riders. But the Americans, who were sixty strong, anticipating the possibility of an attack in crossing the river, left their horses, except those they rode, in the rear with twenty of their number, while forty came ahead to engage the Californians. They were surprised at their numbers, but rushed at once into the encounter. Capt. Foster was killed in the first charge, and Capt. Burrows, who was wounded in the first, fell in leading the second. Two American privates were killed, and a number of Californians. The encounter took place near sunset, and the Americans remained in possession of the ground.

The Delaware Indian, when the firing had slackened, left the field to bring the intelligence to Col. Fremont; but having to turn the enemy's line, he was attacked by three Californians—one of whom he shot with his rifle, another he killed with his tomahawk, and the third fled. His horse broke down before he got in, and he ran the rest of the way on foot. He reports that Thomas O. Larkin, Esq., the American consul, had been captured the night before, while at a rancho between this and San Juan. He had left Monterey to visit a sick child at San Francisco, and stopped for the night, when he was suddenly pounced upon: nor wife nor child will in any probability see him soon again. He will be closely guarded; his life will be considered good for that of several prominent Californian officers who have broken their parol; and not unlikely some half-dozen may, in the event of disaster, be redeemed through his liberation.

TUESDAY, Nov. 17. Col. Fremont, with his three hundred riflemen, took his departure from Monterey this morning. They presented a very formidable line as they wound around the bay and disappeared in the shadows of the hills.

> Spur on my men; the bugle peals
> Its last and stern command,—
> A charge! a charge!—an ocean burst
> Upon a stormy strand.

The artillery is under the command of Capt. McLain, an officer of much private worth and professional merit. He has at present two beautiful brass-pieces, well mounted, and will have two more of the same description on leaving San Juan. With these he will be able to do good execution. Nothing alarms the Californians so much as a piece of flying-artillery. They had rather see the very Evil One come scraggling over the hills.

WEDNESDAY, Nov. 18. The horses which the Californians were endeavoring to reach in their rencounter on the river, were all preserved. Their loss would have been irretrievable in this campaign. The twenty men with whom they were left, declared they would perish to a man sooner than give them up. Rash as this resolution may seem, it would, had the emergency occurred, have been terribly realized. The American engaged in this war puts his life on the die. He must prevail or perish. If there shall be a general engagement between the forces now in the field, it will be one of the most frightful on record. The Americans are outnumbered three to one,—still they are determined to hazard the issue; and would, probably, were the odds much greater. As horsemen, the Californians excel them; but they are greatly their superiors in the use of the rifle and in maneuvering artillery. And these, after all, are the weapons and engines that must decide a hot engagement. Neither party has any veteran cuirassiers to hew their way to triumph through the cloven crests of the foe. The most terrific encounters on the field of Waterloo were between those who wielded the glaive. With them, at least,

"An earthquake might have passed unheededly away."

THURSDAY, Nov. 19. How strangely the lights and shadows of life are blended! As I passed this evening the house of Capt. de la T——, a light strain of music came floating out from the corridor upon the silent air. It was the daughter of the captain whose hand swept the guitar which accompanied the modulations of her melodious voice. Her father and her uncle are both in the ranks of the Californians, leading a forlorn hope, after having broken their parol of honor, and forfeited their lives. And yet she is gay as if her father were only out hunting the gazelle. Just list the numbers as they break from her thoughtless heart :—

> Fly not yet, 'tis just the hour
> When pleasure, like the midnight flower,
> That scorns the eye of vulgar light,
> Begins to bloom for sons of night,
> And maids who love the moon!

And yet that moon before it wanes may gleam upon her father's grave. But she knows it not. She thinks this war will end as other Californian wars— in smoke. But it is a tempest-cloud charged with bolted thunder.

FRIDAY, Nov. 20. A German complained to me this morning that one of the volunteers, a countryman of his, under Col. Fremont, had stolen from him a pair of valuable pistols. He strongly suspected the person who had taken them. I sent for him; he confessed the act, delivered up the pistols, and begged me, as this was his first offence, not to expose him. He was a youth of eighteen or so, slightly built, and with a fair and remarkably ingenuous countenance. I told him he must take heed, as one offence often paves the way to another; but as he was in the campaign, and might soon be on the field of peril and death, his error should rest in silence with his own conscience. The tears stood in his eyes.

SATURDAY, Nov. 21. Capt. Foster, it appears, was not shot in the heat of the engagement on the river. He had rushed forward in advance to reconnoiter, and was suddenly surrounded from an ambush, and fell, bravely fighting to the last. A Delaware Indian, who was hastening to his rescue, finding himself hot-pressed, jumped from his horse behind a tree, from which he shot three of his antagonists, and then effected his escape. His living breastwork now shows in its scathed rind, how well it served him. It looks as if the auger-worm had bored there for an age.

There is something about a tree, with an Indian behind it, armed with a rifle, pointing this way and that, which awkwardly tests a man's nerves. You seem to be shooting at the muzzle of his rifle instead of him; and that is not the worst of it, he is all the while shooting at you. If partial concealment lends a charm to beauty, it also lends terror to an Indian. We think of the brake as much as the serpent coiled in its shadows. Were lightning to fall without thunder, people would put conductors on their bean-poles; and yet the blazing bolt strikes and shivers while the lagging thunder is yet unheard.

SUNDAY, Nov. 22. As soon as it will be prudent to withdraw our men from their posts on the Sabbath, I intend to propose a religious service. We shall soon be able to gather fifty or more. Every house here has a ball-room where the gay may dance, and a Madonna to whom the afflicted may kneel;

but none have a chapel; and if they had, the forms of Protestant worship would be held a profanation. There is only one way to get to heaven here, and that is through the absolving power of the Papal See. Every other path leads to purgatorial pangs and penal fire.

MONDAY, Nov. 23. It is said the Californians are born on horseback; it may also be said they are married on horseback. The day the marriage contract is agreed on between the parties, the bridegroom's first care is to buy or borrow the best horse to be found in his vicinity. At the same time he has to get, by one of these means, a silver-mounted bridle, and a saddle with embroidered housings. This saddle must have, also, at its stern, a bridal pillion, with broad aprons flowing down the flanks of the horse. These aprons are also embroidered with silk of different colors, and with gold and silver thread. Around the margin runs a string of little steel plates, alternated with slight pendants of the same metal. These, as the horse moves, jingle like a thousand mimic bells.

The bride, also, comes in for her share in these nuptial preparations. The bridegroom must present her with at least six entire changes of raiment, nor forget, through any sentiment of delicacy, even the chemise. Such an oversight might frustrate all his hopes; as it would be construed into a personal indifference,—the last kind of indifference which a

California lady will forgive. He therefore hunts this article with as much solicitude as the Peri the gift that was to unlock Paradise. Having found six which are neither too full nor two slender, he packs them in rose-leaves which seem to flutter like his own heart, and sends them to the lady as his last bridal present. She might naturally expect him to come next.

The wedding-day having arrived, the two fine horses, procured for the occasion, are led to the door, saddled, bridled, and pillioned. The bridegroom takes up before him the godmother, and the godfather the bride, and thus they gallop away to church. The priest, in his richest robes, receives them at the altar, where they kneel, partake of the sacrament, and are married. This over, they start on their return,—but now the gentlemen change partners. The bridegroom, still on the pillion, takes up before him his bride. With his right arm he steadies her on the saddle, and in his left hand holds the reins. They return to the house of the parents of the bride, where they are generally received with a discharge of musketry. Two persons, stationed at some convenient place, now rush out and seize him by his legs, and, before he has time to dismount, deprive him of his spurs, which he is obliged to redeem with a bottle of brandy.

The married couple then enter the house, where the near relatives are all waiting in tears to receive them. They kneel down before the parents of the lady, and crave a blessing, which is bestowed with patriarchal solemnity. On rising, the bridegroom makes a signal for the guests to come in, and another for the guitar and harp to strike up. Then commences the dancing, which continues often for three days, with only brief intervals for refreshment, but none for slumber: the wedded pair must be on their feet; their dilemma furnishes food for good-humored gibes and merriment. Thus commences married life in California. This stream, it is to be hoped, is much smoother than its fount.

TUESDAY, Nov. 24. Monterey has been for the last two days remarkably quiet. The excitement occasioned by the battle on the Salinas has sunk into a dead calm. They who fell have received Christian burial; and they who survived have departed, some to find graves elsewhere. The great tragedy of life here is so filled with incident that it requires no stage effect It is the visionary sword which eluded the grasp of Macbeth, turned into flashing steel.

WEDNESDAY, Nov. 25. A Californian in trouble, often disregards the suggestions of national pride and personal resentment, and seeks succor where it can best be had. One of them who had been dangerously wounded in the late engagement, came into Monterey this morning, and applied to our surgeon to have the ball extracted from his hip. He seemed to think that as he had been disabled by one American, it was only right and proper he should be restored by another. He will then probably be off to fight us again. Nor does this in him argue a want of gratitude. He seeks the field to encounter his foes, much on the same principle that you do the wood to hunt wild game. You level your rifle at the hawk, not because he has injured you, but partly to exercise your skill, and partly because he is a saucy fellow, screeching about and frightening the other birds. I never yet saw the little king-bird chase a hawk, or the sword-fish pursue a whale, without a sentiment of delight. Neither have harmed me; but I hate all tyrants, whether they are on wings, fins, or legs.

THURSDAY, Nov. 26. Some of the shopkeepers here have been so long in the habit of smuggling under the former high rate of duties, that now they hardly know how to give up the trick, though there is very little motive for pursuing it. I caught a Frenchman to-day endeavoring to evade the municipal duty on rum. He had a hundred subterfuges, and flew from one to another, like a frightened cat-bird in the bush. His words fell so thick and fast that they quite covered up his falsehoods; the leaves of a wind-shaken tree in autumn conceal the nuts which fall with them to the ground. It is idle to expect honesty in a man who resorts to it only in the failure of his craft and cunning. His integrity is like the religion of some sailors—breaking out in shipwreck.

CHAPTER VII.

SAN JOSÉ GARRISONED.—A CALIFORNIA RAIN.—ESCAPE OF CONVICTS.—SHOOTING EDWARDS.—TWO WASHERWOMEN.—DEATH OF MR. SARGENT.—INDIAN HENS.—HUNTING CURLEW.—THE CALIFORNIA HORSE.—AN OLD EMIGRANT.—THE GRIZZLY BEAR.

FRIDAY, Nov. 27. The prize brig Julia, Lieut. Selden commanding, arrived here to-day from San Francisco. She left there the Savannah and Warren. Fifty of the Savannah's men had been sent by Capt. Mervin to San José, under command of Lieut. Pinkney, where they will form a military post, of sufficient strength, it is believed, to repel any hostile attacks, and maintain the flag. The northern half of California is now pretty safe; the ranchos may suffer from marauding parties of the enemy, and some acts of violence be committed, but no important post can be wrenched from our possession. In the south we hold San Diego, and have an enemy in the field at los Angeles. They will probably break covert at two or three different points; some will fly for Mexico, and some for the sheltered coves of the San Joaquin. Let those catch them who can; I would as soon track a chamois among the clefts and pinnacles of the Alps.

SATURDAY, Nov. 28. It is now near the close of

that month which in other climes is often one of the most unpleasant in the year; but here it has been one of unrivalled brilliancy. The sky has been almost without a cloud, the winds have slept, and the soft air has lain on the landscape like a golden slumber. Such is the tranquil beauty in which the vernal year here sinks to repose.

> "Ah! 'twere a lot too bless'd,
> Forever in thy color'd shades to stray;
> Amid the kisses of the soft southwest
>   To rove and dream for aye;
>
> And leave the vain low strife
> That makes men mad; the tug for wealth and power,
> The passions and the cares that wither life,
>   And waste its little hour."
>   BRYANT.

SUNDAY, Nov. 29. Two Californians called upon me to-day, to decide a difficulty which had arisen between them in some money transactions. I told them to call on some week-day—that I attended to no business matters on the Sabbath. They apologized for interfering with my *recreations;* I told them I had no recreations to be disturbed, but I would not open my office for business on the Sabbath. Had I told them I was going to a cock-fight, their only wonder would have been that they had not heard of the sport; and both would have forgotten their business in hunting their cash for the ring. Such is the moral obtuseness which a perversion of the Sabbath induces. The heart on which the dews of this sacred morn have never melted, will be desolate of moral verdure; though here and there a leaf may spring like flowers in the cleft of a rock.

Monday, Nov. 30. We have had at last a true specimen of California showers. The wind blew a gale from the south. Cloud on cloud was piled into the zenith, till the whole dome of heaven was filled with substantial darkness. The earth lay in an eclipse. A few heavy rolls of thunder, and the rain fell in torrents; it lasted twelve hours. Every roof and frowning cliff became a cascade. Down each ravine rolled an exulting tide. The aquatic bird dashed onward in its foam to the sea. Suddenly the wind veered into the west, and in a few moments the sky was without a cloud. Field and forest flashed out in the splendors of the sun; and on the soft wind came gushes of music from the wild-wood. Instead of bleak November, you would have said:

> " Fairer and brighter spreads the reign of May;
> The tresses of the woods
> With the light dallying of the west wind play·
> And the full briming floods,
> As gladly to their goal they run,
> Hail the returning sun."
>
> PERCIVAL.

Tuesday, Dec. 1. I was startled from my slumbers last night by the report of a musket under my window; and, seizing my rifle, rushed to the door, but could perceive no one near, and only heard, in the darkness, the sound of retreating footsteps. The mystery was soon explained: the convicts had escaped from prison, and the sentry, posted near my residence, had fired upon them as they rushed past. Several of the guard went immediately in pursuit, and succeeded in apprehending two; but seven others, favored by the darkness and storm of the night, had cleared the town.

It appeared, on investigation, that the sentry, posted at the prison, had stolen the keys from the guard-room, where they were kept, unlocked the outer and inner doors, and then run himself with the convicts. Another sentry, by a preconcerted plan, had also joined them. Only one prisoner remained in the apartment which had been unlocked. When asked by me why *he* did not run, he said he would not be seen running from Tophet in such company. This was the funny fellow who stole the money. One of those who escaped, was a great overgrown Californian—a monstrous mass of flesh and bone. He had been shot in the leg in a previous fray, and always affected the cripple, hobbling about on huge crutches, which fairly bent under him. But last night, when his pursuers were close on his trail, he bounded forward like a rabbit. Crutches, and all occasion for them, had been left behind. You would have thought some shape of air were flitting before you, but for the heavy puffs which heaved, at brief intervals, from his laboring trunk. An innocent man escaping from violence has often a hard time of it, but a felon escaping from justice much harder; his guilty conscience will long keep the pursuer at his heels.

WEDNESDAY, DEC. 2. A party, well mounted and armed, started this morning in pursuit of the convicts. They overtook one of them and the two sentries about twenty miles distant. The sentries still had their arms, which they surrendered, and delivered themselves up without resistance. The convict was shot down through the impetuosity of one of the party. There is a degree of ferocity in shooting down an unarmed man at which humanity revolts. We can hardly find an apology for it, even in the brutal instincts of the savage. The fate of the two sentries concerned in liberating the prisoners whom they were posted to guard, is uncertain. If tried by a court-martial, their sentence will be death; if delivered over to the civil authority, they will be sentenced to the public works for a long term of years.

THURSDAY, DEC. 3. The convict Edwards, found with the two sentries, and who had been shot after he had surrendered, was left in a dying condition on the public road. My constable left this morning to find him, but was unable to cross the Salinas river on account of the freshet, and its extreme rapidity. His horse got frightened and refused to swim him over. He fastened him on this side, and, divesting himself of his hat, shoes, and coat, plunged in; but the current, after sweeping him down a mile or more, landed him on the same side from which he had started.

He is a man of great humanity as well as courage and resolution, and it was not with his consent that Edwards was left at night-fall, wounded and dying, exposed to a pitiless storm, and to be devoured by wild beasts. It was inhuman to leave him in this condition, when he might have been brought in, or taken to some house in the neighborhood. Those in fault, now that the wrong has been done, and is irretrievable, would gladly veil it from the public eye. There is a tongue in cruelty, which those who inflict it can never silence. It will speak out and awaken pangs in the most callous conscience. If we have no mercy on others, how can we expect it for ourselves in that day when we most need it ?

" Teach me to feel another's woe,
To hide the faults I see ;
The mercy I to others show,
That mercy show to me."

FRIDAY, DEC. 4. The moment a child is born on a farm in California, and the nurse has had time to dress it, it is given to a man on horseback, who, with its future godfather and godmother, ride post-haste with it to some mission, and present it to a priest for baptism. This ceremony concluded, the party, full of glee, start on their return ; and the little newcomer may now, perhaps, rest a week or two before he starts on another excursion ; but after that, hardly a day will elapse without his being on horseback. He literally rides from his cradle to his grave. Thus, by the time a boy is ten or twelve years of age, he becomes an expert rider, is devoted to the saddle, and looks upon pedestrial motion as a contemptible way of getting through the world. He would sooner travel a hundred miles on horseback than ten on foot, and connect less fatigue and hardship with the result. Most of his labors, too, are on the saddle. He has a farm of twenty or thirty miles to ride over; vast wheat-fields to survey, and, perhaps, ten thousand head of cattle to keep from straying. He would have but little time for repose if he went by steam.

SATURDAY, DEC. 5. Of all the women I have had to deal with here the washer-women are the most unmanageable. Two of them entered my office to-day as full of fight as the feline antagonists of Kilkenny. It seems they had been out washing in one of the little pools created by the recent showers, when one had taken that part of the margin previously occupied by the other. War offensive and defensive immediately commenced. One drew a knife, which had a blade two mortal inches in length, and the other a sharp ivory bodkin. But what their weapons wanted in terror and strength their ungentle anger supplied.

At last one cried out, "the alcalde;" the other echoed it, and so they both rushed down to the office to have their difficulties settled. Both of course commenced talking at the same time; and their stories ran together like two conflicting rivulets forced into the same channel. There was plenty of tumult and bubble. When these had a little subsided, I began cautiously to angle for the truth—a difficult trout to catch in such waters. But one darter after another was captured, till I had enough to form some opinion of those that had escaped. These we discussed till bitter feeling, like biting hunger, became appeased. The rest was very easily settled. Both went away declaring either margin of the pool good enough, and each urging on the other the first choice.

> How gentle is forgiveness! and how sweet
> To feel the severed heart flow back again
> To one we loved, estranged by hasty words!

SUNDAY, DEC. 6. Mr. Sargent, who came out in the Congress in the capacity of clerk to the purser, and who had been left here several weeks since for the restoration of his mind and health, was missed from his quarters on Tuesday last. He has been laboring for some time under mental aberrations which wear a reasoning show, and which alarm only the close observer. His amiable disposition and exemplary life exempted him from all reproach, and have excited a general sympathy and concern for his uncertain fate. He was last seen winding his way through the forest which skirts Monterey, towards a ledge of rocks which overhangs the boiling surf of the bay. I have traversed the beach for miles, and watched each swell as it rolled in, to see if it bore on its crest aught like a human form. But nothing came to the shore or eddied in the surge, to resolve mystery and give a painful certainty to doubt. The sea itself is an awful mystery, and becomes doubly so when the fate of one we loved is locked in the tongueless silence of its unfathomed depths.

> The waves tell not the fate of those
> On whom their hasty waters close;
> But deeper still their secrets spread,
> That travel with their drifting dead.

MONDAY, DEC. 7. The simplest article for the table is often beyond the reach of your money here. I have found it so difficult to procure a few eggs, when required, that I have at last gone to keeping hens. I purchased six of an Indian woman for six dollars, and a rooster for fifty cents. On asking the woman why she charged only half price for the rooster, she replied that the fellow laid no eggs, and as for his crowing that did nobody any good. Sounder reasons than these could not be furnished in a much higher place than a hencoop. The habits of these hens are a little singular. They are perfectly tame, and are as much at home in the kitchen as the cook. They never trouble themselves much about a nest, but deposite their eggs where they find it most convenient; one takes the tea-tray, another the ironing-table, a third the oven, and there is one that always gets into the cradle. She is not at all disturbed by the tossing of the little fellow on whose premises she is obtruding. Neither she nor any of her feathered sisters cackle when they leave the nest. They don't seem to think that any thing worth making an ado about has come to pass. The rooster, it is true, perks up a little, and perhaps feels a feather taller. But this is the vanity of his sex. There are a great many who crow over what others have done.

TUESDAY, DEC. 8. The banditti, that have hovered for some weeks past in the vicinity of Monterey, have made it unsafe to venture out on our hunting excursions, unless in sufficient numbers to repel an attack. But last evening, the want of exercise, and of something to relieve the endless monotony of beef on the table, induced me forth. I took my boy, and put into his hands one of Colt's revolving rifles, and took myself the fowling-piece. We had hardly got a mile from town, when two horsemen broke from the covert of the woods, and dashed down in our direction. I had but little more than time to exchange pieces with my boy, when they were within rifle-shot. Their garb showed them to be Californians. My heart beat a great deal louder than usual. But they suddenly wheeled, and soon disappeared behind one of the hills which look out on the bay. They had no arms, except pistols at the saddle-bow. Whether they had hostile intentions, I know not: their movements had very much that appearance; and I must say I never before experienced so fully those feelings men describe in going into battle. They are not fear so much as an intensity of excitement, which seems as if it would suffocate life: it is dispelled with the first gun. I had once occasion to repel an exasperated Spaniard with a pistol, and though I had anticipated his attack, was prepared for it, and believed that the aim of the pistol would make him sheath his knife; still there was for a moment an intensity of feeling that would, if prolonged, destroy one. We continued our hunting, but changed our ground to the vicinity of the sea, and brought home a dozen curlew, which almost rival in flavor the canvas-back duck.

WEDNESDAY, DEC. 9. The horses of California are of a hardy nature; and it is well for them that they are, considering the inhuman manner in which they are generally treated by the natives. If a man wants to ride forty or fifty miles from his residence, he mounts his horse, and spurs off upon the gallop On arriving at the place of his destination, he ties him to a post, where he stands two or three days, waiting for his master. During this time he is not once fed, and is quite fortunate if he gets a swallow of water. At last, his rider comes, mounts him, and he takes him back again at the same free and easy gait with which he first started. This, of course, is confined to the summer season, when the grass has the most substance and nutriment: still it is almost incredible. Besides the weight of his heavy rider, tne horse generally carries fifty or sixty pounds in the gear of his saddle, and double this in a soaking rain. It requires two large tanned ox hides to fit out a Californian saddle; then add to this, the wooden stirrups, three inches thick, the saddle-tree, with its stout iron rings and buckles, a pair of goat-skins across the pommel, holsters and pistols, and spurs at the heels of the rider, weighing from four to six pounds, and we have some idea of what a Californian horse has to carry. Still he is cheerful and spirited, and never flags till nature sinks with exhaustion. A man who can abuse such an animal, ought to be bitted and saddled himself.

THURSDAY, DEC. 10. The old as well as the young are coming over the mountains. I had an emigrant to dine with me to-day, who has recently arrived, and who is seventy-six years of age. His locks are as free of gray hairs as those of a child, and his eye still flashes with the fires of youth. He is among the volunteers, and you may see him every day on a spirited horse, with a rifle at his saddle-bow. He has four sons with Col. Fremont. They enlisted before they had time to unpack their saddles, and have with them the remnants of the biscuit and cheese which they brought from the United States. I asked the old man what could induce him at his age to come to California. He said his children were coming, and so he determined to come too. I asked him if he had no compunction in taking up arms against the inhabitants the moment of his arrival. He said he had Scripture example for it. The Israelites took the promised land of the East by arms, and the Americans must take the promised land of the West in the same way. I told him that would do, if he could show the same high commission. But I find this kind of parallel running in the imagination of all the emigrants. They seem to look upon this beautiful land as their own Canaan, and the motley race around them as the Hittites, the Hivites, and Jebusites, whom they are to drive out. But they have gone at it with other weapons than ram's horns, except as powder-flasks.

Friday, Dec. 11. The grizzly bear is the most formidable and ferocious animal in California; and yet, with all this ferocity of disposition, rarely attacks a man unless surprised or molested. The fellow never lies in wait for his victim. If the hunter invades his retreat or disputes his path he will fight, but otherwise contents himself with the immunity which he finds in the wildness of his home and the savage grandeur of his nature. It is never safe to attack him with one rifle; for if you fail to hit him in a vital part, he is on you in the twinkling of an eye. Your only possibility of escape is up a near tree, too slender for his giant grasp; and then there is something extremely awkward in being on the top of a tree with such a savage monster at its root. How long he will remain there you cannot tell; it may be a day, and it may be a week. Your antagonist is too shrewd to hand you up your rifle, or let you come down to get it. You are his prisoner, more safely lodged than in a dungeon, and he will set you at liberty when it suits him. He sleeps not himself at his post; day and night his great flashing eyes are fastened upon you. The lyre of Orpheus may have lulled to sleep the sentinel of Hades, but its magic tones have never charmed to slumber the sentinel of the California forest.

The full-grown California bear measures from eight to ten feet in length, and four or five in girth. His strength is tremendous, his embrace death. Had the priest of Apollo fallen into his folds, he would have perished without any of those protracted agonies which the sympathetic muse has wailed round the world. Nature has thrown over him a coat of mail, soft indeed, but impervious to the storm and the arrow of the Indian. The fur, which is of a dark brown color, is nearly a span long, and when the animal is enraged each particular hair stands on end. His food in the summer is chiefly berries, but he will now and then, on some of his feast days, slaughter a bullock. In winter he lives on acorns, which abound in these forests. He is an excellent climber, and will ascend a large oak with the rapidity of a tar up the shrouds of his ship. In procuring his acorns, when on the tree, he does not manifest his usual cunning. Instead of threshing them down like the Indian, he selects a well-stocked limb, throws himself upon its extremity, and there hangs swinging and jerking till the limb gives way, and down they come, branch, acorns, and bear together. On these acorns he becomes extremely fat, yielding ten or fifteen gallons of oil, which is said to be sufficiently pungent and nutritive as a tonic to tuft a statue's marble head.

The she bear has one peculiarity that must puzzle even the philosophical inquirer. As soon as she discovers herself with young, she ceases to roam the forest, and modestly retires from the presence of others, to some secluded grotto. There she remains, while her male companion, with a consideration that does honor to his sex, brings her food. She reappears at length with her twin cubs, and woe to the luckless wight who should attempt to injure or molest them. They are guarded by an affection and ferocity with which it would be madness to trifle. For them she hunts the berries, and dislodges the acorns. Her maternal care is a beautiful trait in her savage nature, and

"Shines like a good deed in a naughty world."

J. C. Frémont

CHAPTER VIII.

LITTLE ADELAIDA.—COL. FREMONT'S BATALLION.—SANTIAGO IN LOVE.—SENTIMENTS OF AN OLD CALIFORNIAN.—THE PRIZE JULIA.—FANDANGO.—WINTER CLIMATE.—PATRON SAINT OF CALIFORNIA.—HABITS OF THE NATIVES.—INSURRECTION IN THE NORTH.—DRAMA IN A CHURCH.—POSITION OF COM. STOCKTON.

SATURDAY, DEC. 12. Our paper, the only one published in California, made its hebdomadal appearance again to-day. It is a little fellow, but is half filled or more with original matter. A paper is much like an infant; the smaller it is, the more anxious the attentions which it requires. My partner promised to stick by me, but has been the greater part of the time since its commencement on the bay of San Francisco. He went there to locate a city, but if rumor speaks truly, has gone off in quest of his Aphrodite before he builds her shrine. I suppose he thinks there is but little use in a cage without a bird, but there is still less in a bird without a cage. Birds, however, always pair before they rear their nests. So that my partner is after all in nature's great line, however wide it may run from the columns of the Californian.

SUNDAY, DEC. 13. I miss very much the light step and laughing eye of my little friend Adelaida, the infant daughter of our consul, Mr. Larkin. She was a sweet child, and beguiled with her gladness, many a moment that had else passed less lightly. But a change came over her brightness, an eclipse whose shadow passes not. We watched its dim veil, and idly dreamed it might still pass, when its faint, inwoven light was lost in spreading darkness. She passed away like a bird from its clouded bower ; and though her flight lay over dark waters, she now sings in the purple land of the blest. There no shadows fall, and death has no trophies. One eternal spring, with its sparkling founts and fragrant blossoms, reigns through the vernal year. The soft airs as they stir, wake the strings of invisible lyres ; and the tender leaves whisper in music. There walk the pure ; there survive the meek who wept with us here. They wait to welcome our flight to their joys and sinless repose. O that I had wings like the dove that I might fly away and be at rest!

MONDAY, DEC. 14. It is now two weeks since Col. Fremont broke up his encampment in the vicinity of San Juan, and commenced his march south. His progress has been retarded by a succession of heavy rains, and it is feared that some of the rivers which he must cross, swollen by torrents from the mountains, have been rendered impassable. His horses may perhaps swim them, but his artillery and ammunition must be floated over on rafts. The construction of these, especially where the material is not at hand, will occasion long and impatient detentions. The condition of the roads, soaked as they are with rain, will still further delay his progress; still, with all these drawbacks, we believe he will reach his destination.

He moves upon no idle or vague object. The great body of the Californians now in arms are at the capital of the southern department, waiting his hostile arrival. They intend to give him battle, and redeem, if possible, some of the laurels which they lost in their precipitate retreat before Com. Stockton. Their forces outnumber his two or three to one; they excel them as horsemen, but fall far short of them in the dexterous use of the rifle. They want that coolness, deliberation, self-reliance, and resolute firmness which appertain to the character of the Americans. We wait the issue of the encounter with a profound interest. Com. Stockton may, perhaps, march from San Pedro and capture los Angeles, as he has done once before; but with the country around in the possession of the enemy, and the cattle driven off upon distant plains, and the wheat and flour removed into the gorges of the mountains, he could not subsist his forces. So at least it would seem; but we shall see. It was the prospect of famine that drove Napoleon from Moscow.

WEDNESDAY, DEC. 16. An old Californian, much respected for his intelligence and patriotic virtues, sent, a few days since, a communication to our paper, written in good, vigorous Castilian, and which will find an echo in the heart of all the considerate portion of the community. He opens his article in these words:—

"The political aspirants in California have inflicted upon her since 1836, only a continued succession of evils. They have seized all the national property and all the missions, as though they were their own patrimony. These riches they have distributed with a prodigal hand among their satellites; a multitude of officers were created, for whom there was no employment; and military grades established more abundantly than in Paraguay, though with this difference in the result. Doctor Francia, when he died, left eight millions of dollars in the public coffers; while the military chieftains in this country, at the close of their brief career, have left the country overwhelmed in debt. And now, to gratify their infatuated ambition, and secure further plunder, have again hoisted the Mexican flag, which they have long hated and cursed. The rash step taken by these men at the town of the Angeles has only compromised their brethren, and ruined many families. The wealth of this country consists in cattle and agriculture; to maintain the one and carry on the other, horses are indispensable; but these frantic men have driven off the horses and cattle to meet the exigencies of war. They have given their afflicted country her death-stroke, merely because they are not permitted to retain those offices which they are not capable of filling. And such outrageous ambition is called by them, love of country! If there ever existed a spark of patriotism in their hearts, they would never have attempted the slightest revolutionary act. They would have seen and felt that it could end only in general disaster and ruin."

Thus writes an old Californian, with the frosts of seventy winters on his head. He understands the condition of this country, and the character of her military chieftains, and has the moral courage to tell the world what he thinks.

THURSDAY, DEC. 17. The United States brig Julia, a prize to the Cyane, left our harbor this morning for the southern coast. She is a beautiful vessel, rides the water like a duck, and sails with the speed of the wind. Her masts rake to an angle that might almost startle a Baltimore clipper. She is commanded by Lieut. Selden, an officer to whose professional attainments she may be safely confided. She goes south to communicate with Col. Fremont at the Rincon, a narrow pass below Santa Barbara. The colonel's route will lead him through this pass, which lies hemmed in between the bluff of a mountain range and the dashing surge of the sea. A small force can defend it against immense odds. Its advantages are well known to the Californians. They have often in their previous revolutions made a stand here, though they have never made it quite a Thermopylæ. Should they post themselves in this pass, the well-trained gun of the Julia may dislodge them, or, at least, act in concert with Col. Fremont on his arrival. A man wants the eyes of Argus in this California war.

FRIDAY, DEC. 18. The ladies of Monterey have so many relatives, near and remote, involved in the issue of the war, that they have had but little heart for their customary amusements. But time, which assuages grief, has slowly quelled a sense of peril, and they are gradually coming back into their more gay and social element. The lively tones of their guitars salute you from their corridors, and often the fandango shakes its light slipper in the saloon. It has been customary here for a person giving a dance to apply to the alcalde for a permit, which was never refused, and which always brought to the purse of this functionary three dollars in the shape of a fee. A similar application was made to me a few days since. To grant it would be to sanction the fandango; to refuse it would be an arbitrary exercise of power. Tack which way I would, I must run on a rock, so I determined not to tack at all, and told the applicant I had nothing to do with his fiddles, fandangoes, or fees, so long as the public peace was not disturbed.

SATURDAY, DEC. 19. The season is now verging towards mid-winter, and we have not yet experienced the first wrinkling frost. The hills and valleys, since the recent rains, are mantled with fresh verdure, and here and there the violet opens its purple eye to the sun. The children are out at play, as in June; their glancing feet are unshod, and their muslin slips but half conceal their pulsing limbs. Even the old men, from whom the ethereal fires have escaped, are abroad in the same garments which covered them in midsummer. Such is the climate of a California winter, or, at least, its interludes, and these will continue to visit us like sunbows between the showering clouds.

MONDAY, DEC. 21. The house of the humbler Californian has often but one apartment, and is without fireplace or floor. Here a family of ten or fifteen tumble in and sleep on the ground. If they have guests, which is often the case, they turn in among the rest. The thicker they lie, of course the less covering they need. The walls of this promiscuous dormitory are formed of rough piles, driven in the ground, just sufficiently to support a roof that is thatched with flag. Through the chinked piles the night-wind whistles in gusty glee; through the roof the star-light falls in broken flakes. The showercloud often pauses over it, and, as if in wanton mischief, empties its floating cistern. But little heed the sleepers these freaks of the elements: they have been familiar with them from their birth. The only beings that seem at all disturbed are the fleas; but they still manage to dodge the shower-drops and secure their nocturnal repast. Those on whom they commit their depredations spring no rattle, raise no cry of alarm. The thief is there, but they know it not. Habit has exempted them from even a perception of their wrongs. Happy flea of California!

> When night-birds fill with waking numbers
>   The star-lit pauses in the storm,
> He deftly springs where Beauty slumbers,
>   And feasts on her seraphic form.
>
> She little knows who shares her pallet,
>   Has heard no lover lift the latch,
> And, waking, only hears the ballet
>   Danced by rain-drops on her thatch.
>
> Were all our ills which others tell us,
>   And all that darken fancy's dream,
> Confined to those we knew befell us,
>   How few our real woes would seem.

TUESDAY, DEC. 22. A courier arrived last evening from the north, with the startling intelligence that forty or fifty mounted Californians had sallied from the hills in the vicinity of San Francisco, and captured several Americans; among them Mr. Bartlett, chief magistrate of that jurisdiction. Capt. Weber, as soon as the news reached him on his station at San José, started with fifty mounted volunteers in pursuit; and fifty more have left Monterey this morning under the command of Capt. Maddox. One party is to come down upon them from the north, and the other is to cut off their retreat to the south. The plan is well laid, and we shall know in a few days if it has been executed with any decisive results.

WEDNESDAY, DEC. 23. It becomes us to keep a

pretty sharp look-out here, or another hostile party may take advantage of the absence of the forces under Capt. Maddox, and pay us a flying visit. No one here can tell when these visits are to be expected; when you feel most secure, they are, perhaps, nearest the door. In all other lands, war bears on its front such a flaring banner that you see its terrific insignia long before you feel its presence; but here, it comes like the descent of the eagle from his mountain eyrie —you hear not his pinions till they beat the air in his reascending: you look for the milk-white lamb that frolicked in your flock, and it is gone. Peril here, like death, borrows half its terrors from the secrecy in which it wraps its footsteps.

THURSDAY, DEC. 24. As soon as the sun had gone down, and twilight had spread its sable shadows over the hills and habitations of Monterey, the festivities of Christmas Eve commenced. The bells rang out a merry chime; the windows were filled with streaming light; bonfires on plain and steep sent up their pyramids of flame; and the sky-rocket burst high over all in showering fire. Children shouted; the young were filled with smiles and gladness; and the aged looked as if some dark cloud had been lifted from the world.

While the bonfires still blazed high, the crowd moved towards the church; the ample nave was soon filled. Before the high altar bent the Virgin Mother, in wonder and love, over her new-born babe; a company of shepherds entered in flowing robes, with high wands garnished with silken streamers, in which floated all the colors of the rainbow, and surmounted with coronals of flowers. In their wake followed a hermit, with his long white beard, tattered missal, and his sin-chastising lash. Near him figured a wild hunter, in the skins of the forest, bearing a huge truncheon, surmounted by an iron rim, from which hung in jingling chime fragments of all sonorous metals. Then came, last of all, the Evil One, with horned frontlet, disguised hoof, and robe of crimson flame. The shepherds were led on by the angel Gabriel, in purple wings and garments of light. They approached the manger, and, kneeling, hymned their wonder and worship in a sweet chant, which was sustained by the rich tones of exulting harps. The hermit and hunter were not among them; they had been beguiled by the Tempter, and were lingering at a game of dice. The hermit seemed to suspect that all was not right, and read his missal vehemently in the pauses of the game; but the hunter was troubled by none of these scruples, staked his soul, and lost! Emboldened by his success, the Tempter shoved himself among the shepherds; but here he encountered Gabriel, who knew him of old. He quailed under the eye of that invincible angel, and fled his presence. The hermit and hunter, once more disenthralled, paid their penitential homage. The shepherds departed, singing their hosannas, while the voices of the whole assembly rose in the choral strain.

FRIDAY, DEC. 25. At our last advices, Com. Stockton was at San Diego; the Congress and Cyane had been warped into the harbor, and a large portion of the officers and crews were in camp near the town. The Californians were in possession of the country, and often presented a formidable force on the surrounding hills. They were well mounted, and had it in their power to dash down at night on the camp of the commodore. Still, it was of the utmost importance to maintain this position; but aggressive movements were deemed here impracticable. The idea has never been seriously entertained here, that the commander-in-chief could march a body of seamen and marines, drilled into an infantry, to los Angeles, in the face of the flying-artillery of the Californians; and still less that he could subsist his forces there with all the resources of the country in the hands of the enemy. The war here is not on a great scale, but it impinges, at certain points, with terrific energy. It is not always the magnitude of the field and of the interests at issue, which test most severely the resources of the general. This California war has to be carried on by means which requires consummate tact, coolness, and courage. A few weeks more will decide the fate of the southern department, and with that, the whole tide of affairs here. That department lost in the pending engagement, our northern positions will be put in imminent peril. It is an idle dream to suppose the Californians will not fight; give them faithful and competent leaders, and they evince a dashing bravery which lifts them immeasurably above contempt. He who presumes on their timidity will learn his error when it may be too late.

SATURDAY, DEC. 26. It is an old custom here for the shepherds, when they have performed their sacred drama in the church, to repeat it, during the holydays, in the residences of some of the citizens. One of the first personages to whom they pay their respects is the chief magistrate of the jurisdiction; I was accordingly saluted this evening with their festive compliment.

The large hall, occupying the centre of the building, was sufficiently ample to accommodate them, and some fifty gentlemen and ladies as spectators. They brought their own orchestral accompaniment, which consisted entirely of violins and guitars. Their prelude had so many sweet harmonies that the listener determined to listen on. The dialogue and chant of the shepherds would have awakened their appropriate associations, but for the obtrusions of the hermit, hunter, and devil, who now gave much freer scope to their characteristic peculiarities than they did in church. The hermit forgot that his lash was intended for himself, and began to use it on others. The hunter left off snaring birds, and commenced setting springes to catch Satan; but his intended victim not only managed to escape, but to decoy the hunter himself into his own net. The hermit tried to disenchant him through the power of his missal; but this having no effect, he threatened to chastise the subtle author of the mischief, but wanted some one to seize and hold him, for fear his horn, hoof, or tail might come in conflict with the life-glass. During this side-acting, the dialogue and chant of the shepherds went on, though it would be difficult to conceive of any two things more wide asunder in their spirit and effect. The whole was concluded with the riata-dance, by the shepherds, who executed its airy movements with a lightness and precision of step that would have thrown enchantment on any occasion less sacred in its associations than the present.

CHAPTER IX.

DAY OF THE SANTOS INNOCENTES.—LETTING OFF A LAKE.—ARRIVAL OF THE DALE WITH HOME LETTERS.—THE DEAD YEAR.—NEWLY-ARRIVED EMIGRANTS.—EGG-BREAKING FESTIVITIES.—CONCEALMENT OF CHAVES.—PLOT TO CAPTURE THE ALCALDE.

SUNDAY, DEC. 27. The dramatic shepherds have just passed my door on their way to the mansion of Gen. Castro, where they are to perform their pastorals. Their drama is ill suited to the sacredness of the Sabbath: its grotesque appendages, in the person of the wild hunter and apocalyptic dragon, are but little short of a burlesque on the devotional chant of the shepherds. Indeed, there is not a truth connected with man's redemption which can derive any force from scenic representation. Every passage in the life of the Redeemer, every act that he performed, and every precept that he inculcated, are invested with a solemnity which should exempt them from the attempts of dramatic art. They have a significancy and force which transcend the evanescent triumphs of the stage. The tragedy of the Cross stands alone; no human passion can approach it; it is shielded in its sorrows by the divinity of the sufferer; its love overwhelmed angels; its agony awoke the dead.

MONDAY, DEC. 28. This is the festival day of the Santos Innocentes, and is devoted by the lovers of fun to every kind of harmless imposition on the simplicity of others. The utmost ingenuity is exercised in borrowing, for every article lent has to be redeemed. Although aware of this, still, in a moment of forgetfulness, one succeeded in borrowing my spurs. A gentleman, who has lived here from his boyhood, lent his cloak, another his saddle and bridle, and a third his guitar. Two ladies performed feats that would have been difficult on any day. One borrowed money of a broker, and the other a rosary of a priest. It is rumored, but not credited, that a client has induced his lawyer to allow his case to be amicably adjusted; that a patient has actually persuaded his physician to permit the aid of nature in throwing off his disease; and that a customer has made a shopkeeper confess an imperfection in his wares. It is said, but doubted, than an old Spanish hidalgo, after being told that his son is engaged in marriage to a peasant girl, will probably sleep before he disinherits him. It is also said, though few believe it, that a wife, whose husband is going to sea, has consented that he shall take the family breeches with him. It is further stated, but on no good authority, that a political partizan has hesitated about voting for his candidate on account of his having been once sentenced to the penitentiary for sheep-stealing. Several other rumors are afloat, but they are not credited. One is, that a disappointed lover has persuaded himself that his suit has been rejected without any parental interference; another is, that a young collegian has written a letter to his grandmother without quoting a word of Greek; another is, that a young clergyman has composed an entire sermon without anything about

"Fixed fate, free will, foreknowledge absolute."

Another is, that a man of giant intellect and profound erudition has selected as his life-partner a woman of sense; another, that a lady who has had an offer of marriage and rejected it, has kept it to herself; another, that an old bachelor has come to the conclusion that he is less captivating with the girls than he was when younger; another, that a young military officer has taken tea with his aunt without having on his regimentals; that a midshipman has entertained a lady fifteen minutes without a gale or disaster; that a sexton had been seen shedding a tear; that a Mormon has confessed Joe Smith's Bible a little less authentic, from the absence of the original plates; that a Millerite has forgiven a debt, on account of the nearness of the last conflagration; that a mesmerite, on account of the death-intelligence conveyed by his clairvoyant, has gone into mourning; that an Englishman has been seen with a smile on his countenance without a plum-pudding in his stomach; that an American has said grace at his table without stopping to expectorate; that a Frenchman has stopped his prattle before death had stopped his breath; and, finally, that a new moon, with a drooping horn, has been followed by a dry month.

While these incredible rumors were afloat, the public ear was startled with the intelligence that a large ship had been driven on the rocks, just behind Point Pinos. The whole population rushed at once in that direction,—the women to see her go to pieces, the men to seize her cargo, and a widow, who has a son at sea, to save the sailors. But the ship proved to be the "Flying Dutchman," with phantom hull and masts, and sails through whose gossamer the setting sun poured its effulgent beam. Some laughed as the spectral fabric dissolved, some grieved in silence over their loss, and one old wrecker hung himself with disappointment. Thus ended the day of the Santos Innocentes.

TUESDAY, DEC. 29. During the rains which prevail at this season of the year, a multitude of small streams rush from the hills which encircle Monterey into the lagoon which lies in the vicinity of the town. This natural basin, replenished by these foaming rivulets, presented this week quite a deep and spacious lake, and began to threaten with inundation the buildings upon its margin. As it lay several feet above the level of the sea, with only an intervening ridge of sand, it occurred to me that it would be a good scheme to cut a channel between the two. The work was easily accomplished; but my channel of two feet soon widened to forty, and the whole lake came rushing down in a tremendous torrent. It swept every thing before it, and carried two boats, which lay on the beach, so far out to sea that they have not been seen or heard of since. Even the sea-birds, that have dashed about here among the breakers ever since they got out of their eggs, seemed frightened, and took wing. Their screams came back on the wind like the howling of wild beasts on a sinking wreck. The lake disappeared; its waters, where the stars had mirrored themselves in tranquil beauty, went off to join the roaring ocean, and left on its sandy bottom only a few floundering fish. How tame is a lake when its bottom is laid bare! It is like the heart of a coquette when the illusions of love have fled.

WEDNESDAY, DEC. 30. The phantom ship, which rounded into our harbor a few weeks since, and departed without token or sign, turns out to be a good sound oak reality, in the shape of a sloop-of-war, honored with the name of Dale, bearing the stars and stripes, and commanded by Wm. W. M Kean. She sailed from New York on the 6th of June, and has stopped on her way out at Rio de Janeiro, Valparaiso, Callao, Payta, and Mazatlan. She has brought a large mail for the Pacific squadron. What an eager breaking of seals there will be!

I am indebted to her for a large package of letters, and for the receipt of one which was written several weeks after she sailed. It was dispatched alone to Jamaica, thence by the mail steamer to Chagres, thence over the Isthmus to Panama, and thence by the steamer to Callao, and then to Lima. Here it came into the care of my esteemed friend, Mr. M'Call, who forwarded it by the Dale. It brings me the intelligence of the birth of a son, and of the safety and happiness of a young mother over her first-born. Had this letter, in one of the many mischances to which it was exposed, failed of reaching me, months might have passed away without any intelligence to relieve my solicitude. There is a Providence, whose care extends to the condition of each one. Not a sparrow falls to the ground without his notice. But a long interval of waning moons must pass, and half the earth's circuit be traversed, before I can see that infant being whose dawning light has shed a gladness on my hearth. In this slow lapse of time what changes may betide, what fearful shadows may fall!

"My child, my child! when I shall reach my door,
If heavy looks should tell me thou art dead,
It seems as I should struggle to believe
Thou wert a spirit, to this nether sphere
Sentenced for some more venial crime to grieve;
Didst sigh, then spring to meet Heaven's quick reprieve,
While we wept idly o'er thy little bier!" COLERIDGE.

THURSDAY, DEC. 31. Com. Stockton is still encamped near San Diego, expecting to march in a few days for the town of the Angels. He has under his command detachments from the crews of the Congress, Cyane, and Portsmouth, with some thirty volunteers, and has with him several pieces of artillery. His plan evidently is, to attack the position of the

Californians from the south at the same time that Col. Fremont comes down upon them from the north. Hemmed in by these encountering forces, they will be obliged to surrender, or attempt a disastrous flight. Public expectation is on the tip-toe to learn the result; but several days must elapse before it can be known here.

FRIDAY, JAN. 1. Last night, while the sentinel stars were on their mid-watch, the old year resigned its sceptre, and departed amid the wailing hours to join the pale shadows of the mighty past. The strong winds, awaking in grief, shook the forest leaves from their slumbers, and poured from cloud and cliff their stormy dirge.

> " As an earthquake rocks a corse
>   In its coffin in the clay,
> So white Winter, that rough nurse,
>   Rocks the death-cold year to-day:
> Solemn hours! wail aloud,
> For your mother in her shroud."   SHELLEY.

But nature never leaves the throne of time vacant. An heir to her wide domain was invested at once with the imperial purple, while woods and water-falls, the organ cloud and the sounding sea, sung his coronation hymn. The great tide of time moved on as before, rolling in events pregnant with the fate of nations. But men, blind to these momentous issues, hail the eventful year—in which perhaps their own coffins swing—with egg-nog! Out on their frivolity!

Their mirth is the bubble that paints the rainbow on Niagara's thundering verge.

SUNDAY, JAN. 3. The deceased year is in its grave, but its deeds remain. But few of them, it is true, are to be found in the archives of earth; they have been sealed up and transmitted, by invisible hands, to Heaven's high chancery. There they will remain, above the ranges of time and the wreck of worlds. When the sun's last ray has expired, every line and letter will flash out in characters of living light. It will then be seen that our minutest action here touches a string that will vibrate forever in the soul; and that issues of happiness or woe, vast as eternity, take their rise in the silent pulses of a hidden thought. We live between two worlds; every impulse we take from this throws an action into the infinitude of the next; we follow it ourselves soon and fast: once beyond the dim veil, we return no more; not a whisper comes back to those we love. We have gone like a shooting-star over the steep verge of night.

MONDAY, JAN. 4. It is mid-winter, and yet the robins are all out, singing as if the buds of May were bursting around them. You miss none of your favorites in meadow or grove. Hill and vale are echoing with their wild numbers. This is not a gush of music that is to be followed soon by silence; it is not an interval of sun-light that is to be succeeded by cloud and hail. All these charms belong to the season, and make you forget that it is winter. You look to the sun, and see that he circles indeed far to the south; but you look around you and find the sparkling streams unfettered by frost, and hear the whistle of the ploughman as he breaks the glebe. You say to yourself, there is no winter in California.

TUESDAY, JAN. 5. Many of the emigrants who have recently arrived, are now with Col. Fremont at the south. By enlisting in this campaign, they will have an opportunity of seeing every important part of California, and will be able to locate themselves with some confidence in their selection of grounds. This will compensate them in some degree in foregoing their first year's tillage. Besides, they generally arrive here with very little means beyond their own enterprise. They are now receiving twenty-five dollars a month, and have but few temptations for spending it; they will consequently find themselves in funds, small to be sure; but there is a period in almost every man's life when a penny takes the importance of a pound. "It is more difficult," said the late Stephen Girard, "to make the first hundred dollars, than the next thousand." But with all due deference to that eminent economist, I have found it extremely difficult to make either, and when made, still more difficult to keep it. It has slipped out of my hands like a squirming eel in its slime. But this has very little to do with the emigrants. They will, it is hoped, soon be able to return to their families, who are now scattered about in the missions, and in shanties on the Sacramento, without the comforts of life. They have suffered greatly from being massed together in these temporary lodgments; and have often, no doubt, wished themselves where they came from. The pioneers of civilization have always a rough path. They force the bear from his covert, not to make room for a palace, but that they may themselves take his jungle.

WEDNESDAY, JAN. 6. As I was sitting in the house of an old Californian to-day, conversing very quietly about the condition of the country, I felt something break on my head, and, starting around, discovered two large black eyes, lighted with their triumph. It flashed upon me, that the annual eggbreaking festival here had commenced. The rules of this frolic do not allow you to take offence, whatever may be your age or the gravity of your profession: you have only one alternative, and that is, to retaliate if you can. You have not to encounter the natural contents of the egg—these are blown out; and the shell is filled with water, scented with cologne, or lavender; or more often, with gold tinsel, and flashing paper, cut into ten thousand minute particles. The tinsel is rubbed by a dash of the hand into your hair, and requires no little combing and brushing to get it out. Ladies will work at it for hours, and find some of the spangles still remaining. When a liquid is used, the apertures are closed with wax, so that the belligerent may carry it about his person. The antagonist is always of the opposite sex. You must return these shots, or encounter a railery, which is even worse. Having finished my chat, I bade my good old Californian friend, and his daughter, my egg-shell opponent, good morning; but turned into a shop, procured an egg or two, and re-entered the mansion of my friend by a side door, where I watched for my victim. A few moments brought her along, all-unconscious of her danger. I slipped from my covert, and, unperceived, dashed the showering egg on her head. Her locks floated in cologne. I was avenged, and now stood square with the world, so far as egg-breaking is concerned. This seems like children's play; but here you are forced into it in self-defence.

THURSDAY, JAN. 7. Two or three of the Californians who were engaged against the Americans on the Salinas, have since been in town; among these, the leader, Chaves, who was wounded on that occasion. Many attempts have been made to take him, but he has always managed to elude the search. Last night, however, he had an extremely narrow escape. The officer in command of the garrison, having been informed that he was in a particular house, silently posted his sentinels around it, and at about eight o'clock in the evening unceremoniously entered. Quick footsteps were heard here and there, and only a part of the ladies were found in the parlor; but these were calm as moonshine, and extremely polite and amiable.

The officers apologized for their abrupt intrusion, and stated, very frankly, what their object was: the ladies assured them that they were quite right, and they should afford them every facility and aid that might lead to the discovery of the obnoxious person. They took lights and piloted them through every apartment of the house, opening every closet, and lifting every bed-curtain. There was no place in garret, cellar, kitchen or out-house on which their tapers did not shed their light; but in none could a trace of the officer whom they sought be found: so they renewed their apologies to the ladies and departed—when out slipped Chaves from between two ladies, who had jumped into a bed for the purpose of concealing him. They had lain there while the officers were in the chamber; their dark locks floating over the pillows, and their large eyes closed in seeming slumber. Between them

> " He had been hid—I don't pretend to say
> How, nor can I, indeed, describe the where:
> Young, slender, and pack'd easily, he lay,
> No doubt, in little compass, round or square"

Friday, Jan. 8. We have as yet no further intelligence in reference to the party of Californians who carried off Mr. Bartlett, of San Francisco. He had gone into the country, it seems, to attend to some of his official duties, when he was captured, and is now detained as a hostage. I came very near falling into a similar trap, a few weeks since. A farmer in Santa Cruze had extended his improvements over the lands of another, which lay contiguous to his own, and it became necessary to go and define the boundaries by the original titles. The day was fixed when I was to be there, and the parties interested were summoned to appear on the spot. But the night before I was to leave, intelligence reached me that an armed party of Californians were encamped close to the road which I should have taken. But for this information, brought in by a citizen of Monterey, I should now be sleeping here and there, under the open heaven, without a change of apparel, and with bandits for bed-fellows: on such slender threads hangs security here. I have been told by Californians, who are my friends, that plans have been laid by their countrymen to slip me quietly out of my house at night, or entrap me in my hunting excursions, on the outskirts of the town. I began to think, last night, that this attempt was to be realized. Quick footsteps and a loud rap came to my door, followed by an excited call for the alcalde. My boy went out, with his pistols swung at his side; but the call proved to be an honest one. A shop had been robbed, and a warrant was wanted for the arrest of the supposed felons.

SATURDAY, JAN. 9. How many inventions a Californian lady has! One who was harboring a

Mexican officer that had broken his parol, wishing to do away with all possible suspicion, got up a far dango to which she took special pains to invite all the American officers. Such open-door hospitality—such challenging of the public eye—threw an air of freedom and frankness over her whole house. Everybody acquitted her at once of the least shadow of suspicion. But while the violins and guitars were trembling and thrilling in concert, and the floor of the old hall was springing to the bounding measures of the fandango, and bright eyes

"Were looking love to eyes that spake again,"

the Mexican officer was snugly taking a nap in the great oven, which, near the cook-house, silently loomed into the moonlight. It must have been a long nap, for the stars that kept the mid-watch were relieved before the company broke up. The officer was then at liberty to leave his oval dormitory to the baker; and creeping forth, had, no doubt, a good laugh with his ingenious hostess over the success of the fandango. There is no disguise so deep as that which seems to seek none.

SUNDAY, JAN. 10. I held service to-day on board the U. S. ship Dale. Though on deck, no inconvenience was experienced from the weather. The air was soft, and hardly a ripple disturbed the mirror of the sea. Capt. McKean, in the absence of a chaplain, reads the service himself. He appreciates the force of moral influences in the government of his crew, and is well sustained in its exertion by his intelligent officers. It is rarely that you meet with a commander in the service who is indifferent to the religious character of his crew. If he has no religion himself, still he respects it in others, and places his greatest reliance where it exerts a controlling influence. Religion, wherever possessed, vindicates its celestial origin.

The captain of a whale-ship applied to Mr. Damon, of Honolulu, to preach on board his vessel, stating very frankly that he had no religion himself, but then he wanted his ship to appear "a little decent." Now when a captain applies for a religious service to give an air of respectability to his vessel, it shows that moral truth is in the ascendancy, at least in the dignity of its claims. There was a time when no such expedient was deemed necessary; but a higher light has struck the mariners who float the great Pacific. Their hosannas will yet be rolled to heaven in concert with the loud anthem of her many-voiced waves.

CHAPTER X.

DESTRUCTION OF DOGS.—THE WASH-TUB MAIL.—THE SURRENDER IN THE NORTH.—ROBBING THE CALIFORNIANS.—DEATH-SCENE IN A SHANTY.—THE MEN WHO TOOK UP ARMS.—ARRIVAL OF THE INDEPENDENCE.—DESTITUTION OF OUR TROOPS.—CAPTURE OF LOS ANGELES.

MONDAY, JAN. 11. I never expected, when threading the streets of Constantinople, where dogs inherit the rights of citizenship, to encounter such multitudes of them in any other part of the world. But California is more than a match for the Ottoman capital. Here you will find in every little village a thousand dogs, who never had a master: every farm-house has some sixty or eighty; and every Indian drives his cart with thirty or forty on its trail. They had become so troublesome, that an order was given a few days since to thin their ranks. The marines, with their muskets, were to be the executioners. The order, of course, very naturally runs into dog-erels.

> The dogs, the dogs! my gallant lads—
>   Let each one seize his gun,
> And lead the battle's fiery van,
>   Though Mars himself should run.
>
> Remember Lodi's blazing bridge,
>   Marengo's shaking plain,
> And Borodino's thunder-clouds,
>   Where Cossacks fell like rain.

Now hurl their howling squadrons down
    To Lethe's silent shore;
They bark so loud, we scarce can hear
    Our sleeping sentries snore.

Lay low the watch-dog first of all;
    For he's a saucy loon,
That bays all night the modest man
    Who figures in the moon.

Then down the pointer: he it is
    That threads the leaves and grass—
To train the sportman's ready fire
    At some poor luckless ass.

Then wing the lap-dog, that pert imp
    Befondled by the fair,
And catching all the tender looks
    Old bachelors should share.

O'er him, who falls in this dread strife,
    The thunder-clouds shall roll,
Through shaking cliffs and caverned hills,
    A requiem to his soul.

And dewy stars shall softly bend
    From their celestial bowers,
To greet the meek-eyed spring, that comes
    To strew his grave with flowers.

TUESDAY, JAN. 12. After three weeks, in which we had a cloudless sky and balmy air, the wind has hauled into the southeast, and a gentle rain has commenced falling. Its having crept upon us so softly, is a symptom that it will continue with us some time. The first break of sunshine may be a week hence.

WEDNESDAY, JAN. 13. We have no intelligence, as yet, from the seat of war. The solicitude of the public to know the result is at the highest pitch. No one doubts that the issue has been very decisive. A report reached us to-day that the town of los Angeles had been taken by our troops, and that a large portion of the Californians had laid down their arms. This rumor comes through the washerwomen of this place. They get their intelligence from the Indians, who cross the streams in which they wash their clothes. Singular as this sort of mail may seem, it very often conveys news, not only with wonderful dispatch, but with extraordinary accuracy.

The first capture of los Angeles, by Com. Stockton, was announced here by these washerwomen; they were also the first to spread the intelligence of the breaking out of the insurrection at the same place, and knew of the retreat of the Americans at San Pedro before any other class of people in Monterey. So much for a wash-tub mail. You may think lightly of it as of the soap-bubbles that break over its rim; but if you are wise you will heed its intelligence. It is an old mail that has long been run in California; and has announced more revolutions, plots, and counterplots, than there are mummies in Memphis. Who, in other lands, would dream of going to an old woman, washing her clothes in a mountain stream, for the first tidings of events in which the destinies of nations tremble? Mr. Morse need hardly come here with his magnetic machine. One of these women would snap the news from a napkin or shirt before his lightning-mail had got under way.

THURSDAY, JAN. 14. The small party of Californians who recently took up arms on the bay of San Francisco, soon increased to two hundred. They were, with few exceptions, men of the better stamp—men who had a permanent interest in the soil, and who had refused to join the rash spirits at the south. They had captured Mr. Bartlett, the chief magistrate of the jurisdiction, and several other Americans, whom they held as hostages.

Capt. Marston, with fifty men from the Savannah, and Capt. Maddox, with a company of mounted volunteers, and Capt. Weber, with another band of resolute spirits, met them. A general and decisive engagement was anticipated; but after a few hours of pretty sharp fighting, the Californians withdrew from Santa Clara, which was entered by our forces. A flag of truce was sent in, and the leading spirits on both sides assembled under the shadows of a great native oak. The Californians stated that they had taken up arms, not to make war on the American flag, but to protect themselves from the depredations of those who, under color of that flag, were plundering them of their cattle, horses, and grain; and that on assurance being given that these acts of lawless violence should cease, they were ready to return quietly to their homes. These demands were not enforced in a spirit of menace, but with that moral firmness which belongs to a deep sense of wrong. They were acceded to, and the parties separated, never again, I hope, to meet as belligerents.

This is a much better mode of settling differences than through the arbitrament of the bayonet. It is an easy thing to dislodge a man's argument by dislodging his life; but this summary process of getting rid of an opponent will generally be followed by something worse. There is terror even in the ghost of a misdeed.

FRIDAY, JAN. 15. We have further intelligence from the seat of war. General Kearny, with his staff and a guard of one hundred dragoons, arrived on the 6th ult. from New Mexico at San Pasqual, about thirty miles from San Diego. Here he encountered a hundred and sixty Californians, under Andres Pico, well mounted, and armed with rifles and lances. A sanguinary engagement ensued, marked by the most daring, determined conduct on both sides. Captain Johnson, with twelve dragoons, led the charge, and was shot dead in the furious onset. Captain Moore, with fifty dragoons, rushed to the front: the enemy wavered—retreated; when this gallant officer, with a few of his men who were better mounted than the the rest, rushed on in pursuit. The enemy suddenly wheeled; and now it was hand to hand between the heavy sword and lance. Captain Moore, on his white charger, was a mark which none could mistake. Lance after lance was shivered by his flashing steel, till, at last, he sunk overpowered. All this lasted but a few minutes, but long enough to reach its tragic results before the remainder of the guard could come up.

The Californians at last retreated, and Gen. Kearny encamped on the disputed field. But what a night it must have been! The camp fire threw its pale light on the countenances of nineteen, who sprung to their saddles at the break of day, but who were now locked in the still embrace of death. The burial rites performed, and another sun in the heavens, the general was again on his way. But another hill bristling with lances obstructs his march; it is stormed, carried, and here again the weary and the wounded require repose. Through the energies of Lieut. Beale, who seems ever to be where the hardiest enterprise demands, a message is conveyed through the beleaguering lines of the enemy to the camp of Com. Stockton, and a detachment of seamen and marines, under Lieut. Gray, of the Congress, is sent out. This fresh force obliged the Californians to relinquish their purpose of another engagement. Had they not arrived, it was the intention of Gen. Kearny to cut his way to San Diego, be the odds against him what they might. His gallant guard had shown the reliance which might be reposed in them, by the desperate valor which they had already evinced. The conduct of Capt. Turner, of Lieut. Emory, and Capt. Gillespie might give a feature to any field where life is perilled and laurels won; while the muse of history would inscribe her glowing eulogy on the tombs of a Johnson, a Moore, and a Hammond. They sleep in the soil of California, where the undying year

"Garlands with fragrant flowers their place of rest."

SATURDAY, JAN. 16. The depredations complained of by those who took up arms in the neighborhood of San Francisco, were committed by some of the volunteers, previous to their joining Col. Fremont on his present campaign. They are a class of persons who have drifted over the mountains into this country from the borders of some of our western states. It is a prime feature in their policy to keep in advance of law and order, and to migrate as often as these trench on their irresponsible privileges. Their connection with our military operations here is a calamity that can only find a relief in the exigencies of war.

Were their lawless proceedings directed against those who are active participators in this revolution, the evils which they inflict would have some palliation. But the principal sufferers are men who have remained quietly on their farms, and whom we are bound in honor, as well as sound policy, to protect. To permit such men to be plundered under the filched authority of our flag is a national reproach. No temporary triumph can redeem the injuries inflicted, or obliterate their stain. But the rash acts committed by one portion of the Californians, and the wrongs endured by another, are fast drawing to a close.

Sunday, Jan. 17. As I was passing this morning one of the little huts sprinkled around the skirts of Monterey, my steps were arrested by the low moans which issued from its narrow door. On entering, I found on a straw pallet a mother whom disease had wasted to a mere shadow, but whose sufferings were now nearly over. She did not notice my entrance, or any thing around; her eyes were lifted, fixed, and glassed in death. A slight motion drew my attention to another corner of the hut, where I discovered, in the dim twilight of the place, a little boy lying on a mat, whom I supposed asleep; his young sister was near him, and trying to cross his hands on his breast She did not seem to notice me, spake not a word, but went on with her baffled task, for the hand which she had adjusted would roll off while she was attempting to recover the other. Now and then she stopped for a moment and kissed the lips which could return none, while her tears fell silently on the face of her dead brother. In a few minutes two women entered, who, it seems, had gone out to call their clergyman to administer the last rites to the mother. He was too late: her spirit had fled. He spoke to her, called her by name—but there was no answer; he turned to the little boy, whispered Raphael, but all was silent and still. Directing the women where to procure grave-clothes at the expense of the alcalde's office, I wended my way home. How little heeds the great stream of life the silent rivulets of sorrow which mingle with its noisy tide!

Monday, Jan. 18. It is deeply to be regretted that the military operations in California should prevent, at this time, an experimental proof of the fertility of her soil. The rain that has already fallen is so abundant, that all the arable land will retain its moisture sufficiently to enable the crops to come to maturity. But this war has broken up every agricultural arrangement, and defeated every possibility of a generous harvest. The calamity will be felt most severely by the emigrants. They arrive here with very slender means; and the idea of paying twenty dollars a barrel for flour covers them with dismay. Instead of having reached a land of plenty, they hastily conclude that they are to suffer the miseries of destitution, and yield to a despondency deeper than that which shook the faith of the Israelites before their wants were miraculously supplied. But there is no manna here, and no quails, except those which are secured by the hunter's skill. The day of miracles is over, even in California.

Tuesday, Jan. 19. One of my boys caught a dove, a few days since, clipped his wing, and placed him in our yard, which has a high wall around it. He looked very lonely at first, but his mate soon came, hovered around on the wall, and finally preferring captivity with him to freedom without, flew down to his side. How beautiful is that affection which never forsakes in adversity, but becomes deeper and stronger as the waves of affliction roll higher over the object of its sympathy and trust!

WEDNESDAY, JAN. 20. There is one feature in our military operations here which is far asunder from that system of order which appertains to a well-disciplined army. Every one who can raise among the emigrants thirty or forty men, becomes a captain, and starts off to fight pretty much on his own hook. Nor is he very scrupulous as to the mode in which he obtains his horses, saddles, and other equipments. He takes them wherever he can find them, and very often without leaving behind the slightest evidence by which the owner can recover the value of his property. He plunders the Californian to procure the means of fighting him. Public exigency is the plea which is made to cover all the culpable features in the transaction. This may justify, perhaps, taking the property, but it never can excuse the refusal or neglect to give receipts. It is due to Com. Stockton and Col. Fremont to say, that this has been done without their sanction. Still, it reflects reproach on our cause, and is a source of vast irritation in the community. No man who has any possible means of redress left will tamely submit to such outrages; and yet we expect the Californians to hug this chain of degradation, and help to rivet its links. Let foreigners land on our own coast, and do among us what Americans have done here, and every farmer, in the absence of a musket, would shoulder his pitchfork and flail. Human nature is the same here as there, and a sense of wrong will burn as deeply in the one place as the other. I utter, for one, my note of remonstrance, though it be as little heeded as the whispers of a leaf in the roar of a storm-swept forest.

THURSDAY, JAN. 21. The scarcity of provisions in Monterey continues. Flour is twenty-five dollars the barrel, and there is hardly a barrel in the place at that. We have in our garrison about a hundred and fifty men, and all are on a short allowance of bread. There is wheat in the interior, but the mules which should be there to grind it have gone to the wars. Even that sorry animal seems here not wholly insensible to military glory. The trump of fame finds an echo even in his long ears.

FRIDAY, JAN. 22. The flag on the fort informed us this afternoon of the approach of a ship within the rim of our bay. As she neared, the signals on the Dale told her to be an American man-of-war. We conjectured at once that she must be the Congress; but as she rounded into her berth we could not recognize, in her majestic form, the features of our old friend. She proved to be the Independence, commanded by Capt. Lavellette, and bearing the broad pennant of Com. Shubrick. She sailed from the U. States on the twenty-ninth of August, and arrived at Rio de Janeiro in fifty-three days; remained there ten days; doubled the Cape and reached Valparaiso in thirty-four days; stopped there seven, and reached here in thirty-eight. This is splendid sailing; but the Independence is one of the fastest, as well as one of the most powerful ships in our service. Though razeed of her carronades, all her effective force remains. Her battery is a frowning mass of thunder. Her officers are men of enterprise and professional merit. They have brought a mail, well filled with letters and papers, from the United States. If you would know the value of a single letter, let an ocean roll between you and your home.

SATURDAY, JAN. 23. The Independence left the Columbus at Valparaiso, under the broad pennant of Com. Biddle, who has instructions to favor us here with a visit. The Columbus was in want of supplies, and would be detained several days in procuring them. She had better lay in all she will require, for there is nothing here. Unless a transport arrives soon, there will not be salt provisions enough on the coast to enable our squadron to go to sea two weeks. There has not been a transport here for six months; our sailors have been living on fresh meat till they hanker for the salt more than they ever did for the fresh. As for clothing, they can hardly muster a shirt a piece, and one pair of shoes among half a dozen is becoming rather a rare sight. This is a hard case, when our markets at home are glutted with these articles. The sailor is required to be faithful to the government, and the government should be faithful to him. He should not be left here barefooted to patter about like a duck in shallow water. It is well for him that it is a California winter through which he is obliged to pass in his destitution; in the same latitude on the Atlantic he would nearly have perished.

SUNDAY, JAN. 24. It is difficult to make the Californians understand why you will not attend to office duties on the Sabbath. The apology that you want it as a day of recreation, would be appreciated; but the plea of its sanctity is with many wholly unintelligible. If you would make a person respect the Sabbath, you must rear him in its sacred observance.

MONDAY, JAN. 25. The wash-tub mail is still further establishing its claims to confidence. Its intelligence is no bubble breaking over its rim, and evaporating into thin air; but a chain of facts carrying with them the destinies of a nation. All that has reached us through this singular mail is confirmed this morning by a California youth who has arrived from below.

He left los Angeles some fourteen days since, and states that previous to his departure, Com. Stockton had entered the town at the head of the American forces from San Diego. He says there had been some pretty hard fighting, in which the Californians had suffered severely. Col. Fremont, he states, was within two days' march of the Pueblo, and in a position to cut off the retreat of the Californians to the north. He believes that most of them have surrendered. This intelligence is, in every essential particular, identical with that which reached us several days since through the washerwomen of this town. They must have obtained it from those who swept through to the north when the rout below first commenced.

TUESDAY, JAN. 26. A Californian made me a present to-day of a wild goose which he had just killed. I value the gift for the giver, rather than any benefit it may be to me. I live mostly on mush; such a thing as a wild goose never floats within the shadows of my domestic dreams. Even the drum of the partridge is rarely heard there Wild geese prevail here in the greatest abundance; every lagoon, lake, and river is filled with them. They fly in squadrons, which, for the moment, shut out the sun; a chance shot will often bring two or three to the ground. The boys will often lasso them in the air. This is done by fastening two lead balls, several yards from each other, to a long line, which is whirled into the air to a great height. In its descent the balls fall on opposite sides of the neck of some luckless goose, and down he comes into the hands of the urchin hunter; sometimes a pair are brought down, but one generally manages to effect his escape. The boy little heeds the domestic relation that may have subsisted between them; and yet there is something in killing the mate of even a goose that might be relieved in the thought that no other goose loved him.

Wm M Gwin

CHAPTER XI.

ARRIVAL OF THE LEXINGTON—THE MARCH TO LOS ANGELES, AND BATTLE OF SAN GABRIEL.—THE CAPITULATION.—MILITARY CHARACTERISTICS OF THE CALIFORNIANS.—BARRICADES DOWN.

THURSDAY, JAN. 28. Our harbor has been enlivened to-day by the arrival of the U. S. ship Lexington, commanded by Lieut. Theodorus Bailey, an officer that might well have been promoted years ago. Capt. Tompkins and his company of one hundred and forty men, and field train of artillery, are on board. She brings out also Capt. Halleck, U. S. Engineer, who is intrusted with the erection of fortifications at this place and San Francisco. The Lexington is laden with heavy battery guns, mortars, shot, shells, muskets, pistols, swords, fixed ammunition, and several hundred barrels of powder. She has also a quantity of shovels, spades, ploughs, pickaxes, saws, hammers, forges, and all the necessary utensils for building fortifications of the first class; and what is better still, she brings with her a saw-mill and a good grist-mill.

FRIDAY, JAN. 29. The U. S. ship Dale, W. W. McKean commander, sailed to-day for Panama. She takes the mail which is to cross the isthmus, and reach the United States by the West India steamers. As soon as her destination was known, a hundred pens were at work, transferring to paper affections, fond remembrances, kind wishes, and a thousand tender, anxious inquiries. How absence melts the heart! The cold is kindled, the indifferent clothed with interest, antipathies melt away, and endearments revive with undying power. I love the very stones over which my truant footsteps ran, and could kiss the birch rod that chastised my youthful follies. What language, then, can portray the love which clings to one who throws sunlight through the shadows of this dark world, or paint the cherished hope that buds into being with—

MY INFANT BOY.

I have not seen thy face, my child;
    They say each look and line,
Which o'er thy father's aspect plays,
    Is miniatured in thine.

They tell me that thy infant voice—
    Its wildly warbled tone,
Seems to thy mother's listening ear
    The echo of my own.

I know it not, but fondly deem
    That such a thing may be,
And trust thy father's better hopes
    May long survive in thee.

I have not seen thy face, my child,
    Though weary moons have set
Since mine and thy glad mother's eyes
    In tender transport met :—

> For ere thy being dawned to light,
>   Or knew what life might mean,
> Our ship had earth's mid circuit swept,
>   And oceans rolled between.
>
> I waft thee back a father's kiss—
>   A pledge of that wild joy,
> Which o'er his yearning heart will rush,
>   To clasp his infant boy.

SATURDAY, JAN. 30. The long-looked for intelligence has come at last in an authentic shape. The American forces, commanded by Com. Stockton, aided by Gen. Kearny, broke camp at San Diego on the 29th ult., and took up the line of march for los Angeles. Their route lay through a rugged country of one hundred and forty miles, drenched with the winter rains, and bristling with the lances of the enemy. Through this the commodore led our seamen and marines, sharing himself, with the general at his side, all the hardships of the common sailor. The stern engagements with the enemy derive their heroic features from the contrast existing in the condition of the two. The Californians were well mounted, are the most expert horsemen in the world, and whirled their flying-artillery to the most commanding positions. Our troops were on foot, mired to the ankle, and with no resource except in their own indomitable resolution and courage. Their exploits may be lost in the shadow of the clouds which roll up from the plains of Mexico, but they are realities here, which impress themselves with a force which reaches the very foundations of social order. The march of the American forces from San Diego to the Pueblo below, and their engagements with the enemy, are vividly described in a letter to me from one of the officers attached to the expedition. This writer says :

" Com. Stockton, at the head of a force amounting to about six hundred men, including a detachment of the 1st regiment of U. S. dragoons, under Gen. Kearny, left San Diego on the morning of the 29th of December, for los Angeles. Our line of march lay through a rough and mountainous country of nearly one hundred and fifty miles, with impediments on every side, and constant apprehensions of an attack from the enemy : our progress was nevertheless rapid ; and though performed mostly by sailor troops, would have done credit to the best disciplined army.

" On the morning of the 8th of January, we found ourselves, after several days' hard marching and fatigue, in the vicinity of the river San Gabriel ; on the north side of which the enemy had fortified themselves to the number of five hundred mounted men, with four pieces of artillery, under Gen. Flores, and in a position so commanding, that it seemed impossible to gain any point by which our troops could be protected from their galling fire. They presented their forces in three divisions—one on our right, another on our left, and a third in front, with the artillery. On reaching the south side of the river, the commodore dismounted, forded the stream, and commanded the troops to pass over, which they did promptly under the brisk fire of the enemy's artillery. He ordered the artillery not to unlimber till the opposite bank should be gained ; as soon as this was effected, he ordered a charge directly in the teeth of the enemy's guns, which soon resulted in the possession of the commanding position they had just occupied. The first gun fired was aimed by the commodore before the charge was made up the hill ; this overthrew the enemy's gun, which had just poured forth its thunder in our midst. Having gained this important position, a brisk cannonading was kept up for some time. We encamped on the spot for the night. The next day we met the enemy again on the plains of the Mesa, near the city. They made a bold and resolute stand; tried our lines on every side; and manœuvred their artillery with much skill. But the firm and steady courage with which our troops continued to defend themselves, repelled their attempts at a general charge, and we found ourselves again victorious. We encamped again near the battle-ground, and on the morning of the tenth marched into the city, while the adjacent hills were glistening with the lances of the enemy."

Sunday, Jan. 31. It is sweet in a land of tumult and strife to see the Sabbath sun come up. Its sacred light melts over the rough aspects of war like melting dew down the frontlet of the crouched lion. May the spirit of devotion, in its ascending flight, bear into a serener element the aspirations of the human heart! There let faith, and hope, and immortal love build their tabernacle. It shall be a dwelling for the soul when the palaces, temples, and towers of earth are in ruins. Over its gem-inwoven roof shall stream the light of stars that never set; flowers that cannot die shall wreath its colonnade, and hang in fragrant festoons from its walls; while the voices of streamlets, as they flash over their golden sands, shall pour unceasing music on the wandering air.

Monday, Feb. 1. The forces under Col. Fremont were within a few leagues of the town of the Angels when Com. Stockton entered it. Their approach cut off the retreat of the Californians to the north. The forces of the commodore were on foot, and of course unable to follow up their brilliant successes. The enemy were mounted, and might have held the country around. If attacked, they had only to retreat, and return again on the retiring footsteps of their foes. But at this critical juncture, Col. Fremont, with his battalion, came down upon them, leaving them no alternative but to capitulate or attempt a disastrous flight into Mexico. They wisely, with the exception of a few, determined to abide the conditions of a treaty. The terms of capitulation are couched in a spirit of great liberality and justice. One would hardly think that men so amiable and confiding in their terms of peace, could have just been on the eve of taking each others lives. But this is one of those exhibitions of forbearance and generosity which not unfrequently relieve the calamities of war.

The articles of capitulation, in substance, were, that the Californians shall surrender their arms to Col. Fremont, return peaceably to their homes, and not resume hostilities during the continuance of the war with Mexico;—that they shall be guaranteed the protection of life and property, and equal rights and privileges with the citizens of the United States. These terms were duly subscribed by the commissioners appointed by the parties to the compact, and ratified by Col. Fremont. They were liberal in their spirit, wise in their purpose, and just in their application. More rigorous terms would have involved a sense of humiliation in one party, without any advantage to the other. The Californians were defeated, but not crushed. They have those salient energies which rebound from misfortune, as their native forests sweep back into the face of heaven, when the tempest has passed. They never took the field out of reverence for the Mexican flag: it was a wild impulse, deriving its life from a love of adventure, and the excitements of the camp. They had had their tragedy, acted their part, and were now willing the dim curtain should drop; and Col. Fremont very wisely clenched it to the stage. A few in the orchestra still piped; but the actors were away, the side-scenes vacant, and the spectators at their homes; and there may they remain, till the sword shall be beaten into the ploughshare, and the spear into the pruning-hook, and the art of war be known no more.

THURSDAY, FEB. 4. The Californians who left Monterey to join the outbreak at the south are now returning to their homes. Every day brings back two or three to their firesides. They look like men who have been out on a hunt, and returned with very little game. Still, it must be confessed that they have materially strengthened their claims to military skill and courage. They have been defeated, it is true, but it has cost their victors many sanguinary struggles, and many valuable lives. They have raised themselves above that contemptuous estimation in which they were erroneously held by many, and secured a degree of respect, which will contribute to mutual forbearance. This result is to be ascribed to the prowess of the few, rather than the conduct of the many. The mass were governed by impulse and the pressure of circumstances. It was not that calm, heroic spirit which disregards personal safety, and exults in the hour of peril; nor was it that deep sense of patriotic duty which makes a man firm in disaster and death. It was rather that recklessness which springs from wounded pride, but which often crowns with laurels a forlorn hope.

FRIDAY, FEB. 5. The outbreak at the north has passed away, and the last wave of commotion perished with it. This result is to be ascribed to the energy of Capt. Mervin, to the moderation and firmness of Capt. Marston and his associates, and to the good conduct of the forces under their command. Nor should it be forgotten that the Californians evinced, on this occasion, a disposition well suited to bring about an amicable treaty. They took up arms, not to make war on the American flag, but in vindication of their rights as citizens of California, and in defence of their property. They had been promised protection—they had been assured that they should not be molested, if they remained quietly at their homes—and these pledges had been glaringly violated. Their horses and cattle had been taken from them, under cover of public exigency, and no receipts given, to secure them indemnification, till at last they determined to have their rights respected, or to die like men. Still, it was necessary to meet them in arms, and in sufficient force to inspire respect. They were, however, well mounted, and might, had they so listed, have prolonged the struggle. But this was not their object, and they sent in a flag of truce. The conditions of the treaty were, that they should lay down their arms, release their prisoners, and that their property should be restored, or such vouchers given as would enable them ultimately to recover its value. This was a reasonable requirement on their part, and the American officers had the good sense to appreciate its force. We must be just before we attempt to be brave. Laurels won through wrong are a dishonor.

SATURDAY, FEB. 6. We have another rain; not a cloud is to be seen; but the whole atmosphere is filled with a thick mist, which dissolves in a soft perpetual shower. It seems as if nature had relinquished every other occupation, and given herself up to this moist business. She calls up no thunder, throws out no lightning; she only squeezes her great sponge, and that as quietly as a mermaid smooths her dripping locks.

SUNDAY, FEB. 7. Com. Shubrick has ordered the barricades removed. Thank God! we are at last relieved of martial law. It is one of the greatest calamities that can fall on a civilized nation. It tramples on private rights, trifles with responsibility, and cuts the conscience adrift from its moorings. Men are thrown into this eddy of excess, and then act like rudderless ships in a tempest-tost sea. Years will elapse before the moral sentiments which have been unhinged by military violence can be restored. Even California, where revolutions come and go like the shadows of passing clouds, will long show the traces of the one which has now passed over her. Its lightning has shivered the tree before the fruit was ripe, and blasted a thousand buds that might have bloomed into fragrant beauty.

MONDAY, FEB. 8. Much to the relief of the citizens, Com. Shubrick has given orders that the volunteers on service here shall be paid off and discharged. They are principally sea-beachers and mountain-combers, and some of them are very good men; but others seem to have no idea of the proprietorship of property. They help themselves to it as canvas-back ducks the grass that grows in the Potomac, or migratory birds the berries which bloom in the forests through which they wander. They hardly left fowls enough here on which to keep Christmas. Could dismembered hens lay eggs, they would have more chickens in their stomachs than they ever had dollars in their pockets.

CHAPTER XII.

RETURN OF T. O. LARKIN.—THE TALL PARTNER IN THE CALIFORNIAN.—MEXICAN OFFICERS.—THE CYANE.—WAR MEMENTOES.—DRAMA OF ADAM AND EVE.—CARNIVAL.—BIRTH-DAY OF WASHINGTON.—A CALIFORNIA CAPTAIN.—APPLICATION FOR A DIVORCE.—ARRIVAL OF THE COLUMBUS.

TUESDAY, FEB. 9. The U. S. ship Cyane, S. F. Dupont commander, is just in from San Diego. She was dispatched to bring up General Kearny and suit, and our consul, T. O. Larkin, Esq. The arrival of the Independence was not known at San Diego when the Cyane sailed. The return of Mr. Larkin was warmly greeted by our citizens. Even the old Californians left their corridors to welcome him back. He was captured by those engaged in the outbreak some three months since, and has been closely guarded as a prisoner of war. Still, in the irregularities of the campaign, and the easy fidelity of those who kept watch, he has had many opportunities of effecting his escape, but declined them all. He was on the eve, at one time, of being taken to Mexico, and got ready for the long and wearisome journey; but some of his captors relented, and he was allowed to remain at the town of the Angels, when the success of the American arms relieved him. He experienced during his captivity many acts of kindness. Even the ladies, who in California are always on the side of those who suffer, sent him many gifts, which contributed essentially to his comfort. But he is once more with his family, and long may it be before he takes another such trip as his last.

WEDNESDAY, FEB. 10. My tall partner in the Californian is back at last from his three months' trip to San Francisco. I excused his long absence, and cheerfully endured all the toil of getting out the paper, with only the assistance of a type-setting sailor, under the vague impression that he was hunting up a wife. But he has come back as single as he came into the world. Whether his solitude is a thing of choice or necessity I have not inquired. A man's celibacy is a misfortune, with which it seems wicked to trifle. It is too selfish for pity and too serious for mirth. But let my partner go; he will get a wife in due time; indeed he has had one already; and that is about the number which nature provides. Some, it is true, take a second, and a few totter on to a third, seemingly that they may have company when they totter into the grave. Go down to your narrow house alone in the majesty of an unshaken faith, and trust to meet the partner of your youth in heaven. She waits there to beckon you to the hills of light. Meet her not with a harem of spirits at your side, but singly, as on earth,

> When first beneath the hawthorn's shade,
> The love she long had veiled from view,
> Her soft, uplifted eyes betrayed,
> As fell their broad, bright glance on you.

THURSDAY, FEB. 11. Two of the officers of Gen. Castro sent through me to-day to Com. Shubrick, applications for permission to return to Mexico. They are very poor, having received no pay since our flag was raised. There are many more in the same situation. They are entitled to our sympathy. They have tried, it is true, to retake the country; but they are not to blame for that : who would not have done the same, situated as they have been? We may call their courage sheer rashness; but even that has higher claims to respect than pusillanimity. They fought for their places, it is true, but I do not see why there is not quite as much honor in a man's fighting for bread with which to feed his children, as for a feather with which to plume his ambition. Very few in these days fight from pure patriotism. Some hope of profit or preferment lights their path and lures them on. There has been, I apprehend, quite as much love of country in the Californian as the American, in the storm of battle which has swept over this land.

FRIDAY, FEB. 12. The Cyane sailed to-day for San Francisco, where she will be allowed a short repose. And truly she merits this indulgence; she has been, under her indefatigable commander, for six months incessantly on duty, and has performed some exploits that will figure in history. All our ships on this coast have been extremely active, and their crews more active still. Wherever they have let go their anchors, it has been for service on shore. They have furled their sails only to unfurl their flags, and have relinquished the rope only to handle the carbine. Not a man of them has been missed in the hour of peril; not a murmur has escaped their lips in privation and fatigue. They have done the duty of soldiers as well as sailors. They have conquered California.

SATURDAY, FEB. 13. The great scarcity of provisions here, and the difficulty experienced in subsisting our forces, has induced Com. Shubrick to issue a circular, throwing the ports open for six months to all necessary articles of food. This step is characterized by sound policy as well as humanity. It will have the effect of lowering the exorbitant prices which we are now paying for these articles, and go far to secure the good will of the citizens. Every measure which relieves the present exigency, will be fully appreciated. The scarcity is the result, in some measure, of the war; in this we have a responsibility, and the least we can do is to relieve, so far as it lies in our power, the calamity which it has entailed.

SUNDAY, FEB. 14. The bones which bleach on the battle-field, and the groans which load the reluctant winds, are not the saddest memorials of war. They lie deeper; they are coffined in decayed virtue, and in the convulsions of outraged humanity. They convert the heart of a nation into a charnel-house, where the gloomy twilight only serves to betray the corruption which festers within. Flowers may bloom over it, and garlands be woven of their fragrant leaves, but within is death. We shudder at a recollection of the Deluge, and still gaze with wonder and fear at its ghastly memorials: *that* catastrophe, however, swept the earth but once, and then departed; but war has for ages trampled over it in blood, followed by the shrieks of fatherless children, and the wail of ruined nations.

> Where'er the blood-stained monster trod
> Fell deep and wide the curse of God.

MONDAY, FEB. 15. We have had the drama of Adam and Eve as a phase in the amusements, which have been crowded into the last days of the carnival. It was got up by one of our most respectable citizens, who for the purpose converted his ample saloon into a mimic opera-house. The actors were his own children, and those near akin. They sustained their parts well except the one who impersonated Satan; he was of too mild and frank a nature to represent such a daring, subtle character. It was as if the lark were to close his eyes to the touch of day, or the moon to invest herself with thunder. But Eve was beautiful, and full of nature as an unweaned child. She rose at once into full bloom, like the Aphrodite of Phidias from the sparkling wave. Every sound and sight struck on her wondering sense, as that of a being just waked to life. Her untaught motions melted into flowing lines, soft and graceful as those of a bird circling among flowers.

> "Her eyes as stars of twilight fair;
> Like twilight's too her dusky hair:
> But all things else about her drawn,
> From May-time and the cheerful dawn."

The features of Adam betrayed his affinity to Eve. It was a brother's pride hovering over a sister's loveliness. This imparted the highest moral charm to the association. No unhallowed thought cast an ambiguous shadow on the purity of their bliss. It was dashed by the evil one while yet untouched by sorrow. When all was lost, Adam sustained himself in his irreparable calamity with majestic resignation. In a moment of forgetfulness he cast the blame on his companion, but her silent tears instantly subdued him, and he clasped her to his heart. There is no affection so deep as that which springs from sympathy in sorrow. Tears fell here and there among the spectators, as the exiled pair left forever their own sweet Eden. The birds became silent as if they had sung only for the ear of Eve; the flowers would not lift themselves from the light pressure of her departing footstep; and the streamlet trembled in its flow, as if afraid it might lose the image, which her disappearing form had cast upon its crystal mirror.

TUESDAY, FEB. 16. It is past midnight, and I have just come from the house of T. O. Larkin, Esq., where I left the youth, the beauty, the wisdom, and worth of Monterey. There are more happy hearts there than I have met with in any other assemblage since I came to California. This is the sunshine that has followed the war-cloud. This being the last night of the carnival, every one has broken his last egg-shells. But few of them contained cologne or lavender; nearly all were filled with golden tinsel. Ladies and gentlemen too are covered with the sparkling shower, and the lights of the chandeliers are thrown back in millions of mimic rays. Two of the young ladies, remarkable for their sprightliness and beauty, broke their eggs on the head of our commodore, and got kissed by way of retaliation. They blushed, but still enjoyed their triumph. I did not venture the *lex talionés* in this form, but I had eggs, and came off pretty even in the battle. The hens will now have a little peace, and be allowed to hatch their chickens. The origin of this egg-breaking custom I have not been able to learn. It seems lost in the twilight of antiquity. I must leave it to those walking mummies, who love to grope among the catacombs of perished nations: should they discover it, their shouts will almost shake down the Egyptian pyramids.

Wednesday, Feb. 17. A convict on our public works managed to escape to-day, carrying off his ball and chain. Well, if he only will stop stealing, he may run to earth's utmost verge. I always like to see a fellow get out of trouble, and sometimes half forget his crimes in his misfortunes. This is not right, perhaps, in one situated as I am; but I cannot help it; it is as much beyond my will as the pulses which throb in my veins.

FRIDAY, FEB. 19. The volunteers, who accompanied Col. Fremont to the south, are beginning to return to their homes on the Sacramento. Several of them have stopped here on their way up, and report every thing tranquil below. They murmur in deep undertones over their failure to reach the Pueblo before the forces under Com. Stockton, and ascribe their disappointment to a want of confidence in their courage and skill. I know not how this may be; but, certainly, many and most of them could have had but very little experience in California modes of warfare. They may have been as brave as Cæsar, and their very daring have contributed to their defeat. The secret of success here, where lances are used, lies in a commander's keeping his troops compact; but this is almost a moral impossibility where men are well mounted and as full of enthusiasm as a Cape Horn cloud of storms; without the severest discipline, they will dash ahead, and take consequences however fatal. It was this error which cost Capt. Burrows and his brave companions their lives.

SATURDAY, FEB. 20. We have had a fresh stir today, in the arrival of Lieut. Watson, of the navy, with dispatches for Com. Shubrick and Gen. Kearny, and with private letters to many of the officers. I have one dated quite into November, and from my own hearth and home. I rushed into the middle of it, then to each end, to ascertain that all were well; and felt there was still one spot of earth covered with golden light.

Mr. Watson sailed from New York, November twelfth, in the brig Sylvan, landed at Chagres, and reached Panama on the twenty-seventh of the same month; was detained there waiting for a conveyance till December the twenty-fifth, when he took passage in an English steamer for Callao, fell in with the U. S. storeship Erie, at Payta, on January third, went on board of her, and arrived at San Francisco in thirty-nine days. But for the detention in Panama, he would have reached here from New York in sixty-seven days. But even this passage may be still further abridged by a line of steamers. The day is not distant when a trip to California will be regarded rather as a diversion than a serious undertaking. It will be quite worth the while to come out here merely to enjoy this climate for a few months. It is unrivalled, perhaps, in the world.

Sunday, Feb. 21. The American Tract Society has sent me out, by the Lexington, a large box of their publications. Nothing could be more timely. I have not seen a tract circulating in California. Emigrants are arriving, settling here and there, without bringing even their Bibles with them. The same is true of the United States troops. All these are to be supplied from home, and by those two great institutions which are now throwing the light of life over continents and isles. It remains for the Missionary Society to do its duty, and dispatch to this shore the self-denying heralds of the Cross.

MONDAY, FEB. 22. This is the birth-day of Washington. The Independence and Lexington are brilliantly dressed; the flags of all nations stream over them in a gorgeous arch. A salute of twenty-eight guns from the Independence has expressed the homage of each state to the occasion. Even here, and among the native population, Washington is known, and his virtues are revered. People speak of him as a being exempted from the weaknesses of our nature —as one commissioned of Heaven for a great and glorious purpose, and endowed with the amazing powers requisite for its accomplishment. It is the character of Washington that will never die. His achievements will long survive on the page of history, but his character is embalmed in the human heart. It is not a man's deeds that of themselves render him immortal. There must be some high consecrating motive. He who reared the most gigantic of the pyramids has perished. He sought an eternal remembrance in his monument, and not in any virtues which it was to perpetuate. The monument remains, but where is its builder?

"Gone, glimmering through the twilight of the past."

TUESDAY, FEB. 23. We are eagerly looking for the arrival of store-ships from the United States. Our squadron is without provisions, except fresh grub from the shore. Our ships, as far as sea-service is concerned, are of about as much use as so many nautical pictures. They look stately and brave, as they ride at anchor in our bay; but let them go to sea, and they would carry famine with them. It is a strange policy that keeps a squadron on this coast in such a disabled condition. One would suppose the Department had concluded men could live at sea on moonshine.

WEDNESDAY, FEB. 24. A Californian woman complained to me, several months since, of very ill-treatment from her husband. He was thoroughly indolent, cross, and abusive. She had him and the children to feed and clothe, while he did nothing but lounge about, find fault, and abuse her. She asked for a divorce; but I told her she must be satisfied, for the present, with a separation. So I called him before me, and ordered him to gather up his traps, and leave the house for six months. He grumbled a little, but obeyed the order.

To-day, the woman returned, and said she would try to live with her husband again; that he often now walked past the house, and looked very lonely and dejected; that she felt sorry for him, and, if I was willing, she would try him again. I told her, with all my heart; that this was good Christian conduct in her, and much better than a divorce. She seemed gratified with this warm commendation; so did her husband with the permission to return. How the restoration will turn out, remains to be seen. But how forgiving is the heart of woman! Where she has once loved, the affection never dies. Neglect may chill it, but it will bud again, as plants, over which the snows of winter have been spread.

THURSDAY, FEB. 25. A courier arrived to-day from los Angeles. Every thing continues quiet there. The Californians had entirely dispersed, and retired to their ranchos, with the exception of those few who had gone upon a forlorn hope to Sonora. They will never be able to raise a force there sufficient to make any impression here. Mexico has enough to do in her own borders, without an attempt to retake California.

FRIDAY, FEB. 26. A captain of artillery in the Californian army, said to me a few days since, that his military career was now over, that he had a numerous family to maintain, and he thought of engaging in making adobes, if I would sell him a small patch of ground for that purpose, belonging to the municipality; but stated that he had no money, and was not a little puzzled to know how he was to pay for it, unless I would suggest some method by which he could work it out with his boys and team. I told him I was drawing stone for a prison; that he could engage in this, and should be allowed the highest cash price. To-day I found him, with his boys, at the quarry, lifting the stone into his cart. To show him that I connected no idea of degradation with the work, I turned to and assisted in heaving in one of the hugest in the pile. He wanted to know if the people in the United States generally worked. I told him all, except a few loafers and dandies, who were regarded as a public nuisance. He said he was glad to hear it; for he must now work himself, and it would be an easier lot with others to share it with him. I assured him he would have company enough, as the emigration poured in over the mountains. I must say, I have more respect for this working captain of artillery, than for forty of his rank clinging to the shreds of office, and shrinking from honest labor.

SATURDAY, FEB. 27. The weather continues bright and beautiful. The air is soft, the sky clear, the trees are in bud, and the fields are medallioned with flowers. A bouquet of these floral offerings was sent me to-day by a California lady, with a little note in liquid Castilian, that I would accept them as emblems of those hopes, which were timidly expanding into life for California. Long may those hopes remain, and long the gentle being who has sent these tokens live to walk in their light. She is one, over whom adversity has swept; but she breaks from its gloomy veil, bright as a star from the shadow of the departed cloud.

SUNDAY, FEB. 28. It is Lent; and the family that live the next door to mine, are at their evening prayers. They were merry as a marriage-bell during carnival, and now they are in sackcloth and ashes. Religion has a wide vibration to reach these extremes of mirth and melancholy. But life itself is made up of vicissitudes; wealth disappears in poverty; smiles dissolve in tears; and the light of our mortal being goes out in the night of the grave. But there is a higher life that is never overcast—a spirit-home, where sorrow and change come not. Thither let the weary lift the eye of faith, and forget the cares which environ their pilgrimage here.

MONDAY, FEB. 29. Our harbor has been thrown into some commotion again by another of the great leviathans of the deep. The U. S. ship of the line Columbus, commanded by Capt. Wyman, and bearing the broad pennant of Com. Biddle, entered our bay in stately majesty this morning. She came in before a light breeze, under a vast cloud of canvas, and rounded to in splendid style, near the Independence. She is the largest ship that has ever been on this coast. Ladies and gentlemen watched from hill-top and balcony her approach. She is last from Callao; her crew have recovered from the effects of the East India climate, and her officers are all in excellent spirits. They preferred, of course, a more immediate return home, but evinced no want of alacrity in obeying the mandate that has brought them here. I find among them my esteemed friend, the Rev. Mr. Newton, highly and justly respected in the service. We separated in Philadelphia to meet in California! After this we may expect to encounter each other at the North Pole!

TUESDAY, MARCH 3. The U. S. ship Warren, under Commander Hull, is in from San Francisco. She is now in the fourth year of her cruise, and has hardly copper enough on her to make a warming-pan. Some say she will tumble to pieces if an attempt is made to get her around Cape Horn. But she has weathered many stormy headlands, and would undoubtedly weather that. Still, she may be detained here as a harbor-ship; but wiser heads than mine will determine that question. Her crew ought to be permitted to return; it is cruel to keep men out as they have been. The sailor's lot is hard enough, indeed, when every suitable effort is made to relieve it. There are but few drops of real happiness in his cup of sorrow. He has his pastimes, it is true, but they partake more of insanity than sober gladness. He is cradled in adversity, reared in neglect, and dies in the midst of his days; and over his floating bier the ocean thunders its dirge.

WEDNESDAY, MARCH 4. The convict that escaped a short time since was overtaken by my constable ninety miles distant, and brought back to-day. He looked like one whose last desperate hope had been baffled. I asked what he attempted to run away for. He said the devil put it into his head. I told him the poor old devil had enough to answer for without being charged with his offences, and doubled the time of his sentence, which was only for six months, and sent him back to the public works. He is rather a hardened character, but if he has got a good vein in him, I will try to find it. And in the mean time I shall set the prisoners quarrying stone for a school-house, and have already laid the foundations. The building is to be sixty feet by thirty—two stories, suitably proportioned, with a handsome portico. The labor of the convicts, the taxes on rum, and the banks of the gamblers, must put it up. Some think my project impracticable; we shall see.

CHAPTER XIII.

THE PEOPLE OF MONTEREY.—THE GUITAR AND RUNAWAY WIFE.—MOTHER ORDERED TO FLOG HER SON.—WORK OF THE PRISONERS.—CATCHING SAILORS.—COURT OF ADMIRALTY.—GAMBLERS CAUGHT AND FINED.—LIFTING LAND BOUNDARIES.

SATURDAY, MARCH 6. I have never been in a community that rivals Monterey in its spirit of hospitality and generous regard. Such is the welcome to the privileges of the private hearth, that a public hotel has never been able to maintain itself. You are not expected to wait for a particular invitation, but to come without the slightest ceremony, make yourself entirely at home, and tarry as long as it suits your inclination, be it for a day or for a month. You create no flutter in the family, awaken no apologies, and are greeted every morning with the same bright smile. It is not a smile which flits over the countenance, and passes away like a flake of moonlight over a marble tablet. It is the steady sunshine of the soul within.

If a stranger, you are not expected to bring a formal letter of introduction. No one here thinks any the better of a man who carries the credentials of his character and standing in his pocket. A word or an allusion to recognized persons or places is sufficient. If you turn out to be different from what your first impressions and fair speech promised, still you meet with no frowning looks, no impatience for your departure. You still enjoy in full that charity which suffereth long, and is kind. The children are never told that you are a burden; you enjoy their glad greetings and unsuspecting confidence to the last. And when you finally depart, it will not be without a benison; not perhaps that you are worthy of it; but you belong to the great human family, where faults often spring from misfortune, and the force of untoward circumstances. Generous, forbearing people of Monterey! there is more true hospitality in one throb of your heart, than circulates for years through the courts and capitals of kings.

TUESDAY, MARCH 16. Met Com. Biddle and Gen. Kearny to-day by appointment, and gave them a history of California affairs from the time the flag was raised. Both expressed a little surprise at some of the events that had occurred, but neither called in question the wisdom of the policy which had been pursued. The report of a disposition on the part of these distinguished officers to cast reproach on events in California, are without a shadow of foundation. Com. Biddle has not come, it is true, to prosecute the measures of his predecessors, nor has he come to repudiate them. He desires, so far as his instructions will permit, to let them remain as he found them, and leave to time, that moral touchstone of wisdom and folly, the tests of their expediency.

WEDNESDAY, MARCH 17. I met a Californian to-day with a guitar, from which he was reeling off a merry strain, and asked him how it was possible he could be so light-hearted while the flag of his country was passing to the hands of the stranger. Oh, said the Californian, give us the guitar and a fandango, and the devil take the flag. This reveals a fact deeper than what meets the eye. The Californians as a community never had any profound reverence for their nominal flag. They have regarded it only as an evidence of their colonial relation to Mexico; a relation for which they have felt neither affection nor pride.

THURSDAY, MARCH 18. A poor fellow came to me to-day, and complained that his wife had run away with another man, and wanted I should advise him what to do. I asked him if he desired her to come back; he said he did, for he had five children who required her care. I told him he must then keep still: the harder he chased a deer, the faster it would run; that if he kept quiet she would soon circle back again to him.

He hardly seemed to understand the philosophy of inaction: I told him there was hardly an animal in the world that might not be won by doing nothing; that the hare ran from us simply because we had chased it; that a woman ran for the same reason, though generally with a different motive: the one ran to escape, the other to be overtaken. He consented to try the do-nothing plan, and in the mean time I shall try to catch the villain who has covered an humble family with disaster.

THURSDAY, MARCH 25. A California mother complained to me to-day, that her son, a full grown youth, had struck her. Usage here allows a mother to chastise her son as long as he remains unmarried and lives at home, whatever may be his age, and regards a blow inflicted on a parent as a high offence. I sent for the culprit; laid his crime before him, for which he seemed to care but little; and ordered him to take off his jacket, which was done. Then putting a riata into the hands of his mother, whom nature had endowed with strong arms, directed her to flog him. Every cut of the riata made the fellow jump from the floor. Twelve lashes were enough; the mother did her duty, and as I had done mine, the parties were dismissed. No further complaint from that quarter.

MONDAY, APRIL 12. The old prison being too confined and frail for the safe custody of convicts, I have given orders for the erection of a new one. The work is to be done by the prisoners themselves; they render the building necessary, and it is but right they should put it up. Every bird builds its own nest. The old one will hold an uninventive Indian, but a veteran from Sidney or Sing Sing would work his way out like a badger from his hole, which the school urchin had obstructed. I had an experiment with one a few nights since, and he went through the roof with ball and chain. How he ever reached the rafters, unless the man in the moon magnetized him, I cannot conjecture. But out he got, and it cost me a California chase to catch him.

THURSDAY, APRIL 16. Six of the crew of the Columbus ran from one of her boats this morning. They cleared the town in a few minutes, and plunged into a forest which shadows a mountain gorge. The officer of the boat came with a request from Capt. Wyman that I would have them caught and brought back. My constables were both absent, and I ordered three Californians who were well mounted to go in pursuit. The native people are always inclined to aid a sailor in his attempt to escape; they seem to think he is of course running from oppression or wrong, when in nine cases out of ten he is running upon some sudden impulse, and continues the race because he has begun it.

In this instance an order was given and it was obeyed; the sailors were promptly apprehended and brought back. But had I offered a reward of fifty dollars each for them, and left the Californians to pursue or not as they preferred, not one of them would have been apprehended. I have never known a Californian to molest a runaway sailor or soldier to secure the reward offered. He will obey my order to arrest him, and he would do the same if ordered to arrest his own brother, but he will not do it to secure any pecuniary consideration. He seems to look upon it as a breach of national hospitality. Were the De'il himself to call for a night's lodging, the Californian would hardly find it in his heart to bolt the door. He would think they could manage against his horn hoof and tail in some way.

SATURDAY, APRIL 18. The Pacific squadron having captured several prizes not in a condition to be sent round the cape for adjudication in the United States, the necessity of a court of admiralty here to determine upon them, has induced Com. Biddle and Gen. Kearny to take the responsibility of its organization. They have installed me in this new office, invested with the authority which emanates through them from the national executive, and the still higher sanctions derived *ex necessitate rei.* And now comes the task of looking up those legal authorities which may serve as guiding lights and safe precedents. But even here, on this dim confine of civilization, loom to light all the bright particular stars which have shed their rays on the intricacies of national law and admiralty jurisprudence. We have the eloquent commentaries of Kent, the able dissertations of Wheaton, the lucid expositions of Chitty, and the authoritative decisions of Sir William Scott. These, with half a dozen young lawyers ready to throw in their own effulgent beam, as the glow-worm turns the sparkle in its tail to the sun, will enable us perhaps to escape the breakers, where much richer argosies than ours have been wrecked. But one thing is pretty certain, my journal in the midst of all these perplexing duties will find some breaks in it. I must hunt my rabbits, quail, and curlew, or stagnate on beef; a sirloin may regale the hungry for a time, but even that, if confined to it, palls on the appetite worse than a one-stringed fiddle on the ear, or the low, wordless, monotonous grumble of a discontented wife.

WEDNESDAY, MAY 12. A nest of gamblers arrived in town yesterday, and last evening opened a monté at the hotel honored with the name of the Astor House. I took a file of soldiers, and under cover of night reached the hotel unsuspected, where I stationed them at the two doors which afforded the only egresses from the building. In a moment I was on the stairs which lead to the apartment where the gamesters were congregated. I heard a whistle and then footsteps flying into every part of the edifice. On entering the great chamber, not a being was visible save one Sonoranian reclining against a large table, and composedly smoking his cigarito. I passed the compliments of the evening with him, and desired the honor of an introduction to his companions.

At this moment a feigned snore broke on my ear from a bed in the corner of the apartment.—"Ha! Dutre, is that you? Come, tumble up, and aid me in stirring out the rest." He pointed under the bed, where I discovered, just within the drop of the valance a multitude of feet and legs radiating as from a common centre. "Hallo there, friends—turn out!" and out came some half-dozen or more, covered with dust and feathers, and odorous as the nameless furniture left behind. Their plight and discovery threw them into a laugh at each other. From this apartment, accompanied by my secretary, I proceeded to others, where I found the slopers stowed away in every imaginable position—some in the beds, some under them, several in closets, two in a hogshead, and one up a chimney. Mr. R——, from Missouri—known here under the soubriquet of "the prairie-wolf"—I found between two bed-ticks, with his coat and boots on, and half smothered with the feathers. He was the ringleader, and raises a monté table wherever he goes as regularly as a whale comes to the surface to blow. All shouted as he tumbled out from his ticks. Among the rest I found the alcalde of San Francisco, a gentleman of education and refinement, who never plays himself, but who, on this occasion, had come to witness the excitement. I gathered them all, some fifty in number, into the large saloon, and told them the only speech I had to make was in the shape of a fine of twenty dollars each. The more astute began to demur on the plea of not guilty, as no cards and no money had been discovered; and as for the beds, a man had as good a right to sleep under one as in it. I told them that was a matter of taste, misfortune often made strange bedfellows, and the only way to get out of the scrape was to pay up. Dr. S—— was the first to plank down. "Come, my good fellows," said the doctor, "pay up, and no grumbling; this money goes to build a schoolhouse, where I hope our children will be taught better principles than they gather from the example of their fathers." The "prairie-wolf" planked down next, and in ten minutes the whole, Chillanos, Sonoranians, Oregonians, Californians, Englices, Americanos, delivered in their fines. These, with the hundred dollar fine of the keeper of the hotel, filled quite a bag. With this I bade them good night, and took my departure. I hope the doctor's prediction will prove true; certainly it shall not be my fault if it turns out a failure. In all this there was not an angry look or petulant remark; they knew I was doing my duty, and they felt that they atoned in part for a violation of theirs through their fines. If you must hold office be an alcalde, be absolute, but be upright, impartial, and humane.

THURSDAY, MAY 27. A ranchero, living some forty miles distant, not liking his own land, had lifted his boundary line, and projected it some six miles over that of his neighbor. Quite a lap this would be among farmers in the United States, but a small slice here. I was called upon to decide the difficulty. Taking with me from the public archives a certified copy of the original grant to each of the rancheros, I proceeded to the spot, where I found some twenty men under the shadow of a great oak-tree, and each ready to locate the boundaries agreeably to the interests of the party that had summoned him. I listened to the stories of each, and then asked the ranchero, who had lifted his line, to show me his grant. He drew it from his pocket—a document signed, sealed, and delivered with all the formalities of law. I then drew out the original, and found their topographical lines as much alike as the here and there of an unresting squatter. The fact was, the man had two grants; but the last one being a palpable invasion of his neighbor's domain, as secured to him under the seal of the state, he must of course retreat within the limits of the first. A township of land being thus judicially and justly disposed of, I started on my return; fell in with a grizzly bear—levelled and fired—but without waiting to see if the ball took effect, dashed on. A loadless rifle, with an enraged bear at your heels, makes you value a fleet horse in California.

CHAPTER XIV.

A CONVICT WHO WOULD NOT WORK.—LAWYERS AT MONTEREY.—WHO CONQUERED CALIFORNIA.—RIDE TO A RANCHO.—LEOPALDO.—PARTY OF CALIFORNIANS.—A DASH INTO THE FORESTS.—CHASING A DEER.—KILLING A BEAR.—LADIES WITH FIREARMS.—A MOTHER AND VOLUNTEER.

FRIDAY, JUNE 18. One of the prisoners, who is an Englishman, ventured a criticism on the stonework of another prisoner, which revealed the fact of his being a stonecutter himself. I immediately sat him at work at his old trade. But he feigned utter ignorance of it, and spoiled several blocks in making his feint good. I then ordered him into a deep well, where the water had given out, to drill and blast rocks. He drove his drills here for several days, and finding that the well was to be sunk some twenty or thirty feet deeper, concluded it was better for him to work in the upper air, and requested that he might be permitted to try his chisel again. Permission was given, and he is now shaping stones fit to be laid in the walls of a cathedral. He was taken up for disorderly conduct, and he is now at work on a schoolhouse, where the principles of good order are the first things to be taught.

SATURDAY, JUNE 19. We have at this time three young lawyers in Monterey, as full of legal acuteness as the lancet cup of a phlebotomist. All want clients, and fees, and the privilege of a practice in this court. Mexican statutes, which prevail here, permit lawyers as counsel, but preclude their pleas. They may examine witnesses, sift evidence, but not build arguments. This spoils the whole business, and every effort has been made to have the impediment removed, and the floodgate of eloquence lifted. I should be glad to gratify their ambition, but it is impossible. I should never get through with the business pressing on my hands in every variety of shape which civil and criminal jurisprudence ever assumed. I tell them after the evidence has been submitted, the verdict or decision must follow, and then if any in the court-room desire to hear the arguments, they can adjourn to another apartment, and plead as long as they like. In this way justice will go ahead, and eloquence too, and the great globe still turn on its axle.

SATURDAY, JULY 17. Com. Stockton has left us on his return home over the continent. His measures in California have been bold and vigorous, and have been followed by decisive results. He found the country in anarchy and confusion, and the greater part under the Mexican flag, and has left it in peace and quietness beneath the stars and stripes. His position in the march of the American forces from San Diego, and in the battle of San Gabriel, has not been changed by any subsequent information in the judgment of the candid and impartial. He tendered the command of the expedition to Gen. Kearny, which that gallant officer deferred to the commodore, out of regard to his position at the head of the naval forces upon which the success of the enterprise must depend. The propriety of this arrangement is seen in the fact that the general had but sixty dragoons at his command, and those on foot, while the Pacific squadron poured six hundred seamen and marines upon the field. There was no confusion of orders or evolutions on the route; every general movement emanated from Com. Stockton, with the good understanding and harmonious action of Gen. Kearny.

It is deeply to be regretted that any thing subsequently occurred to disturb this spirit of mutual deference and generous devotion to the crisis which pressed upon our ams. It is not my purpose to comment on this feature in the affairs of California; but it is due to truth that history should be set right; that facts warped from their true position should be reinstated on their own pedestals. The army has covered itself with laurels on the plains of Mexico, and might have won honors here with an adequate force; but to rely on sixty dragoons in the face of a thousand Californians, armed with the rifle and lance, and accustomed to the saddle from their birth, is to trifle with the stern solemnities of war. It is requiring too much of us, who have lived here through the war, and are conversant with its history, to claim our assent to the allegation, that California has been conquered through the achievements of the army. *That* unshrinking arm of the nation has done its work well and fast elsewhere, but only the vibrations of its blows have trembled across the confines of California. For matter of these the Mexican flag would still be flying over these hills and valleys. The seamen of the Pacific squadron, as reliable on land as faithful on the deck, and the emigrants, who have come here to find a home, have wrenched this land of wealth and promise from the grasp of Mexico, and unfurled the stars and stripes, where they will wave evermore. Let the laurel light where it belongs.

TUESDAY, AUG. 10. An Indian galloped to my door this morning, having in lead a splendid pied horse, richly caparisoned, and with an invitation from a ranchero, forty miles distant, that I would come and spend a few days with him at his country-seat; so I placed the office in the hands of Don Davido, well competent to its duties, and with my secretary, Mr. G——, mounted on another noble animal, started for the mansion of my old friend from the mountains of Spain, now in the winter of age, but with a heart warm as a sunbeam. The town, with its white dwellings, soon vanished behind the pine and evergreen oak, which crown the hills, that throw around it their arms of waving shade. The little lakes, navelled in the breaks of the forest, flashed on the eye; the water-fowl, in clouds, took wing; the quail whirled into the bushes; and the deer bounded off to their woodland retreats. A grizzly bear, with a storm of darkness in his face, stood his ground, and never even blinked at the crack of our pistols.

We were now on the bank of the Salinas, through which we dashed, allowing our horses a taste of its yellow waters, then up the opposite bank, and away over the broad plain, which stretches in vernal beauty beyond. Our horses required no spur, were in fine condition, high spirits, never broke their gallop, and swept ahead, like a fawn to its covert. Mine belonged to the daughter of the Don, to whose hearth we were bound, and had often rattled about among these hills beneath his fair owner, whose equestrian graces and achievements might throw a fresh enchantment on the chase that had gathered to its rivalries the beauty and bravery of Old England. Another mountain stream—a dash through its foaming tide, and away again through a broad ravine, which bent its ample track to the steep hills, which threw the shadows of their waving trees over a thousand echoing caverns. Where the forests broke, the wild oats waved, like golden lakes, and mirrored the passing cloud; while the swaying pines rolled out their music on the wind, like the dirge of ocean. And now another luxuriant plain, where cattle, and horses, and sheep gambolled and grazed by thousands; and on the opposite side the white mansion of our host, crowning the headland, and glimmering through the waving shade, like the columns which consecrate Colonna. Here we alighted without weariness to ourselves or our spirited animals, though we had swept through the forty miles in three hours and a half. The señorita, who had sent me her horse, vaulted into the saddle, which I had just relinquished, and patting the noble fellow, whom she called Leopaldo, induced him to exhibit a variety of his cunning evolutions. He knew his rider as well as a Newfoundlander his mistress, or an eagle his mountain mate.

It was a festive eve at the Don's; youth and beauty were there; and as the sable hues of night sunk on silent tree and tower, the harp and guitar woke into melodious action; the hour was late when the waltz and song resigned their votaries to the calmer claims of slumber. My apartment betrayed the rural diversions of some fairy, one whose floral trophies threw their fragrance from every variety of vase. The air was loaded with perfume, and could hardly be relieved by the visits of the night-wind through the lifted window. My dreams ran on tulips and roses. Morn blazed again in the east; the soaring lark sung from its cloud; the guests were up, glad voices were heard in the hall; light forms glanced through the corridors, and a *buenos dios* rolled in sweet accents from lips circled with smiles. Coffee and tortillas went round, mingled with salutations and those first fresh thoughts which spring from the heart like early birds from the tree, which the sunlight has touched, while the dew yet sparkles on its leaves. The horses of the Don were now driven to the door— a sprightly band—vieing in their hues with the flowers that sprinkled the meadows where they gambolled, and the guests were invited to make their selection. My choice fell, of course, on Leopaldo, who had brought me from Monterey; but his fair owner would want him; no, he was delivered to me, as the señorita took another quite as full of fire.

The ladies were now tost into their saddles, and the gentlemen, belted and spurred, vaulted into theirs. We all struck at once into a hand gallop, and swept over the broad plain which stretches from the acropolis of the Don, to the broken line of a mountain range. Here we spurred into a broad shadowy ravine, overhung with toppling crags, and breaking through the bold ranges of rock, which threw their steep faces in wild fantastic forms on the eye. "A coyote!" shouted those in the van, and started in chase; but this prairie-wolf had his den near at hand, and soon vanished from sight. Another, and a third, but the chasm yielded its instant refuge. A fourth was started, who gave us a longer pursuit; but he soon doubled from sight around a bold bluff into a jungle. Here the horse of señorita S—— dashed ahead of the whole caballada, with his dilated eye fastened on a noble buck, and swept up the sloping side of the ravine to gain the ridge, and cut off his escape in that direction, while the whole troop spurred hot and fast upon his retreat below. We were now in for a chase, brief though it might be. The buck seemed confused; and no wonder, with such a shouting bevy at his heels, and with the señorita streaming along the ridge, and dashing over chasm and cliff like the storm-swept cloud where "leaps the live thunder." But the proud buck was not be captured in this way; and as soon as the other side of the ravine began to slope from its steep line, up its bank he sprung, and bounded along its ridge as if in exulting rivalry at the rattling chase of the señorita. "Two *deers*," shouted one of the caballeros, "and neither of them to be caught."

We here wheeled into another mountain gorge, which opened into a long irregular vista of savage wildness. A gallop of two or three miles brought us to a spot where the rocky barriers retreated on either hand, shaping out a bowl, in the centre of which stood a cluster of oaks. On the lower limb of one, which threw its giant arm boldly from the rough trunk, a dark object was descried, half lost in the leaves. "A bear, a bear!" shouted our leader, and dashed up to the tree, which was instantly surrounded by the whole troop, "Give us pistols," exclaimed the señoritas, as bravely in for the sport as the rest. Click, crack! and a storm of balls went through the tree-top. Down came old bruin with one bound into the midst, full of wrath and revenge. The horses instinctively wheeled into a circle, and as bruin sprung for a death-grapple, the lasso of our baccaros, thrown with unerring aim, brought him up all standing. He now turned upon the horse of his new assailant; but that sagacious animal evaded each plunge, and seemed to play in transport about his antagonist. The pistols were out again, and a fresh volley fell thick as hail around the bear. In the smoke and confusion no one could tell where his next spring might be; but the horse of the baccaro knew his duty and kept the lasso taught. Bruin was wounded, but resolute and undaunted; the fire rolled from his red eyes like a flash of lightning out of a forked cloud. Foiled in his plunges at the horse, he seized the lasso in his paws, and in a moment more would have been at his side, but the horse sprung and tripped him, rolling him over and over till he lost his desperate hold on the lasso. The pistols were reloaded, and señoritas and caballeros all dashed up for another shower of fire and lead. As the smoke cleared, bruin was found with the lasso slack, a sure evidence that the horse who managed it knew his antagonist was dead.

This was sport enough for one day; we galloped on through the defile, which wound round a mountain spur, till it struck a precipitous stream, which sent into the green nooks the wild echoes of its cascades. Following the ravine through which it poured its more tranquil tide, we debouched at length upon the plain, crowned with the hospitable mansion of our host. The feats of the morning astonished even the old Don, who offered his favorite roan to the one whose bullet had killed the bear. The meed was challenged by each and all, but no one could make good and exclusive claim. The gentlemen relinquished their claim, but that only made the matter worse, as it narrowed the contest to the circle of the señoritas. Dinner was announced; then came the siesta, followed by the soft twilight, with the harp, guitar, and song, which melted away into sweet sleep. In the morning Mr. G. and myself, with the glorious Leopaldo, waved our adieu, and returned to Monterey.

MONDAY, SEPT. 6. A mother, who lives with a man out of wedlock, applied to me this morning to take her two daughters from an aunt, with whom they were living, and place them in another family. When asked for her reasons, she stated that this aunt had not a good reputation, and though bad herself, she did not want to see her daughters so. I told her she could hardly expect me to make her daughters better than their mother; that parental example was stronger than law; that if she wanted to keep her daughters pure, she must be so herself. She shed tears: I said no more; but ordered her daughters into the family where she desired.

TUESDAY, SEPT. 7. One of the volunteers broke into my coral last night, with the intention of reaching the hen-roost, but was frightened nearly to death by a discharge of mustard-seed from an old fowling-piece, with which my servant had armed himself, for the protection of his poultry. Some of the volunteers, and I hope much the larger portion, are upright, honest men, but there are others who will steal any thing and every thing, from a horse to a hen. One of the evils of a soldier's lot is, that the good are often confounded with the bad. But every profession suffers in the same way.

FRIDAY, SEPT. 10. Our bay is full of sardines; an Indian jumped into the surf and scooped up for me, with his blanket, half a peck in a few minutes. The pelican follows these small fish, and pounces down upon them with a savage ferocity. There is something in such a sudden destruction of life, even in a minnow, which you don't like. I have often wished the bird just shot again on the wing.

We are looking every moment for the return of the Cyane, under Commander Du Pont, from the Sandwich Islands, where she has been on important service. She is the water-witch of the Pacific—if ceaseless motion can claim that honor. Her commander enjoys so thoroughly the confidence and affection of his officers and crew, they go with him through all this exhausting service without a murmur. It is a happy tact that can maintain discipline and wield at any moment the whole moral and physical power of such a ship.

CHAPTER XV.

A CALIFORNIA PIC-NIC.—SEVENTY AND SEVENTEEN IN THE DANCE.—CHILDREN IN THE GROVE.—A CALIFORNIA BEAR-HUNT.—THE BEAR AND BULL BATED.—THE RUSSIAN'S CABBAGE HEAD.

WEDNESDAY, SEPT. 22. The lovers of rural pastimes were on an early stir this morning with their pic-nic preparations. Basket after basket, freighted with ham, poultry, game, pies, and all kinds of pastry, took their course in the direction of a wood which stands three miles from town, and shades a sloping cove in the strand of the sea. The sky was without a cloud, and the brooding fog had lifted its dusky wings from the face of the bright waters. At every door the impatient steed, gayly caparisoned, was waiting his rider. Into the saddle youth and age vaulted together, while the araba rolled forward with its living freight of laughing childhood. The dogs swept on before, barking in chorus, and flaring the gay ribbon which some happy child had fastened round the neck.

This mingled tide of health and social gladness flowed on to the grove of pine and birch, which threw their branching arms in a verdant canopy over a plat of green grass, which had been shorn close to the level earth. Around this arena strayed every variety of twig-inwoven seat, where matron and maiden, in

A California party on a Pic-nic excursion.

the flow of the heart, forgot their disparity of years. The children wreathed each other's locks with coronals of flowers, the soft breeze whispered in the pines, and the little billow murmured its music on the strand. And now the violin, the harp, and guitar woke the bounding dance. Forth upon the green the man of seventy, still erect and tall, led the blooming girl of sixteen. Age had whitened his locks, but the light of an unclouded spirit still rolled in his eye, and the salient bound of youth still dwelt in his limbs. His young partner, with her tresses of raven darkness, inwoven with snow-white flowers,—with a cheek, where the mantling tide of health was curbed into a blush—and a step light and elastic as that of the gazelle, seemed as one of Flora's train, just lighted there to swim in youth and beauty in the wild woodland merriment. By the side of these, others, in mingled youth and age, lead down the double files, and balance and whirl in the mazy measures which roll from the orchestral band. As these retire, others still spring to the arena, and the dance goes on, ever changing, and still the same. No faltering step delays its feathered feet, no glance of envy disturbs its love-lit smiles, no look of clouded care overshadows its real mirth:

> "The garlands, the rose-odors, and the flowers,
> The sparkling eyes, and flashing ornaments,
> The white arms and the raven hair, the braids
> And bracelets, swan-like bosoms, the thin robes
> Floating like light clouds 'twixt our gaze and heaven."

And now they glide to the tables, which stretch away under the embowering trees, and where the rich larder has emptied its choicest stores. There the savory venison scents the still air, and the wild strawberries blush between the green leaves. There the domestic fowl, the swift-footed hare, and the timid quail have met in strange brotherhood. There the juice of the native grape, and the cool wave of the gushing rock, sparkle in the flowing goblet. These were discussed, and the festive board was relinquished to the children, who were too full of glee to note if aught more than the fruit and confectionery remained. The ripe berry sought in vain to add color to their lips, or rival the bloom which lent its rosy hue to the round cheek. Golden locks floated around eyes which sparkled with light and love, and the accents of gladness rung out in joyous peals, like the song of birds when the storm-cloud has passed.

"Theirs was the shout! the song! the burst of joy!
Which sweet from childhood's rosy lip resoundeth;
Theirs was the eager spirit naught could cloy,
And the glad heart from which all grief reboundeth."

The music from the harp and guitar streamed out again, and the green plat was full of glancing forms, where youth and age, maternal dignity and maiden charms, led down the merry dance. As these glided to their seats, childhood crowned with wild-flowers sprung to the arena, with motions light as the measures through which it whirled its infantile forms. A sylvan Pan might have fancied his fays had left their green-wood covert to frolic on the green beneath the soft light of the dying day. But ere the evening star ascended its watchtower the merry groups were on their fleet steeds, bounding over hill and valley to their homes. The shadows of the moonlit trees fell in softness and silence where all this mirth had been; only the silver tones of the streamlets were heard as they murmured their music in the ear of night. The echoes of our voices will all cease in the places that have known us as we glide at last to the "dim bourn," nor will a leaflet tremble long in the breath of memory. The myriads who people the past are still, the stir of their existence is over, the great ocean of their being is at rest. The wandering wind only sighs over their tombless repose.

FRIDAY, OCT. 10. Captain Hull, who has been out here nearly four years in command of the Warren, left us to-day for the United States. He has rendered good service to the country during his long exile. May prosperous breezes waft him safely to his distant home. Lieut. J. B. Lanman succeeds to the command of the Warren; an officer justly esteemed for his gentlemanly deportment and professional intelligence. It is this foreign duty that puts the competency and fidelity of an officer to the test. It is easy to carry on duty at a navy yard, but duty on board ship with a heterogeneous crew, is another thing; it calls for the last resources of the officer, in the maintenance of discipline, harmony, and efficiency.

For a person who has been but a few months in a man-of-war, and never been at sea in any other situation, to attempt to enlighten the public on the discipline of the navy, or any of the duties which belong on board ship, is an exhibition of impertinent vanity. He has no practical knowledge of the subjects upon which he is delivering his sage lecture. He has a certain theory with which he proposes to test the wisdom or folly, the humanity or cruelty, of every thing in the service; and when this theory gets snagged, which is often the case, he is for rooting out the whole concern. He don't reflect that his land theory is as much out of its element at sea as a stranded porpoise would be out of his. All the habits and usages of a man-of-war, are heaven wide of those which obtain on land. They require rules and regulations suited to their genius. Reforms must necessarily be of slow growth; they must take root in the service itself, and not in the novelties of any land theory.

THURSDAY, OCT. 28. The king of all field-sports in California is the bear-hunt: I determined to witness one, and for this purpose joined a company of native gentlemen bound out on this wild amusement. All were well mounted, armed with rifles and pistols, and provided with lassoes. A ride of fifteen miles among the mountain crags, which frown in stern wildness over the tranquil beauty of Monterey, brought us to a deserted shanty, in the midst of a gloomy forest of cypress and oak. In a break of this swinging gloom lay a natural pasture, isled in the centre by a copse of willows and birch, and on which the sunlight fell. This, it was decided, should be the arena of the sport: a wild bullock was now shot, and the quarters, after being trailed around the copse, to scent the bear, were deposited in its shade. The party now retired to the shanty, where our henchman tumbled from his panniers several rolls of bread, a boiled ham, and a few bottles of London porter. These discussed, and our horses tethered, each wrapped himself in his blanket, and with his saddle for his pillow, rolled down for repose.

At about twelve o'clock of the night our watch came into camp and informed us that a bear had just entered the copse. In an instant each sprung to his feet and into the saddle. It was a still, cloudless night, and the moonlight lay in sheets on rivulet, rock, and plain. We proceeded with a cautious, noiseless step, through the moist grass of the pasture to the copse in its centre, where each one took his station, forming a cordon around the little grove. The horse was the first to discover, through the glimmering shade, the stealthful movements of his antagonist. His ears were thrown forward, his nostrils distended, his breathing became heavy and oppressed, and his large eye was fixed immovably on the dim form of the savage animal. Each rider now uncoiled his lasso from its loggerhead, and held it ready to spring from his hand, like a hooped serpent from the brake. The bear soon discovered the trap that had been laid for him; plunged from the thicket, broke through the cordon, and was leaping, with giant bounds, over the cleared plot for the dark covert of the forest beyond. A shout arose—a hot pursuit followed, and lasso after lasso fell in curving lines around the bear, till at last one looped him around the neck and brought him to a momentary stand.

As soon as bruin felt the lasso, he growled his defiant thunder, and sprung in rage at the horse. Here came in the sagacity of that noble animal. He knew, as well as his rider, that the safety of both depended on his keeping the lasso taught, and without the admonitions of rein or spur, bounded this way and that, to the front or rear, to accomplish his object, never once taking his eye from the ferocious foe, and ever in an attitude to foil his assaults. The bear, in desperation, seized the lasso in his griping paws, and hand over hand drew it into his teeth: a moment more and he would have been within leaping distance of his victim; but the horse sprung at the instant, and, with a sudden whirl, tripped the bear and extricated the lasso. At this crowning feat the horse fairly danced with delight. A shout went up which seemed to shake the wild-wood with its echoes. The bear plunged again, when the lasso slipped from its loggerhead, and bruin was instantly leaping over the field to reach his jungle. The horse, without spur or rein, dashed after him. While his rider, throwing himself over his side, and hanging there like a lampereel to a flying sturgeon, recovered his lasso, bruin was brought up again all standing, more frantic and furious than before; while the horse pranced and curveted around him like a savage in his death-dance over his doomed captive. In all this no overpowering torture was inflicted on old bruin, unless it were through his own rage,—which sometimes towers so high he drops dead at your feet. He was now lassoed to a sturdy oak, and wound so closely to its body by riata over riata, as to leave him no scope for breaking or grinding off his clankless chain; though his struggles were often terrific as those of Laocoon, in the resistless folds of the serpent.

This accomplished, the company retired again to the shanty, but in spirits too high and noisy for sleep. Day glimmered, and four of the baccaros started off for a wild bull, which they lassoed out of a roving herd, and in a few hours brought into camp, as full of fury as the bear. Bruin was now cautiously unwound, and stood front to front with his horned antagonist. We retreated on our horses to the rim of a large circle, leaving the arena to the two monarchs of the forest and field. Conjectures went wildly round on the issue, and the excitement became momently more intense. They stood motionless, as if lost in wonder and indignant astonishment at this strange encounter. Neither turned from the other his blazing eyes; while menace and defiance began to lower in the looks of each. Gathering their full strength, the terrific rush was made: the bull missed, when the bear, with one enormous bound, dashed his teeth into his back to break the spine; the bull fell, but whirled his huge horn deep into the side of his antagonist. There they lay, grappled and gored, in their convulsive struggles and death-throes. We spurred up, and with our rifles and pistols closed the tragedy; and it was time: this last scene was too full of blind rage and madness even for the wild sports of a California bear-hunt.

TUESDAY, Nov. 2. Byron says, a hog in a high wind is a poetical object. Had he lived here, he might have put a mischievous boy on the top of that grotesque animal, and it would have helped out the poetical image immensely. The boys here begin their equestrianism on the back of a hog or bullock, and end it on the saddle, to which they seem to grow, like a muscle to a rock.

WEDNESDAY, Nov. 3. A Russian, who carries on a farm at Santa Cruz, called at my office a few days since, and presented me with a cabbage-head. I was sure from this garden gift, the old Cossack had something in tow yet out of sight; but it soon came in the shape of a request that I would summon a debtor of his, and order payment.

The creditor of the Russian proved to be a young Frenchman, who had run away with the old man's daughter, married her, and then quartered himself and wife on her father. I told the Frenchman he must pay board, or run away again with his wife; but if he came back he must satisfy arrears: so he concluded to run. This running before the honeymoon is pleasant enough; but running after that sweet orb has waned, is rather a dismal business.

Col. Burton, with his command, is in Lower California, where he has maintained the flag against desperate odds. His officers and men have acquitted themselves with honor. The powder and ball of the enemy were smuggled in by an American—a wretch who ought to be shot himself.

Monday, Nov. 8. After being six months without rain, the first shower of the season fell this evening. Its approach had been announced for several days by a dim atmosphere, which was filled with a soft, thick vapor, that swung about, like a limitless cloud. The rain itself was warm, and sunk into the earth, like flattery into the heart of a fool.

CHAPTER XVI.

A CALIFORNIAN JEALOUS OF HIS WIFE.—HOSPITALITY OF THE NATIVES.—HONORS TO GUADALUPE.—APPLICATION FROM A LOTHARIO FOR A DIVORCE.—CAPTURE OF MAZATLAN.—LARCENY OF CANTON SHAWLS.—AN EMIGRANT'S WIFE CLAIMING TO HAVE TAKEN THE COUNTRY.—A WILD BULLOCK IN MAIN-STREET.

SATURDAY, Nov. 20. I was tumbled out of my dreams last night by a succession of rapid and heavy knocks at my office door. Unbarring it, I found Giuseppe, a townsman, who stated, under an excitement that almost choked his voice, that he had just returned from the Salinas; that on entering his house he had discovered, through the window in the door leading to his bedroom, by the clear light of the moon, which shone into the apartment, a man reposing on his pillow by the side of his faithless spouse, and desired me to come and arrest him. I had understood that the sposa had not the reputation of the "icicle that hung on Dian's temple," and had no great confidence in Giuseppe's domestic virtues either; but that was no valid reason why he should be so unceremoniously ousted of his domestic claims. I therefore ordered the constable, whom this midnight noise had now awoke, to go with him and bring the culprit before me.

Off they started, well armed with batons and revolvers. On reaching the premises the house was carefully reconnoitred, and every egress from the building securely bolted. They were now inside, and had conducted their operations so silently they were unsuspected. The door leading to the bedroom was at the other end of the hall; they crept over the floor with steps so low and soft, each heard his heart beat, and the clock seemed to strike instead of ticking its seconds. Giuseppe's thoughts ran—

"I'll see before I doubt; when I doubt, prove;
And, on the proof, there is no more but this."

Through the panes of glass which relieved the panels of the door, they saw in the faint moonlight, which fell through the opposite window, the dark locks of the guilty intruder flowing over the husband's pillow. "I have a mind," whispered Giuseppe, "to rush in and plunge my knife at once to his cursed heart." "No, no;" returned my faithful constable, "we are here to execute the orders of the alcalde, and if you are going to take the law into your own hands I will leave you. Hush! hark! he stirs! No; it was the shadow of the tree that frecks the moonlight." All was still and waveless again. The door was on the jar, and drawing one good long relieving breath, in they rushed, and seized—— what? A muff! The husband could not believe his own eyes, and mussed the muff up, jerking it this way and that, as if to ascertain if there was not a man inside of it. "You return late, Giuseppe," murmured his wife, scarce yet awake. "Oh, yes, yes, my dear, late, late," stammered the husband. "You have a friend with you," continued the unsuspecting sposa. "Yes, my darling; a friend from the Salinas, whom I have invited to take a night's lodging," replied Giuseppe. "Well, you will find a bed for him in the opposite room, and a candle and matches on the table," rejoined the sposa. So the twain went out, and having disturbed the bed assigned the friend sufficiently to give it the appearance of having been slept in, my constable slipped out and came home, denouncing all jealous husbands and ladies' muffs. This fluster cost me two hours' sleep, and Giuseppe a fee of three dollars to the constable. He would have paid forty times that sum to get free of the joke. Nothing so completely confounds a Californian as to find himself the dupe of his suspicions. It is more vexatious than the wrong which his mistaken anger sought to avenge. Mutual confidence is the basis of all domestic endearment, and the cause which is allowed to disturb it, should be as weighty as the happiness it wrecks. So reads my homily.

TUESDAY, DEC. 7. There are no people that I have ever been among who enjoy life so thoroughly as the Californians. Their habits are simple; their wants few; nature rolls almost every thing spontaneously into their lap. Their cattle, horses, and sheep roam at large—not a blade of grass is cut, and none is required. The harvest waves wherever the plough and harrow have been; and the grain which the wind scatters this year, serves as seed for the next. The slight labor required is more a diversion than a toil; and even this is shared by the Indian. They attach no value to money, except as it administers to their pleasures. A fortune, without the facilities of enjoying it, is with them no object of emulation or envy. Their happiness flows from a fount that has very little connection with their outward circumstances.

There is hardly a shanty among them which does not contain more true contentment, more genuine gladness of the heart, than you will meet with in the most princely palace. Their hospitality knows no bounds; they are always glad to see you, come when you may; take a pleasure in entertaining you while you remain; and only regret that your business calls you away. If you are sick, there is nothing which sympathy and care can devise or perform which is not done for you. No sister ever hung over the throbbing brain or fluttering pulse of a brother with more tenderness and fidelity. This is as true of the lady whose hand has only figured her embroidery or swept her guitar, as of the cottage-girl wringing from her laundry the foam of the mountain stream; and all this from the *heart!* If I must be cast in sickness or destitution on the care of the stranger, let it be in California; but let it be before American avarice has hardened the heart and made a god of gold.

Monday, Dec. 13. A Californian, who had been

absent some two years in Mexico, where he had led a gay irregular life, finding or fancying on his return grounds for suspecting the regularity of his wife, applied to me for a decree of divorce, *a vinculo matrimonii*. I told him that it was necessary, that on so grave a subject, he should come into court with clean hands; that if he would swear on the Cross, at the peril of his soul, that he had been faithful himself during his long absence, I would then see what could be done with his wife. He wanted to know if that was United States law; I told him it was the law by which I was governed—the law of the Bible—and a good law, too—let him that is without sin cast the first stone. "Then I cannot cast any stone at all, sir," was the candid reply. "Then go and live with your wife; she is as good as you are, and you cannot require her to be any better." He took my advice, is now living with his wife, and difficulties seem to have ceased. Nothing disarms a man like the conscious guilt of the offence for which he would arraign another.

TUESDAY, DEC. 21. The old church bell has been ringing out all the morning in honor of Guadalupe, the patron saint of California. Her festivities commenced last evening in illuminated windows, bonfires, the flight of rockets, and the loud mirth of children. I wonder if Guadalupe knows or cares much about these exhibitions of devotional glee. Can the shout of boyhood around the crackling bonfire reach to her celestial pavillion? can the flambeau throw its tremulous ray so far? will she bend her ear from the golden lyres of heaven to catch the sound of a torpedo vibrating up over the cloud-cataracts which thunder between? If Guadalupe be in heaven, where I hope she is, she has done with the crackers and bonfires of earth, and heeds them as little as the glow-worm that glimmers on her grave. But let the old bell peal on; it matters but little whether it be for this saint or that; it is only a metallic hosanna to either. There is more true homage in one silent prayer, breathed from the depths of a meek confiding heart, than in all the peals ever rung from cathedral towers. The only worship which approaches that of a resigned heart is the hymn of the forest, as its leaves in the fading twilight softly tremble to rest. He who can listen unmoved to these vesper melodies, can have no sensibility in his soul, and no God in his creed. When this fevered being shall sink to rest, let me be laid beneath some green tree, whose vernal leaves shall whisper their music over my sleep. And yet it would be lonely were there none beloved in life to linger there in death.

> When the bright sun upon that spot is shining
> With purest ray,
> And the small shrubs their buds and blossoms twining,
> Burst through that clay,
> Will there be one still on that spot refining
> Lost hopes away?

WEDNESDAY, DEC. 22. We are now carrying the

war into the enemy's camp; the Pacific squadron, under the broad pennant of Com. Shubrick, is in front of Mazatlan. That important position was captured on the twelfth ult., and is now garrisoned by three hundred and fifty seamen and marines. Capt. Lavelette, well qualified by his intelligence, urbanity, and moral firmness for the post, is governor of the town. The country around, and all the great avenues leading through it, are in the hands of the enemy, who can, at any moment, bring two thousand horsemen into the field. They only want a leader of sufficient resolution, and they might force our garrison upon the last resource of their courage and strength. But Gen. Telles is weak and vacillating, and has not the confidence even of the troops which he commands; while many of the citizens, who have property at issue, prefer the protection extended to them under the flag, to the anarchy and confusion into which they might be thrown by the success of their own arms. It was a bold and decisive movement on the part of our commodore, and executed with a vigor that has impressed itself on the apprehensions of Mexico. Our flag now waves from ocean to ocean, through the plains and mountain fastnesses of that dismayed country.

FRIDAY, JAN. 7. The captain of a merchant ship complained to me this morning, that one of his crew had taken a package of rich Canton shawls on shore, and clandestinely disposed of them. I had the sailor before me, and wormed out of him the name of every person, as he alleged, with whom he had communicated; but he omitted the name of one suspicious character. I took the constable, and went immediately to her house, and demanded the shawls: she seemed shocked, and denied all knowledge of them. Her manner half staggered me; but I told the constable to take her to prison, not intending, however, to put her in without some evidence of her guilt; but she had not gone many steps from her door before her resolution, which had been as firm as adamant, broke down, and she told where the shawls might be found. They were secreted in the mattress of her bed; and the whole fifteen were recovered. Had the sailor mentioned her name among the rest, I should have been extremely puzzled. A seeming frankness is often the deepest disguise.

SATURDAY, JAN. 8. An assistant alcalde, residing at San Juan, in reporting a case that came before him, states that one of the witnesses, not having a good reputation for veracity, he thought it best to swear him pretty strongly; so he swore him on the Bible, on the cross, by the holy angels, by the blessed Virgin, and on the *twelve* Evangelists. I have written him for some information about eight of his evangelists, as I have no recollection of having met with but four in my biblical readings.

MONDAY, JAN. 10. A woman, from our western

border, who had drifted into California over the mountains, and looking as if she had well survived the hardships of the way, walked into my office this morning, and rather demanded, than invoked, a decree, that her husband might cut timber on the lands of Señor M——. I asked her if her husband had rented the land. "No." If he had any contract or agreement with the owner. "No." "Why then, my woman, do you claim the right of cutting the timber?" "Right, sir!" she exclaimed; "why, have we not taken the country?" I told her it was true, we had taken the country; but we had not taken the private land titles with it: she seemed to think that was a distinction without a difference. This anecdote will furnish a clue to the spirit with which the patient Californians have had to contend.

TUESDAY, JAN. 18. Main-street was thrown into confusion this morning by a wild bullock, who had broken the lasso of his keeper. He plunged down the peopled avenue in foaming fury, clothed with all the terrors of the Apocalyptic beast: men, women, and children fled in every direction. I was standing at the moment in the portico of our Navy Agent, and before I could clear it, he swept through a corner, dashing to the earth a huge stanchion. His next rencounter was with the high paling which protected a shade-tree, and which he carried off as Samson the gates of Gaza. Something attracted his flashing eyes to the door of a small dwelling; in an instant it flew into fragments before his impetuous strength; fortunately it contained no tenant except the wild monster himself, who soon issued from the door, and seemed for a moment lost in his phrensy. A caballero, mounted on a spirited horse, and with his lasso whirling high in air, now rushed up; I expected for a moment to see a desperate plunge from the beast at the courser's side, but the rider and his steed understood their occupation too well; the lasso fell over his horn, and in an instant he was tumbling in the sand. He recovered himself, but it was only to be thrown again, till a second lasso secured his flying heels, and the knife of the Indian finished the rest. A wave of lava let loose from its crater, an avalanch that has slipped from its Alpine steep, and a wild bull that has broken his lasso, are among the most terrific objects that dash on human vision.

CHAPTER XVII.

RAINS IN CALIFORNIA.—FUNCTIONS OF THE ALCALDE OF MONTEREY.—ORPHANS IN CALIFORNIA.—SLIP OF THE GALLOWS ROPE.—MAKING A FATHER WHIP HIS BOY.—A CONVICT AS PRISON COOK.—THE KANACKA.—THOM. COLE.—A MAN ROBBING HIMSELF.—A BLACKSMITH OUTWITTED.

MONDAY, FEB. 7. The rains in California are mostly confined to the three winter months—a few showers may come before, or a few occur after, but the body of the rain falls within that period. The rain is relieved of nearly all the chilling discomforts of a winter's storm in other climes; it falls only when the wind is from a southern quarter, and is consequently warm and refreshing. It is by no means continuous; it pays its visits like a judicious lover—with intervals sufficient to keep up the affection; and like the suitor, brings with it flowers, and leads the fair one by the side of streamlets never wrinkled with frost, and into groves where the leaf never withers, and where the songs of birds ever fill the warbling air.

THURSDAY, FEB. 10. By the laws and usages of the country, the judicial functions of the Alcalde of Monterey extend to all cases, civil and criminal, arising within the middle department of California. He is also the guardian of the public peace, and is charged with the maintenance of law and order, whenever and wherever threatened, or violated; he must arrest, fine, imprison, or sentence to the public works, the lawless and refractory, and he must enforce, through his executive powers, the decisions and sentences which he has pronounced in his judicial capacity. His prerogatives and official duties extend over all the multiplied interests and concerns of his department, and reach to every grievance and crime, from the jar that trembles around the domestic hearth, to the guilt which throws its gloom on the gallows and the grave.

THURSDAY, FEB. 17. There is no need of an Orphan Asylum in California. The amiable and benevolent spirit of the people hovers like a shield over the helpless. The question is not, who shall be burdened with the care of an orphan, but who shall have the privilege of rearing it. Nor do numbers or circumstances seem to shake this spirit; it is triumphant over both. A plain, industrious man, of rather limited means, applied to me to-day for the care of six orphan children. I asked him how many he had of his own; he said fourteen as yet. "Well, my friend," I observed, "are not fourteen enough for one table, and especially with the prospect of more?" "Ah," said the Californian, "the hen that has twenty chickens scratches no harder than the hen that has one." So I told him I would inquire into the present condition of the children, and then decide on his application. His claim lay in the fact that his wife was the godmother of the orphans.

WEDNESDAY, FEB. 23. One of my Indian prisoners, sentenced to the works for theft, managed this morning to effect his escape, but was overtaken by the constable on the Salinas, and brought back. When asked by me what he ran for, he said the devil put it into his head. I asked him if he thought a ball and chain would keep the evil one off; he said it might, but then if he once got at him, he should stand no chance with one of his legs chained. I told him I should let his leg go for the present, but if he attempted to run again, I should chain both of them. "And my hands too," said the Indian, to assure me of his good conduct.

FRIDAY, MARCH 3. There is an old Mexican law, or usage, here, which has sometimes exempted from death the murderer who has reached the sanctuary of the church, or been favored with some accident, in the execution of the extreme sentence. Two desperadoes, of Mexican and Indian blood, were brought before me, charged with a wilful, deliberate murder. A jury of twelve citizens, the largest scope of challenge having been allowed, was empanneled. The prisoners were convicted and sentenced to be hung. But by some strange accident, or design, both knots slipped, and down they came, half imagining themselves still swinging in the air. The priest who confessed them, and who was present among the great crowd, immediately declared the penalty paid and the criminals absolved, and started post-haste to

Gen. Mason for his mandate to that effect. The general told him the prisoners were sentenced to be hung by the neck till dead, and when this sentence had been executed, the knot-slipping business might perhaps be considered. This may seem to have been dictated by a want of humanity, but had the accident or stratagem in question rescued the criminals, not a noose in California would have held. The murderers were executed, and the crime for which they suffered vanished from the future records of the court.

Wednesday, March 15. A lad of fourteen years was brought before me to-day charged with stealing a horse. The evidence of the larceny was conclusive; but what punishment to inflict was the question. We have no house of correction, and to sentence him to the ball and chain on the public works, among hardened culprits, was to cut off all hope of amendment, and inflict an indelible stigma on the youth; so I sent for his father, who had no good reputation himself, and placing a riata in his hand, directed him to inflict twenty-four lashes on his thieving boy. He proceeded as far as twelve, when I stopped him; they were enough. They seemed inflicted by one attempting to atone in this form for his own transgressions. "Inflict the rest, Soto, on your own evil example; if you had been upright yourself, you might expect truth and honesty in your boy; you are more responsible than this lad for his crimes;

you can never chastise him into the right path, and continue yourself to travel in the wrong." With these remarks I dismissed the parties.

SATURDAY, MARCH 18. Horse-stealing has given me more trouble than any other species of offence in California. It has grown out of a loose habit of using the horses of other people without their consent, at a time when they were of very little account; and what was once a venial trespass has become a crime. It is very difficult to arrest it; much must be left to time, the higher influences of moral sentiments, and the administration of more specific laws. Nor are the Americans here a whit better than the natives; they have a facility of conscience which easily suits itself to any prevailing vice. Many of them appear to have left their good principles on the other side of Cape Horn, or over the Rocky Mountains. They slide into gambling, drinking, and cheating, as easily as a frog into its native pond. They seem only the worse for the restraints, which law at home partially exerted. They are like a froward urchin who retaliates the wholesome visits of the birch by some act of fresh audacity the moment he is beyond its reach. But they will find a little law even in California, and this little enforced with some steadiness of purpose. It is not the law which threatens loudest that always exerts the greatest restraint. Thunder, with all its uproar, don't strike; it is the lightning that cleaves the gnarled oak.

THURSDAY, MARCH 23. A clergyman, who had just arrived in California, called on me to-day, with letters of introduction from several of the first rectors in New York. They spoke of him in high terms of commendation, and invited that confidence and regard which might secure him success in his foreign adventure; while they knew him to be a loquacious shallow booby. They had probably been so much annoyed by him in one shape and another, that they had taken this method of getting rid of him, thinking that the afflictions of Providence, like his blessings, should be more equally distributed.

SATURDAY, MARCH 25. To-day I remitted the sentence of my prison cook. He is a Mulatto, a native of San Domingo; had drifted into California; was attached, in a subordinate capacity, to Col. Fremont's battalion; and while the troops were quartered in town, had robbed the drawer of a liquor shop of two hundred dollars. For this offence, I had sentenced him to two years on the public works. Discovering early some reliable traits about the fellow, I began to confide in him, soon made him cook to the rest of the prisoners, and allowed him the privileges of the town, so far as his duties in that capacity required. He has never betrayed my trust, and has always been the first to communicate to me any stratagem on the part of the prisoners to effect their escape. I have trusted him with money to purchase provisions, and he has faithfully accounted for every shilling. He has always been kind and attentive to the sick. For these faithful services, I have remitted the remainder of his sentence, which would have confined him nine months longer, and have put him on a pay of thirty dollars per month as cook. There is a string in every man's breast, which, if you can rightly touch, will "discourse music."

THURSDAY, APRIL 6. I met a little California boy to-day in tattered garments, and without hat or shoes. He had a small fish in his hand, which he had just hooked up from the end of the wharf. I offered him half a dollar for it; he said no, he wanted it himself. I offered him a dollar; he still said no, he was going to make a dinner on it. The result would probably have been the same had I offered him five dollars. No one here is going to catch fish for you or any one else while he wants them himself.

SATURDAY, APRIL 15. I made another pounce this evening on the gamblers, and captured their bank; but most of the players had slipped their money into their pockets before I could reach the table. No one rescued a dollar after my cane, with its alcalde insignia, had been laid on the boards. The authority of that baton they always respect. How comfortable it is for one to carry his moral power on the top of his cane. It almost justifies the Roman Catholic exegesis—and Jacob worshipped the top of his staff.

MONDAY, APRIL 17. I had sent one of my constables to the Salinas river, and the other to San Juan, and retired to rest; but about midnight was startled from my dreams, by a loud rap at my office door. Throwing my cloak around me, I unbolted the portal, and there stood, in the clear moonlight, a tall Kanacka, who reverently lifted his hat, and observed, " The town, sir, is perfectly quiet." I thanked him for the information, and closed the door. The fellow had been drinking, and in the importance which liquor sometimes imparts, had imagined himself at the head of the police.

THURSDAY, APRIL 27. Thom. Cole, whose moral vision could never yet discover any difference between possession and ownership, where a horse was concerned, was brought before me this morning, mounted on a fleet steed belonging to a citizen of the town. He had removed the brand of the rightful owner and substituted his own; but the disguise was easily penetrated, and the horse identified. Thom. averred the horse was found on his rancho; but he was ordered to deliver him to his proper owner, who stood by to receive him. At this moment Thom. sprung into his saddle and was off, horse and all, in the twinkling of an eye. I applied to Gen. Mason for a file of soldiers; they were promptly ordered, and stationed on the three streets, through one of which Thom. must make his egress from town. He soon came sweeping on at the top of his speed, when he suddenly found three **muskets** levelled at him, with an order to dismount. There was no discharge in that war, and down he jumped, and was soon delivered over to me. How changed! a moment before setting the whole world at defiance; and now praying to be saved from the fleas of the prison. As the flea could only punish him without benefiting the town, I determined to reach him through another channel, by which both purposes should be answered; and fined him fifty dollars for contempt of court. So Thom. lost his horse and fifty dollars, and got a lesson of humiliation which quelled his spirit like a wet blanket thrown on a flaxen flame.

TUESDAY, MAY 2. I was roused from my sleep last night by a loud, hurried knocking at my door, and a voice exclaiming, "Alcalde, alcalde!" On reaching the door I found there a young Mexican, the clerk of a store near by, without hat or shoes, and only a blanket wrapped around him. He told me the volunteers had broken into his store, and were robbing the money-chest. By this time my constable was up, and, throwing on our clothes, we hastened with the clerk to his store; but not a human being was to be seen. He showed us the bolt that had been forced, the chest that had been broken, the pistol that he had snapped, and the wound that he had received on the head. I sent the constable to the captain of the volunteers, who immediately searched his quarters, where he found every man in his berth, except those on guard. With these unsatisfactory results I returned to my office and bed, and directed the constable to keep an eye on the clerk.

WEDNESDAY, MAY 3. This morning I examined into all the circumstances connected with the robbery. The wound of the clerk, which he says he received from a cudgel, is a slight cut, apparently made by some sharp instrument. The chisel, with which the chest was forced, corresponds in width to one for sale on the shelf. Of the thousand dollars locked up in the chest and drawers, not one, it seems, escaped; not a quarter or fip fell to the floor; all went into the sack of the robbers, though they worked in the dark. And then, as he alleges, the robbers were volunteers without their uniform, and with their faces blacked. If so thoroughly disguised, how could he know they were volunteers? From these circumstances I have no doubt the rogue robbed himself, and raised the hue and cry to cover the transaction. But we shall see; the thing will out yet.

SUNDAY, MAY 9. This is my birth-day. I am on the shaded side of that hill which swells midway between the extremities of life. The past seems but a dream, and the future will soon be so. To what has been and to what may be, I seem to myself almost indifferent. I know the vanities in which human hopes end; I know that life itself is only a bubble that has caught the hues of some falling star. And yet this airy phantom is not all such as it would seem; there is something besides shadow in its evanescent form. Our visions of happiness may prove an illusion, but our sorrows are real. It is no fancied knell that shakes the bier; no imaginary pall that wraps the loved and the lost. The grave is invested with the awful majesty of the real.

MONDAY, MAY 10. I had directed the constable to get a pair of iron hinges made for one of the doors of the prison. He gave the order to a blacksmith, a crabbed old fellow, who charged eight dollars for his coarse work. As the charge was an imposition, I told the constable not to take the hinges; when up came the blacksmith with them to the office, and, in a fit of passion, hurled them at my feet, as I stood in the piazza. I handed the constable eight dollars, and told him to call on the blacksmith, pay him for the hinges, take his receipt, and then bring him before me. All which was done, and before me stood the smith, with his choler yet up. I told him that his violence and indignity would not be passed over; that I should fine him ten dollars for the benefit of the town, which he might pay or go to prison. After a few moments' hesitation, he laid the ten dollars on the table, and took his departure without uttering a word. When clear of the office he grumbled out to the constable, "For once in my life I have been outwitted; that Yankee alcalde has not only got my hinges for nothing, but two dollars besides. I don't wonder he can swing his prison doors at that rate; I would have tried the calaboose but for the infernal fleas." The constable told him the next time he made hinges he must charge what they were worth, and curb his towering temper.

WEDNESDAY, MAY 17. The ire of a Californian of hidalgo extraction flashes from his dark eyes like heat-lightning on a July cloud—you see the blaze, but hear no thunder; while the wit of a California lady glances here and there like the sun-rays through the fluttering leaves of a wind-stirred forest. We have several ladies here celebrated for their brilliant sallies, but Donna Jimeno carries off the palm. A friend showed her this morning a picture of the Israelites gathering manna. "Ah! they are the Californians," said the Donna, "they pick up what heaven rains down." He showed her Moses smiting the rock. "And there," said the Donna, "is a Yankee; he can bring water out of a rock." But humor and wit are not the highest characteristics of this lady. She possesses a refinement and intelligence that might grace any court in Europe; and withal, a benevolence that never wearies in reaching and relieving the sick. Her care of Lieut. Miner, one of the officers attached to this post, will long live in grateful remembrance. She hovered over him till his spirit fled, and wept as she thought of his mother.

CHAPTER XVIII.

FIRST DISCOVERY OF GOLD.—PRISON GUARD.—INCREDULITY ABOUT THE GOLD.—SANTIAGO GETTING MARRIED.—ANOTHER LUMP OF GOLD.—EFFECTS OF THE GOLD FEVER.—THE COURT OF AN ALCALDE.—MOSQUITOES AS CONSTABLES.—BOB AND HIS BAG OF GOLD.—RETURN OF CITIZENS FROM THE MINES.—A MAN WITH THE GOLD CHOLIC.—THE MINES ON INDIVIDUAL CREDIT.

MONDAY, MAY 29. Our town was startled out of its quiet dreams to-day, by the announcement that gold had been discovered on the American Fork. The men wondered and talked, and the women too; but neither believed. The sibyls were less skeptical; they said the moon had, for several nights, appeared not more than a cable's length from the earth; that a white raven had been seen playing with an infant; and that an owl had rung the church bells.

SATURDAY, JUNE 3. The most faithful and reliable guard that I have ever had over the prisoners, is himself a prisoner. He had been a lieutenant in the Mexican army, and was sentenced, for a flagrant breach of the peace, to the public works for the term of one year. Being hard up for funds, I determined to make an experiment with this lieutenant; had him brought before me; ordered the ball and chain to be taken from his leg, and placed a double-barrelled gun, loaded and primed, in his hands. "Take that musket, and proceed with the prisoners to the stone quarry; return them to their cells before sunset, and report to me." "Your order, Señor Alcalde, shall be faithfully obeyed," was the reply. I then ordered one of the constables, well mounted and armed, to reconnoitre the quarry, and, unseen by the prisoners or guard, ascertain how things went on. He returned, and reported well of their regularity. At sunset, the lieutenant entered the office, and reported the prisoners in their cells, and all safe. "Very well, José; now make yourself safe, and that will do." He accordingly returned to his prison, and from that day to this, has been my most faithful and reliable guard.

MONDAY, JUNE 5. Another report reached us this morning from the American Fork. The rumor ran, that several workmen, while excavating for a mill-race, had thrown up little shining scales of a yellow ore, that proved to be gold; that an old Sonoranian, who had spent his life in gold mines, pronounced it the genuine thing. Still the public incredulity remained, save here and there a glimmer of faith, like the flash of a fire-fly at night. One good old lady, however, declared that she had been dreaming of gold every night for several weeks, and that it had so frustrated her simple household economy, that she had relieved her conscience, by confessing to her priest—

"Absolve me, father, of that sinful dream."

TUESDAY, JUNE 6. Being troubled with the golden dream almost as much as the good lady, I determined to put an end to the suspense, and dispatched a messenger this morning to the American Fork. He will have to ride, going and returning, some four hundred miles, but his report will be reliable. We shall then know whether this gold is a fact or a fiction—a tangible reality on the earth, or a fanciful treasure at the base of some rainbow, retreating over hill and waterfall, to lure pursuit and disappoint hope.

SATURDAY, JUNE 10. My boy Santiago has taken it into his head to get married; and being a Protestant, finds it extremely difficult to get through the ecclesiastical hopper. Were the person whom he wishes to wed of the same faith with himself, there would be but little impediment; but as she is a Roman Catholic, it is necessary that he should become one too. He has been to the presiding priest to see if he could not get his permission to retain a few articles of his own religion, just enough to save his conscience. But his reverence told him he must give it up in toto, renounce it as a heresy, and come without a scruple into the mother church. Iago is not much of a theologian, but has sense enough to know that conscientious scruples are not things of which a man can free himself at will. His love, none the less deep and sincere for his humble condition, urges him to a compliance with the canonical requirement, but these very scruples hold him back. How he will extricate

One of the "upper ten" in the diggings, and a California savan—"My charge for examination is exactly one pound of gold. Science is extremely rare in these parts, and I have the only spy-glass."

himself I know not. He will probably compound the matter with his conscience by some mental reservations, as Galileo did when awed into the indignant confession that the earth was flat. Verily, if a man cannot marry in this world without becoming a hypocrite or apostate from the faith of his fathers, the sooner Miller's conflagrating dream becomes a reality the better. Perhaps some shape of flame might emerge from its drifting embers, that would dare glimmer towards heaven without the leave of a pragmatic priest. I wonder if Adam asked Eve if she were a Roman Catholic before they celebrated their nuptials. This is an important question, and ought to be looked into, though now rather late in the day. I commend it to my venerable friend, the Bishop of New York, who has recently issued an edict that no Protestant shall marry a Roman Catholic without first passing his children, prospectively, through his baptismal font.

Monday, June 12. A straggler came in to-day from the American Fork, bringing a piece of yellow ore weighing an ounce. The young dashed the dirt from their eyes, and the old from their spectacles. One brought a spyglass, another an iron ladle; some wanted to melt it, others to hammer it, and a few were satisfied with smelling it. All were full of tests; and many, who could not be gratified in making their experiments, declared it a humbug. One lady sent me a huge gold ring, in the hope of reaching the truth by comparison; while a gentleman placed the specimen on the top of his gold-headed cane and held it up, challenging the sharpest eyes to detect a difference. But doubts still hovered on the minds of the great mass. They could not conceive that such a treasure could have lain there so long undiscovered. The idea seemed to convict them of stupidity. There is nothing of which a man is more tenacious than his claims to sagacity. He sticks to them like an old bachelor to the idea of his personal attractions, or a toper to the strength of his temperance ability, whenever he shall wish to call it into play.

THURSDAY, JUNE 15. Found an Indian to-day perfectly sober, who is generally drunk, and questioned him of the cause of his sobriety. He stated that he wished to marry an Indian girl, and she would not have him unless he would keep sober a month; that this was but his third day, and he should never be able to stand it unless I would put him beyond the reach of liquor. So I sentenced him to the public works for a month; this will pay off old scores, and help him to a wife, who may perhaps keep him sober, though I fear there is little hope of that.

TUESDAY, JUNE 20. My messenger sent to the mines, has returned with specimens of the gold; he dismounted in a sea of upturned faces. As he drew forth the yellow lumps from his pockets, and passed them around among the eager crowd, the doubts, which had lingered till now, fled. All admitted they were gold, except one old man, who still persisted they were some Yankee invention, got up to reconcile the people to the change of flag. The excitement produced was intense; and many were soon busy in their hasty preparations for a departure to the mines. The family who had kept house for me caught the moving infection. Husband and wife were both packing up; the blacksmith dropped his hammer, the carpenter his plane, the mason his trowel, the farmer his sickle, the baker his loaf, and the tapster his bottle. All were off for the mines, some on horses, some on carts, and some on crutches, and one went in a litter. An American woman, who had recently established a boarding-house here, pulled up stakes, and was off before her lodgers had even time to pay their bills. Debtors ran, of course. I have only a community of women left, and a gang of prisoners, with here and there a soldier, who will give his captain the slip at the first chance. I don't blame the fellow a whit; seven dollars a month, while others are making two or three hundred a day! that is too much for human nature to stand.

Saturday, July 15. The gold fever has reached every servant in Monterey; none are to be trusted in their engagement beyond a week, and as for compulsion, it is like attempting to drive fish into a net with the ocean before them. Gen. Mason, Lieut.

Lanman, and myself, form a mess; we have a house, and all the table furniture and culinary apparatus requisite; but our servants have run, one after another, till we are almost in despair: even Sambo, who we thought would stick by from laziness, if no other cause, ran last night; and this morning, for the fortieth time, we had to take to the kitchen, and cook our own breakfast. A general of the United States Army, the commander of a man-of-war, and the Alcalde of Monterey, in a smoking kitchen, grinding coffee, toasting a herring, and pealing onions! These gold mines are going to upset all the domestic arrangements of society, turning the head to the tail, and the tail to the head. Well, it is an ill wind that blows nobody any good: the nabobs have had their time, and now comes that of the "niggers." We shall all live just as long, and be quite as fit to die.

TUESDAY, JULY 18. Another bag of gold from the mines, and another spasm in the community. It was brought down by a sailor from Yuba river, and contains a hundred and thirty-six ounces. It is the most beautiful gold that has appeared in the market; it looks like the yellow scales of the dolphin, passing through his rainbow hues at death. My carpenters, at work on the school-house, on seeing it, threw down their saws and planes, shouldered their picks, and are off for the Yuba. Three seamen ran from the Warren, forfeiting their four years' pay; and a whole platoon of soldiers from the fort left only their colors behind. One old woman declared she would never again break an egg or kill a chicken, without examining yolk and gizzard.

SATURDAY, JULY 22. The laws by which an alcalde here is governed, in the administration of justice, are the Mexican code as compiled in Frebrero and Alverez—works of remarkable comprehensiveness, clearness, and facility of application. They embody all the leading principles of the civil law, derived from the institutes of Justinian. The common law of England is hardly known here, though its rules and maxims have more or less influenced local legislation. But with all these legal provisions a vast many questions arise which have to be determined *ex cathedra*. In minor matters the alcalde is often himself the law; and the records of his court might reveal some very exquisite specimens of judicial prerogative; such as shaving a rogue's head—*lex talionis*—who had shaved the tail of his neighbor's horse; or making a busybody, who had slandered a worthy citizen, promenade the streets with a gag in his mouth; or obliging a man who had recklessly caused a premature birth, to compensate the bereaved father for the loss of that happiness which he might have derived from his embryo hope, had it budded into life. This last has rather too many contingencies about it; but the principle, which reaches it and meets the offender, does very well out here in California, and would not be misapplied in some of those pill-shops which slope the path to crime in the United States.

THURSDAY, JULY 27. I never knew mosquitoes turned to any good account save in California; and here it seems they are sometimes ministers of justice. A rogue had stolen a bag of gold from a digger in the mines, and hid it. Neither threats nor persuasions could induce him to reveal the place of its concealment. He was at last sentenced to a hundred lashes, and then informed that he would be let off with thirty, provided he would tell what he had done with the gold; but he refused. The thirty lashes were inflicted, but he was still stubborn as a mule.

He was then stripped naked and tied to a tree. The mosquitoes with their long bills went at him, and in less than three hours he was covered with blood. Writhing and trembling from head to foot with exquisite torture, he exclaimed, "Untie me, untie me, and I will tell where it is." "Tell first," was the reply. So he told where it might be found. Some of the party then, with wisps, kept off the still hungry mosquitoes, while others went where the culprit had directed, and recovered the bag of gold. He was then untied, washed with cold water, and helped to his clothes, while he muttered, as if talking to himself, "I couldn't stand that anyhow."

FRIDAY, JULY 28. A little laughing girl tripped into the office to-day, and handed me a bunch of flowers, which she said her mother sent me. "And who is your mother, my sweet one?" I inquired. She told me, and I then remembered that I had recovered for her a silver cup, which an Indian had stolen; and these flowers had now come as a memento.

"Fee me with flowers, they hold no sordid bribe."

SATURDAY, AUG. 12. My man Bob, who is of Irish extraction, and who had been in the mines about two months, returned to Monterey four weeks since, bringing with him over two thousand dollars, as the proceeds of his labor. Bob, while in my employ, required me to pay him every Saturday night, in gold, which he put into a little leather bag and sewed into the lining of his coat, after taking out just twelve and a half cents, his weekly allowance for tobacco. But now he took rooms and began to branch out; he had the best horses, the richest viands, and the choicest wines in the place. He never drank himself, but it filled him with delight to brim the sparkling goblet for others. I met Bob to-day, and asked him how he got on. "Oh, very well," he replied, "but I am off again for the mines." "How is that, Bob? you brought down with you over two thousand dollars; I hope you have not spent all that: you used to be very saving; twelve and a half cents a week for tobacco, and the rest you sewed into the lining of your coat." "Oh, yes," replied Bob, "and I have got *that* money yet; I worked hard for it; and the diel can't get it away; but the two thousand dollars came asily by good luck, and has gone as asily as it came." Now Bob's story is only one of a thousand like it in California, and has a deeper philosophy in it than meets the eye. Multitudes here are none the richer for the mines. He who can shake chestnuts from an exhaustless tree, won't stickle about the quantity he roasts.

THURSDAY, AUG. 16. Four citizens of Monterey are just in from the gold mines on Feather River, where they worked in company with three others. They employed about thirty wild Indians, who are attached to the rancho owned by one of the party. They worked precisely seven weeks and three days, and have divided seventy-six thousand eight hundred and forty-four dollars,—nearly eleven thousand dollars to each. Make a dot there, and let me introduce a man, well known to me, who has worked on the Yuba river sixty-four days, and brought back, as the result of his individual labor, five thousand three hundred and fifty-six dollars. Make a dot there, and let me introduce another townsman, who has worked on the North Fork fifty-seven days, and brought back four thousand five hundred and thirty-four dollars. Make a dot there, and let me introduce a boy, fourteen years of age, who has worked on the Mokelumne fifty-four days, and brought back three thousand four hundred and sixty-seven dollars. Make another dot there, and let me introduce a woman, of Sonoranian birth, who has worked in the dry diggings forty-six days, and brought back two thousand one hundred and twenty-five dollars. Is not this enough to make a man throw down his leger and shoulder a pick? But the deposits which yielded these harvests were now opened for the first time; they were the accumulation of ages; only the foot-prints of the elk and wild savage had passed over them. Their slumber was broken for the first time by the sturdy arms of the American emigrant.

TUESDAY, AUG. 28. The gold mines have upset all social and domestic arrangements in Monterey; the master has become his own servant, and the servant his own lord. The millionaire is obliged to groom his own horse, and roll his wheelbarrow; and the hidalgo—in whose veins flows the blood of all the Cortes—to clean his own boots! Here is lady L——, who has lived here seventeen years, the pride and ornament of the place, with a broomstick in her jewelled hand! And here is lady B—— with her daughter—all the way from "old Virginia," where they graced society with their varied accomplishments—now floating between the parlor and kitchen, and as much at home in the one as the other! And here is lady S——, whose cattle are on a thousand hills, lifting, like Rachel of old, her bucket of water from the deep well! And here is lady M. L——, whose honeymoon is still full of soft seraphic light, unhouseling a potatoe, and hunting the hen that laid the last egg. And here am I, who have been a man of some note in my day, loafing on the hospitality of the good citizens, and grateful for a meal, though in an Indian's wigwam. Why, is not this enough to make one wish the gold mines were in the earth's flaming centre, from which they sprung? Out on this yellow dust! it is worse than the cinders which buried Pompeii, for there, high and low shared the same fate!

SATURDAY, SEPT. 9. I met a Scotchman this morning bent half double, and evidently in pain. On inquiring the cause, he informed me that he had just seen a lump of gold from the Mokelumne as big as his double fist, and it had given him the cholic. The diagnosis of the complaint struck me as a new feature in human maladies, and one for which it would be difficult to find a suitable medicament in the therapeutics known to the profession; especially in the allopathic practice, which has stood still for three thousand years, except in the discovery of quinine for ague, and sulphur for itch. The gentlemen of this embalmed school must wake up; their antediluvian owl may do on an Egyptian obelisk, but we must have a more wide-awake bird in these days of progress. Here is a man bent double with a new and strange disease, taken from looking at gold: your bleeding, blistering, and purging won't free him of it. What is to be done? shall he be left to die, or be delivered over to the homœopathics? They have a medicament that acts as a specific, on the principle that the hair of the dog is good for the bite. If you burn your hand, what do you do—clasp a piece of ice?—no, seize a warm poker; if you freeze your foot, do you put it to the fire?—no, dash it into the snow; and so if you take the gold-cholic, the remedy is, *aurum—similia similibus curantur.*

SATURDAY, SEPT. 16. The gold mines are producing one good result; every creditor who has gone there is paying his debts. Claims not deemed worth a farthing are now cashed on presentation at nature's great bank. This has rendered the credit of every man here good for almost any amount. Orders for merchandise are honored which six months ago would have been thrown into the fire. There is none so poor, who has two stout arms and a pickaxe left, but he can empty any store in Monterey. Nor has the first instance yet occurred, in which the creditor has suffered. All distinctions indicative of means have vanished; the only capital required is muscle and an honest purpose. I met a man to-day from the mines in patched buckskins, rough as a badger from his hole, who had fifteen thousand dollars in yellow dust, swung at his back. Talk to him of brooches, gold-headed canes, and Carpenter's coats! Why he can unpack a lump of gold that would throw all Chesnut-street into spasms. And there is more where this came from. *His* rights in the great domain are equal to yours, and his prospects of getting it out vastly better. With these advantages, he bends the knee to no man, but strides along in his buckskins, a lord of earth by a higher prescriptive privilege than what emanates from the partiality of kings. His patent is medallioned with rivers which roll over golden sands, and embossed with mountains which have lifted for ages their golden coronets to heaven. Clear out of the way with your crests, and crowns, and pedigree trees, and let this democrat pass. Every drop of blood in his veins tells that it flows from a great heart, which God has made and which man shall never enslave. Such are the genuine sons of California; such may they live and die.

> " They will not be the tyrant's slaves,
> While heaven has light, or earth has graves."

CHAPTER XIX.

TOUR TO THE GOLD-MINES.—LOSS OF HORSES.—FIRST NIGHT IN THE WOODS.—ARRIVAL AT SAN JUAN.—UNDER WAY.—CAMPING OUT.—BARK OF THE WOLVES.—WATCH-FIRES.—SAN JOSÉ.—A FRESH START.—CAMPING ON THE SLOPE OF A HILL.—WILD FEATURES OF THE COUNTRY.—VALLEY OF THE SAN JOAQUIN.—BAND OF WILD HORSES.

WEDNESDAY, SEPT. 20. A servant of James McKinley, Esq., led to my door this morning a beautiful saddle-horse, with a message from his master, desiring me to accept the animal as a token of his regard. The gift was most opportune, as I was on the eve of a trip to the gold-mines. To guard against contingencies I purchased another, and, to prevent their being stolen, placed them both in the government coral, where a watch is posted night and day. My companions on the trip were to be Capt. Marcy, son of the late secretary of war, Mr. Botts, naval storekeeper, and Mr. Wilkinson, son of our ex-minister to Russia.

Having procured a suitable wagon, we freighted it lightly with provisions, articles of Indian traffic, tools for working in the mines, cooking utensils, and blankets to sleep in. To this we attached four mules, but little used to the harness, and of no great power, but they were the best that could be got at the time. The whole was put under the charge of a man who was half sailor and half teamster, and not much of either. Thus accoutred, the team was sent ahead, and we were to follow the next day.

THURSDAY, SEPT. 21. The hour for starting having arrived, I sent my man to the government coral for my horses. He returned in a few moments with the intelligence that a party of the volunteers had broken into the coral during the night, and carried off ten horses, and among them both of mine! There was no time now for ferreting out thieves, or hunting stolen animals. Our wagon was on the way, and my companions were mounted and waiting. I hurried to Mr. S——, who I knew had a fine horse in his yard, and offered him two hundred dollars for the animal, but he declined parting with him. My only resource now was with Mr. T——, who had three horses in his coral, but they were off a long journey the night before. I struck a bargain at a hundred dollars for one of them, and throwing on my saddle, was under way in a few minutes.

My horse held out pretty well for twenty miles, and then suddenly broke down. We were on the plain of the Salinas, and there was but little prospect of my being able to procure a substitute. But just at this crisis the mail rider hove in sight, with a horse in lead. I arranged with him for the spare animal, transferred my saddle to him, and with a farewell to my wearied steed, started again. We had directed our wagoner to proceed to San Juan, and expected to overtake him at that place before dark. But night set in while we were eight or ten miles distant, and it was a night of Egyptian darkness. We lost our way, and brought up in the woods. To proceed was impossible; so we dismounted, tied our horses together, felt for some dry leaves, and fired them with a lucifer which had been given us by a traveller an hour before.

With brush and bits of bark we managed to sustain our fire, but our prospect for the night was rather gloomy—without a drop of water, without any food, without an overcoat or blanket to cover us, with heavy thunder over head, and the wolves barking around. But we divided ourselves into four watches; one was to keep up the fire while the other three slept, and each take his turn in feeding the flame. My watch came first, and it was the longest two hours I ever experienced. Every old snag I drew to the fire seemed to exhaust the little strength that remained. My eyelids would fall, and it seemed impossible to lift them. I heard the wolves bark, but it was like a noise in one's dream. But my relief came at last, and throwing myself down close to the fire, I slept too sound even for the thunder. It was the cold dim gray of advancing morn when I awoke. A ride of an hour brought us to San Juan, where we found our baggage-wagon at a stream, the mules tethered, and whistling a piteous welcome to our steeds, and the driver blowing into a bundle of reeds and straw, from which a slender thread of smoke was rising into the chill atmosphere.

San Juan is thirty-four miles from Monterey; the only buildings are a gigantic church and the contiguous dwelling—once occupied by the priests and their Indian neophytes. The sanctuary remains; but the priests are gone, and the Indians are on the four winds, save those over whom the pine sings its requiem. We broke our long fast on hard bread, broiled pork, and coffee without milk. The sun was high when our mules were harnessed, and the crack of the driver's whip told that we were on the way. A few miles brought us to the foot of a hill; when half-way up our mules balked, and the wagon began to travel backward. We blocked the wheels, and tried to cheer and force them on; but a mule has that peculiar virtue which is insensible alike to flatteries and frowns. Still we coaxed, and whipped, and cheered, but in vain—there stuck our old wagon, fast as a thunder-cloud on a mountain's bluff. We had to turn lighters, and carry the greater part of the load, by hand, to the top of the hill. One of the mules whistled out in seeming derision; while his fellow looked sorry, as if smitten with compunction. This delay consumed several hours, and the sun was far down his western slope when we reached a few shanties on a plain covered in spots with the surviving verdure of the year: here we camped for the night. One tethered the animals; two brought wood and water; and one turned cook. We made our supper by the light of our watch-fire, smoked our cigars, and turned down upon the earth, with our saddles for our pillows. A blanket served to protect each from the dews and the night air. How little man wants here! His palace seems to tower in idle grandeur, between a cradle and a coffin.

FRIDAY, SEPT. 22. Day glimmered over the hills and we were up; the gathered brands of our watch-fire kindled again under our camp-kettle. Our breakfast was soon dispatched, our mules in harness, our blankets stowed, and we were on the way. Ten miles farther, and my third horse, which I had procured at San Juan, began to give out, and I was thrown upon my feet, till relieved by the opportune arrival of a gentleman with a spare horse, which I purchased at his own price, leaving my own to shift for himself. When on my feet, my thoughts ran bitterly back to the two fine horses with which I had expected to leave Monterey. We are the least forgiving when we feel most the need of that of which we have been robbed.

Our road lay through a level plain, into which the spur of a mountain range had thrown its bold terminus. Doubling this, we wound into a deep cove, where wild oats waved, and a copious spring gushed from a cleft of the rock. It was yet two hours to sunset; but the next stream lay ten miles ahead, and we decided to camp where we were. Our horses and mules were turned into the ample cove untethered; and in half an hour we had gathered sufficient wood for a strong fire through the night. We were near the rancho of Mr. Murphy, and the kind old gentleman called, and invited us to his house; but we deemed it more prudent to stay by our animals. Our supper of hard bread, broiled pork, and coffee was quickly prepared, and as quickly disposed of. The shadows of eve fell fast; we arranged our watches for the night; and each, in his blanket wound, composed himself to sleep. Mine was the mid-watch: I found the camp-fire bright, and the cliffs around lit with its rays. I numbered the animals to see that none had strayed, and then sat down to watch the motions of a wolf, who was reconnoitering our camp, with step as soft and low—

"As that of man on guilty errand bent."

SATURDAY, SEPT. 23. We broke camp, were up and away while the dew was yet fresh on the grass. Ten miles brought us to Fisher's rancho, where we procured soft bread and fresh milk. But our animals fared hard; the grasshoppers had been there before them. We had yet three hours of sun when we reached the lagoon near San José, but camped there on account of the grass. A shanty stood near by, where we procured a few potatoes and onions, and a piece of fresh meat, with which we made a stew—quite a luxury on a California road. The owner of the shanty invited me to a night's lodging, which I accepted, but found my host much more hospitable than his fleas, for I was driven back to my camp before midnight. A California flea is not be trifled with; his nippers drive you into spasms.

SUNDAY, SEPT. 24. This is the Sabbath, and we are in San José, in the house of Dr. Stokes, to whose hospitality we are indebted for a good table and quiet apartments. I must here relate a domestic incident in the doctor's family, which fell under my eye while he resided at Monterey, and which pictured itself strongly on my mind. It was evening, and the hour for rest with the children, when six little boys and girls knelt around the chair of their father, repeating the Lord's prayer, and closing with the invocation—"God bless our dear parents, and brothers, and sisters, and grant that we meet in heaven at last." Then came the good-night, and the cheerful footsteps to the chamber of soft sleep. What are gold mines to this? A glow-worm's light beneath a star that shall never set!

MONDAY, SEPT. 25. San José is sixty-five miles from Monterey, and stands in the centre of a spacious valley which opens on the great bay of San Francisco. It is cultivated only in spots, but the immense yield in these is sufficient evidence of what the valley is capable. A plough and harrow, at which a New England crow would laugh, are followed by fields of waving grain. Within this valley lie the rich lands of Com. Stockton, and they will yet feel the force of his vivifying enterprise. The mission buildings of

Santa Clara lift their huge proportions on the eye. The bells that swing in their towers are silent, but they will yet find a tongue and fill the cliffs with their glad echoes. The Anglo-Saxon blood will yet roll here as if in its first leap.

Such are the representations of the roads between this and the mines, that we have concluded to part with our wagon and pack our mules. Mr. Botts, one of our companions, has received intelligence which requires his return to Monterey. We must proceed without his agreeable society. Wm. Stewart, Esq., secretary of Com. Jones, and Lieut. Simmons, of the Ohio, have just arrived, on their way to the mines. Two of our mules were now packed, the third mounted by our wagoner, and the fourth driven, to guard against contingencies. Thus equipped, we started again for the mines; but we had hardly cleared the town when one of our mules took fright, plunged over the plain, burst his girth, and scattered on the winds the contents of his pack. Capt. Marcy and Mr. Wilkinson, with the mules and their driver, returned into town to repack, and I proceeded on in the company of Mr. Stewart and Lieut. Simmons.

We passed the mission of San José, which stands three leagues from the town. The massive proportions of the church lay in shadow, but the crowning cross was lit with the rays of the descending sun. No hum of busy streets or jocund voice of childhood saluted the ear. No eye regarded us but that of the owl gazing in wise wonder from his ivy tower. He seemed to marvel at the vanity that had brought us here; and as we hurried past on our gold destination, sent after us an ominous hoot! The purple twilight was settling fast when we reached a stream singing along between the slopes of two hills. Here we camped for the night. The grass was scanty and the ground uneven, but it was now too late to look for other spots. The dry willows, which skirted the stream, furnished us with fuel. The lid of our coffee kettle was soon trembling over the steam, while the fresh steaks, curling on the coals, scented the evening air. Our supper over, we talked of friends far away, and spread our blankets for the night. The ground was so descending I put a stone at my feet to keep from slipping down, but must have rolled from my pedestal, for on awaking at daybreak, I found myself at the foot of the slope, and close on the verge of the bubbling stream. My ground-blanket remained where it had been spread, though it seemed higher up the hill, as I clambered back to it from my somnambulic roll.

TUESDAY, SEPT. 26. My companions, who had returned to San José to repack the mules, arrived at our camp about mid-day, accompanied by W. R. Garner, so long my secretary in the office of alcalde. Our own horses were soon saddled, and we were off, all the more light-hearted for this accession to our numbers. Our road lay through a rolling country covered with live-oak and pine, and through small prairies, cradled in emerald repose among the hills. It was quite dark when we reached the small farm-house of Mr. Livermore. Here we camped. A snag-fence supplied us with fuel, and Mr. L. furnished us with a sheep ready dressed. Our large camp-fire sent up its waving flame, which threw its red light over a group gathered around in every attitude which hunger and culinary care could assume. What was the howl of the wolves on the hills to us, engaged in picking the bones of that sheep? A camp-life teaches you the value of three things—meat, salt, and fire; with these you can travel the globe round.

WEDNESDAY, SEPT. 27. The night had been dark, the wind bleak, and the rack was driving on the sky, when the first rays of the sun kindled the soaring cliffs. We had the great Tularé plain to pass, and lost no time in finishing our breakfast and effecting an early start. Crossing the plain attached to the rancho, which we had left, our road lay among steep conical hills feathered with pine, and pyramids of rock piled in naked majesty. From these we opened on the great plain of the San Joaquin, stretching away like a Sahara, and without an object on which the eye could rest. The sun was hot, and not a breath of wind crept over the cheerless expanse. A column of cloud, soaring on the distant horizon, showed where the fearful flame was at work.

We were now in the midst of the plain, when a moving object, dim and distant, rapidly advanced into more distinct vision. It was a band of wild horses, rushing down the plain like a foaming torrent to the sea.

> "With flowing tail and flying mane,
> With nostrils never stretched by pain,
> Mouths bloodless to the bit or rein;
> And feet that iron never shod,
> And flanks unscarred by spur or rod,
> A thousand horse—the wild, the free—
> Like waves that follow o'er the sea—
> Came thickly thundering on."

We instantly seized the halters of our pack-mules, and not knowing whether to advance or retreat, waited the issue where we stood. They swept past us but a short distance ahead, heeding us as little as the Niagara the reeds that tremble on its bank. The very ground shook with the thunder of their hoofs. Their arching necks and flowing mane, their glossy flanks and sinewy bound made you begrudge them their freedom. You thought what a flight you might make on them into the mines. It seemed a pity that so much celerity and strength should be thrown away upon a stampede.

As we advanced the line of the horizon began to lift itself into irregular shapes, like a broken coast at sea. These emerging forms proved to be the broad tops of a belt of trees, which seemed not more than half a league distant, but which retreated as we advanced, like the bow which childhood pursues. It was a weary ride before we reached them, but the tedium of the way was relieved by several adventures among the wild geese, which hovered near our path in immense flocks. Mr. Stewart, who is an excellent shot, brought several to the ground: with these trophies we camped for the night. Some watered and tethered the animals, others gathered wood, and others ground the coffee and picked the geese. Having in our panniers a few onions and potatoes, with a piece of pork, we prepared for a stew. But our geese must have been the goslins of those that went into the ark, for neither fire nor steam could make an impression on their sinewy forms. We tried them with the puncture of our long knives; found them tough as ever, and then swung off the pot. There was enough, with bread and coffee, without the geese, and as we threw the legs and wings this way and that, an owl watched the flying fragments, as much as to say, it is an ill wind that blows nobody any good.

CHAPTER XX.

THE GRAVE OF A GOLD-HUNTER.—MOUNTAIN SPURS.—A COMPANY OF SONO-RANIANS.—A NIGHT ALARM.—FIRST VIEW OF THE MINES.—CHARACTER OF THE DEPOSITS.—A WOMAN AND HER PAN.—REMOVAL TO OTHER MINES.—WILD INDIANS AND THEIR WEAPONS.—COST OF PROVISIONS.—A PLUNGE INTO A GOLD RIVER.—MACHINES USED BY THE GOLD-DIGGERS.

Thursday, Sept. 28. We slept soundly last night. The sun had been up an hour before we finished our coffee and vaulted into our saddles. A short ride brought us to the San Joaquin river, which we crossed in the primitive way. We threw our saddles and packs into a boat, and then getting in ourselves, rowed off, leading at the stern one of our little mules, called Nina. The horses being driven in, followed in her wake and swam to the opposite bank. The moment they reached the shore, every one lay down and rolled, covering himself with a layer of sand. My own for once seemed to have caught the mine fever, and without waiting for the saddle, much less his rider, went snorting up the bank.

A mile or two further on, and we passed the grave of one whom I had known well in Monterey. He was a young man of many amiable and excellent qualities; was on his way to the mines; but in crossing a gulch, now entirely dry, but through which a freshet then swept, became entangled with the gearing of his horses, and was drowned. An evergreen tree throws its perpetual shadows on the mound where he rests, and the wild birds sing his requiem. His widowed mother, who dwells by the rushing tide of the Missouri, will long look for his return, and still doubt in her grief the story of his death. But never will her eyes again rest on his. Till the heavens be no more he shall not awake, nor be raised out of his sleep.

Our road for ten miles lay through a level plain corresponding in its cheerless aspect to that we had passed on the other side of the San Joaquin. We encountered a drove of wild elk with their forest of branching horns, but they kept beyond the range of our rifles, and our horses were too tired to be put on the pursuit. We had only the satisfaction of venting, in words, our spleen on their speed, but little cared they for that. They run away at times, as it would seem, from their own horns, for our road was strewn with these cast-off coronets.

Leaving the plain we ascended into a rolling country lightly timbered with oak, pine, and birch. We wound rapidly forward, till we encountered a stream, and a plot of green grass which had escaped the fire that had been straggling about among the hills. We were without a guide, and on a trail which at times became rather faint and difficult, and no one knew where we might next meet with water, so we tethered, collected our wood for the night, and lit our camp-fire. We had no more potatoes or onions for a stew, and made our supper on broiled pork, hard bread, and coffee. We had our saddles for our pillows, the green earth for our couch, and the bright stars to light us to our rest.

Friday, Sept. 29. One of our company discovered near our camp this morning a little lake, with fish darting about in its lucid waters. Our twine was soon out and hooked, the alder supplied us with poles, and we answered exactly to Dr. Johnson's definition of angling—" Line and rod, with a worm at one end and a fool at the other," for not a fish would bite; they were not to be caught with a poor wriggling worm, when golden flies were floating about. They were fish of a better taste; and we had to breakfast as we had done before, on broiled pork, hard bread, and coffee. A famished crow, as if in sympathy with our wants, rattled his bones near by on a dry limb.

The trail which we were following accommodated itself to the wild country through which it lay. The bold bluff and deep chasm bent it into a constant succession of quick circles and sharp angles. The head of our train was never in sight of those who occupied the rear, except when we wound over those more gradual slopes which here and there relieved the ruggedness of the landscape. We met a company of Californians about mid-day, on their return from the mines, and a more forlorn looking group never knocked at the gate of a pauper asylum. They were most of them dismounted, with rags fastened round their blistered feet, and with clubs in their hands, with which they were trying to force on their skeleton animals. They inquired for bread and meat: we had but little of either, but shared it with them. They took from one of their packs a large bag of gold, and began to shell out a pound or two in payment. We told them they were welcome; still they seemed anxious to pay, and we were obliged to be positive in our refusal. This company, as I afterwards ascertained, had with them over a hundred thousand dollars in grain gold. One of them had the largest lump that had yet been found; it weighed over twenty pounds; and he seemed almost ready to part with it for a mess of pottage. What is gold where there is nothing to eat?—the gilded fly of the angler in a troutless stream.

SATURDAY, SEPT. 30. We camped last night in a forest, where a small opening let in the sun's rays upon a plot of green grass and a sparkling spring. Our slumbers were broken in the night by the discharge of a pistol by one of our company, who saw, or thought he saw, a wolf snuffling about his blanket. We seized our arms, thinking the wild Indians were upon us, but found no enemy. It was probably the phantom of a disturbed dream. We scolded the young man soundly who gave the alarm, and turned down on the earth again to finish our night's repose.

The scenery, as we advanced, became more wild and picturesque. The hills lost their gentle slopes, and took the form of steep and rugged cones : the mountain ranges were broken by dark and rugged gorges ; over crags that toppled high in air, the soaring pine threw its wild music on the wind; while merry streams dashed down the precipitous rocks, as if in haste to greet the green vale below. A short distance beyond us lay the richest gold mines that had yet been discovered ; and nature, as if to guard her treasures, had thrown around them a steep mountain barrier. This frowning wall seemed as if riven in some great convulsion. The broad chasm, like a break in a huge Roman aqueduct, dropped to the level plain ; while the bold bluffs of the severed barrier gazed at each other in savage grandeur. Beyond this gateway, a valley wandered for some distance, and then expanded into a plain, in the midst of which stood a beautiful grove of oak and pine. Crossing this, we wound over a rough, rocky elevation, and turned suddenly into a ravine, up which we discovered a line of tents glittering in the sun's rays. We were in the gold mines ! I jumped from my horse, took a pick, and in five minutes found a piece of gold large enough to make a signet-ring.

We had the unexpected pleasure of meeting here Gov. Mason and Capt. Sherman, who had arrived the evening before in their tour of observation ; and Dr. Ord, recently of the army, and Mr. Taylor, of Monterey. They invited us to their camp and a supper which we enjoyed with a keen relish. If you want to know what it is to have an appetite, which scruples at nothing and enjoys every thing, travel on horseback and sleep in the open air. Railroads and hotels are the graves of invalids. But I forgot our horses: we could find no grass; there was a poor pasture several miles distant; but it was now near sunset; we gathered acorns for them, which a horse will eat when pinched with hunger. Our camp-fire was kindled, and we rolled down for the night.

Sunday, Oct. 1. Another Sabbath, and our first in the mines. But here and there a digger has resumed his work. With most it is a day of rest, not so much perhaps from religious scruples, as a conviction that the system requires and must have repose. He is a blind philosopher, as well as a stupid Christian, who cannot see, even in the physical benefits of the Sabbath, motives sufficient to sanctify its observance. He must be a callous soul, who, with the hope of heaven in his dreams, can wantonly profane its spirit.

Monday, Oct. 2. I went among the gold-diggers; found half a dozen at the bottom of the ravine, tearing up the bogs, and up to their knees in mud. Beneath these bogs lay a bed of clay, sprinkled in spots with gold. These deposits, and the earth mixed with them, were shovelled into bowls, taken to a pool near by, and washed out. The bowl, in working, is held in both hands, whirled violently back and forth through half a circle, and pitched this way and that sufficiently to throw off the earth and water, while the gold settles to the bottom. The process is extremely laborious, and taxes the entire muscles of the frame. In its effect it is more like swinging a scythe than any work I ever attempted.

Not having much relish for the bogs and mud, I procured a light crowbar and went to splitting the slate-rocks which project into the ravine. I found between the layers, which were not perfectly closed, particles of gold, resembling in shape the small and delicate scales of a fish. These were easily scraped from the slate by a hunter's knife, and readily separated in the wash-bowl from all foreign substances. The layers in which they were found generally inclined from a vertical or horizontal position, and formed an acute angle with the bank of the ravine, in the direction of the current. In the reverse of this position, and where the inclination was with the current, they rarely contained any gold. The inference would seem to be, that these deposits are made by the currents when swelled by the winter rains, and poured in a rushing tide down these channels. It is only the most rapid stream that can carry this treasure, and even that must soon resign it to some eddy, or the rock that paves its footsteps.

There are about seventy persons at work in this ravine, and all within a few yards of each other. They average about one ounce per diem each. They who get less are discontented, and they who get more are not satisfied. Every day brings in some fresh report of richer discoveries in some quarter not far remote, and the diggers are consequently kept in a state of feverish excitement. One woman, a Sonoranian, who was washing here, finding at the bottom of her bowl only the amount of half a dollar or so, hurled it back again into the water, and straightening herself up to her full height, strode off with the indignant air of one who feels himself insulted. Poor woman! how little thou knowest of those patient females, who in our large cities make a shirt or vest for ten cents! Were an ounce of diamonds to fall into one of our hands every day, we should hold out the other just as eager and impatient as if its fellow were empty. Such is human nature; and a miserable thing it is, too, especially when touched with the gold fever.

Tuesday, Oct. 3. We parted to-day with the society of Mr. Stewart and Mr. Simmons: they were on a tour of observation; were bound to Sutter's Fort, and availed themselves of the company of Gov. Mason and Capt. Sherman, who were going in the same direction; may they have an agreeable journey, and each find a lump of gold as big as Vulcan's anvil. We ordered up our own horses, packed our mules, and started for a ravine some seven miles distant. Our path lay over the spur of a mountain, so rugged and steep that we were obliged to dismount. The soaring masses were piled around us in the wildest sublimity, presenting those thunder-scarred fronts which the volcano in its terrific energy throws into the eye of the sun. You had a dim persuasion that some fearful charm, some unseen treasure lurked in the sunless recesses of these stupendous piles; and so it seemed, for out walked a grizzly bear from a mountain gorge, and fixed his burning eyes steadfastly on us. Not being certain of our rifles, as we had not used them for several days, we deemed prudence the better part of valor, and gave the old monarch of the woods a pretty wide berth.

We examined several spots on our route for gold, but found none, either on the table-rock, or in the channels of the mountain streams. If it ever existed there, it had been swept below, or remained in the veins of the rock beyond the reach of pickaxe and spade. On the plain we fell in with the camp of Mr. Murphy, who invited us into his tent, and set before us refreshments that would have graced a scene less wild than this. His tent is pitched in the midst of a small tribe of wild Indians who gather gold for him, and receive in return provisions and blankets. He knocks down two bullocks a day to furnish them with meat. Though never before within the wake of civilization, they respect his person and property. This, however, is to be ascribed in part to the fact that he has married the daughter of the chief—a young woman of many personal attractions, and full of that warm wild love which makes her the Haide of the woods. She is the queen of the tribe, and walks among them with the air of one on whom authority sets as a native grace,—a charm which all feel, and of which she seems the least conscious.

The men and boys were busy with their bows and arrows. A difficulty had arisen between this tribe and one not far remote, and they were expecting an attack. Though the less powerful tribe of the two, they seemed not the least dismayed. The old men looked stern and grave, but the boys were full of glee as if mustering for a deer-hunt. The mothers with Spartan coolness were engaged in pointing arrows with flint stones, so shaped that they easily penetrate and break off in the effort to extract them, and always leave an ugly wound. They project these arrows from their bows with incredible force, often burying them to the feather in the luckless elk; the deer gives his last life-bound and falls, while the unsuspecting foe drops unwarned from his saddle. I saw no signs of intoxication among these Indians, and was told by Mr. Murphy that he allowed no liquors in the camp. He said a trader brought there a few days since a barrel of rum, and that he gave him exactly five minutes in which to decide whether he would quit the grounds, or have the head of the barrel knocked in. He of course took his fire-curse to some other place.

WEDNESDAY, OCT. 4. Our camping-ground is in a broad ravine through which a rivulet wanders, and which is dotted with the frequent tents of gold-diggers. The sounds of the crowbar and pick, as they shake or shiver the rock, are echoed from a thousand cliffs; while the hum of human voices rolls off on the breeze to mingle with the barking of wolves, who regard with no friendly eyes this intrusion into their solitude. They resemble their great progenetrix, trembling in stone, as the Vandals broke into Rome. But little care the gold-diggers about the wolves, it is enough for them to know that this ravine contains gold; and it must be dug out, though an earthquake may slumber beneath. If you want to find men prepared to storm the burning threshold of the infernal prison, go among gold-diggers.

The provisions with which we left San José are gone, and we have been obliged to supply ourselves here. We pay at the rate of four hundred dollars a barrel for flour; four dollars a pound for poor brown sugar, and four dollars a pound for indifferent coffee. And as for meat, there is none to be got except jerked-beef, which is the flesh of the bullock cut into strings and hung up in the sun to dry, and which has about as much juice in it as a strip of bark dangling in the wind from a dead tree. Still, when moistened and toasted, it will do something towards sustaining life; so also will the sole of your shoe. And yet I have seen men set and grind it as if it were nutritious and sweetly flavored. Oh ye who lose your temper because your sirloin has rolled once too much on the spit, come to the mines of California and eat jerked-beef!

THURSDAY, OCT. 5. The rivulet, which waters the ravine, collects here and there into deep pools. Over one of these a low limb had thrown itself, upon which I ventured out with an apparatus for scooping up the sand at the bottom. But just as I had lowered my dipper the limb broke, and down I went to the chin in water. It was some minutes before I could extricate myself, and when I did there was not a dry thread on my body. The chill of the stream reduced the gold fever in me very considerably. I had brought no outward garments but those in which I stood; I wrung out the water and hung them up in the sun to dry, and wound myself, like an Indian, in my blanket. But I was not more savage in my aspect than in my feelings. This, however, soon passed off, and I could laugh with others at the gold plunge. But nothing is a novelty here for more than a minute; were a man to cast his skin or lose his head, no one would stop to inquire if he had recovered either, unless they suspected foul play, and then they would arraign and execute the culprit before one of our lawyers could pen an indictment.

FRIDAY, OCT. 6. The most efficient gold-washer here is the cradle, which resembles in shape that appendage of the nursery, from which it takes its name. It is nine or ten feet long, open at one end and closed at the other. At the end which is closed, a sheet-iron pan, four inches deep, and sixteen over, and perforated in the bottom with holes, is let in even with the sides of the cradle. The earth is thrown into the pan, water turned on it, and the cradle, which is on an inclined plane, set in motion. The earth and water pass through the pan, and then down the cradle, while the gold, owing to its specific gravity, is caught by cleets fastened across the bottom. Very little escapes; it generally lodges before it reaches the last cleet. It requires four or five men to supply the earth and water to work such a machine to advantage. The quantity of gold washed out must depend on the relative proportion of gold in the earth. The one worked in this ravine yields a hundred dollars a day; but this is considered a slender result. Most of the diggers use the bowl or pan; its lightness never embarrasses their roving habits; and it can be put in motion wherever they may find a stream or spring. It can be purchased now in the mines for five or six dollars; a few months since it cost an ounce—sixteen dollars for a wooden bowl! But I have seen twenty-four dollars paid for a box of seidlitz-powders, and forty dollars for as many drops of laudanum.

CHAPTER XXI.

LUMP OF GOLD LOST.—INDIANS AT THEIR GAME OF ARROWS.—CAMP OF THE GOLD-HUNTERS.—A SONORANIAN GOLD-DIGGER.—SABBATH IN THE MINES.—THE GIANT WELCHMAN.—NATURE OF GOLD DEPOSITS.—AVERAGE PER MAN.—NEW DISCOVERIES.

SATURDAY, OCT. 7. I had come to the mines without a pick, but this morning fell in with a trader who had one for sale: his price was ten dollars in specie, or eighteen in gold dust. I gave him the specie; the pick weighed about four pounds, was of rude manufacture, and without a handle; but this appendage was readily supplied from the limb of an ash. Thus accoutred I strode down the ravine, not doubting but what I should, before night, strike upon some deposit which would fill my pockets. Passing groups who were engaged in digging into this bank and that, I fell in with a sailor, whom I recognized as one of the men who had been honorably discharged from the Savannah. He was groping about as if in quest of something he had lost. "What is the matter, Jones?" I inquired; he sprung to his feet, gave me his rough hand, and pointed to a cliff which overhung the glen. "There, on that crag," said he, "I have been at work ever since the peep of day, and got out several bits of gold, and one good-sized lump: I put them in my tin cup, when, striking away again, my pick glanced, struck the cup, and knocked it, gold and all, half-way across this ravine; and I might as well hunt a clam in the Pacific as that gold, though it was a jewel of a piece—the biggest I have seen here." So I laid down my pick, ascended the cliff, ascertained, as near as possible, the direction in which the cup flew, and commenced the search. Every bunch of leaves, every hole and gulley were examined, and the cup recovered, but the gold was not in it.

Fatigued, I threw myself into the shade of a scrub-oak, and went to sleep; but the gold of poor Jones glanced through my dreams. I saw, in that fantastic realm, a small birch-tree, a bubbling spring at its root, and in its fount a piece of gold. I seemed to know at the time it was only a dream; still the picture remained in my mind so clear, so distinct, that on awaking I identified at a glance the birch, and springing to its root found the little fount, and with a hoe fetched up the piece of gold!—the same that had been lost, for none other could answer so exactly to the description which had been given. It weighed about three ounces, but did not seem larger than the sparkling eye of the sailor as I placed it in his hand. They may laugh who will at dreams, but now and then some Sibyl leaf floats through them. I tried to dream again where gold might be found; saw plenty of birch-trees and fountains, but never discovered an ingot in either.

MONDAY, OCT. 9. On returning to our camping-tree this afternoon, I found three wild Indians quietly squatted in its shade. They had been attracted there by a red belt, which hung from one of the limbs. They could speak only their native dialect, not a word of which could I understand. We had to make ourselves intelligible by signs. They wanted to purchase the belt, and each laid down a piece of gold, which were worth in the aggregate some two hundred dollars. I took one of the pieces, and gave the Indian to whom it belonged the belt. They made signs for a piece of coin; I offered them an eagle, but it was not what they wanted,—a Spanish mill dollar, but they wanted something smaller,—a fifty-cent piece, and they signified it would do. Taking the coin they fastened it in the end of a stick, so as to expose nearly the entire circle, and set it up about forty yards distant. They then cast lots by a bone, which they threw into the air, for the order in which they should discharge their arrows. The one who had the first shot, drew his long sinewy bow and missed; the second, he missed; the third, and he missed,—though the arrow of each flew so near the coin it would have killed a deer at that distance. The second now shot first and grazed the coin; then the third, who broke his string and shot with the bow of the second, but missed; and now the first took his turn, and struck the coin, whirling it off at a great distance. The other two gave him the belt, which he tied around his head instead of his blanket, and away they started over the hills, full of wild life and glee, leaving the coin, as a thing of no importance, in the bushes where it had been whirled.

TUESDAY, OCT. 10. My companions, who have been out on a gold-hunt for several hours, have just returned, bringing with them about an ounce of gold each. They are so thoroughly fatigued they prefer sleep to a dinner, connected with the trouble of preparing it. And there is no other way here; every man is obliged to be his own cook. We have our henchman, it is true, but he is in a ravine some four miles distant, in charge of our horses and mules. If he will keep them from straying, or being stolen by the wild Indians, we shall be content to wait on ourselves. Several of the persons at work in the ravine turned their horses adrift on their arrival, which they might safely do, for the poor things have not got strength enough to climb its steep sides. They subsist on the acorns which they gather, and a few tufts of grass as dry and scorched as the clover over which the flames of Sodom rolled. But what think men of the hunger or thirst of dumb animals, when the gold fever is throwing its circle of fire around the soul.

WEDNESDAY, OCT. 11. It is near sunset, and the gold-diggers are returning from their labors, each one bearing on his head a brush-heap, with which he will kindle his evening fire. Their wild halloos, as they come in, fill the cliffs with their echoes. All are merry, whatever may have been the fortunes of the day with them. Not one among the whole can anticipate a more luxurious supper than a cake baked in the ashes, with a cup of coffee and a bit of jerked-beef, except in the case of a new-comer, who has brought with him a few pounds of buckwheat flour; he can have a pancake, that is if he has any thing with which to grease his pan, which is extremely doubtful. There is not a bottle of liquor in the ravine, and every one must, per force, turn in sober. Every streamlet preaches temperance, and the wind-stirred pine sings its soft eulogy on the charmed air.

THURSDAY, OCT. 12. I found near our camp this morning a boulder of trap and quartz which had evidently travelled some distance, as nothing of the kind existed in the ravine. I had no means of demolishing the mass, and could with my pick only dislodge a few of the quartz: these I found veined with gold. But it is the only specimen of this combination with which I have met. Where the fellow came from, I know not; but had he tumbled into New York or Philadelphia, instead of this cañada, the whole community would have been filled with prattling wonders. How much the marvellous depends on circumstances!

FRIDAY, OCT. 13. I passed a few days since a Sonoranian at work against a steep bank of decomposed granite and clay, which was so firm that he could hardly make an impression upon it with a heavy sharp-pointed crowbar. "And what, my friend," I inquired, "are you going to get out there?" to which he replied, "A pocket of gold, sir, as soon as I can reach it." "And what makes you think," I continued, "that you will find a deposit there?" to which he responded, "Do you see that blow-hole on the other side of the ravine, where the slate rock stands out so rough, with a savage mouth in the centre? Well, sir, *that* was the devil's blow-hole, and he blowed the gold straight across the ravine into this bank, where I will find it, if I work long enough." I thought him some half-crazy fellow, and passed on. He dug away all that day without reaching his pocket; but on the following day took out two pounds of gold, in small pieces, resembling in shape the seeds of the watermellon. As soon as this was known, four of the New York volunteers struck in each side of the Sonoranian, and dug him out; and the old man very quietly retired. The intruders dug away through the remainder of the day, but found no gold, and then quit the spot, concluding that the Sonoranian had got out the only pocket which existed there. The next morning, however, the Sonoranian renewed his attack on the bank, and with his sharp-pointed crowbar and pick, penetrated beyond the layer where the volunteers had knocked off. Before night he struck another pocket, and took out a pound and a half of gold of the same shape and size as the other. The volunteers were now roused, and returned to the spot, determined to dig down the whole bank; but one day of hard work, unrewarded by a single particle of gold, was enough. They quitted the bank in disgust. The old Sonoranian told me it contained no more pockets. His theory about the blow-hole is by no means confined to his own wild imagination; a man by the name of Black, who is one of the most successful gold-hunters in the ravine, is guided, in his researches, by the same seemingly absurd theory. It is possible that these blow-holes, as they are called, were the vents of volcanoes, performing the same functions as those found beneath the shaking cone of Etna.

SATURDAY, OCT. 14. A party of seven Americans are just in from the higher slopes of the Sierra, where they have been prospecting for gold. They penetrated to the snow, tearing up roots, overturning rocks, and draining fountains, but discovering no gold. It is the foot range of the Sierra that contains the deposits; this has been cut into segments by rapid streams, rising higher up, and which have sunk their channels into deep gorges. The larger portion of the gold, subjected to the action of these torrents, has been swept out upon the plain, or buried deep in some nearer undulation, where it will remain undisturbed till the deposits nearer the surface have been exhausted. These deeper treasures, like the inhumed remains of a Herculaneum, will then be brought to light.

SUNDAY, OCT. 15. A quiet day among the gold-diggers; but few are at work with pick or pan;

An Alcalde at the mines examining a lump of gold—catches the fever—drops his staff of office, and tells his sheriff to go home and hang the prisoner whom he left at the bar, and he will sentence him afterwards

small parties have gone over the hills "prospecting," but the masses are beneath the oak and pines, which shadow the cañadas. Missionaries might find a field here in this rolling population; the waving grain, as well as the still, falls before the sickle of the reaper There is something inspiring in wild-wood worship; you are with nature and nature's God: every thing around you trembles in the breath of the Almighty: the glad rivulet whispers his name, and the pine-grove pours its sweeping anthem; your spirit soars on lighter wings, and religion becomes, as another has beautifully expressed it, the play of the soul in the sunbeams of God.

MONDAY, OCT. 16. I encountered this morning, in the person of a Welchman, a pretty marked specimen of the gold-digger. He stood some six feet eight in his shoes, with giant limbs and frame. A leather strap fastened his coarse trowsers above his hips, and confined the flowing bunt of his flannel shirt. A broad-rimmed hat sheltered his browny features, while his unshorn beard and hair flowed in tangled confusion to his waist. To his back was lashed a blanket and bag of provisions; on one shoulder rested a huge crowbar, to which were hung a gold-washer and skillet; on the other rested a rifle, a spade, and pick, from which dangled a cup and pair of heavy shoes. He recognized me as the magistrate who had once arrested him for a breach of the peace. "Well, Señor Alcalde," said he, "I am glad to see you in these diggings. You had some trouble with me in Monterey; I was on a burster; you did your duty, and I respect you for it; and now let me settle the difference between us with a bit of gold: it shall be the first I strike under this bog." I told him there was no difference between us; that I knew at the time it was rum which had raised the rumpus. But before I had finished my disclaiming speech, his traps were on the ground, and his heavy pick was tearing up bog after bog from the marl in which it had struck its tangling roots. These removed, he struck a layer of clay: "Here she comes!" he ejaculated, and turned out a piece of gold that would weigh an ounce or more. "There," said he, "Señor Alcalde, accept that; and when you reach home, where I hope you will find all well, have a bracelet made of it for your good lady."

He continued to dig around the same place, but during the hour I remained with him found no other piece of gold—not a particle. This is no uncommon thing; I have seen a piece weighing six ounces taken from some little curve in a bank undulating in its bed, while not another of any size, after the most laborious search, could be found in its vicinity. This holds true of the larger pieces, but rarely of the scale gold. Where you find half an ounce of that, you may be pretty sure there is more near by. The same law which deposited that, has carried its results much further; and you will find a clue to them in the curves of the channel, or the character and position of the rocks which project into it. If the projection is smooth, or forms an obtuse angle with the current, there is no gold there, and you must look to the eddy directly below it. This eddy, or its deposit, can be examined only when the water has subsided. During the rainy season, and when the snows are melting on the Sierra, no such investigations can be successfully prosecuted. Of all metals the most difficult to reach and secure under water is gold. It has a thousand modes of eluding your search, and escaping your scooping implements.

TUESDAY, OCT. 17. A German this morning, picking a hole in the ground, near our camping-tree, for a tent-pole, struck a piece of gold, weighing about three ounces. As soon as it was known, some forty picks were flying into the earth all around the spot. You would have thought the ground had suddenly caved over some human being, who must be instantly disenhumed or die. But the fellow sought was not the companion of the digger, but the mate of the yellow boy accidentally found by the German. But no such mate was discovered; the one found had slumbered thus alone like Adam before the birth of Eve. How solitary that couch, though in Paradise! Think of that, ye devotees of celibacy, who people your dreams with fairies, and imagine a bliss amid the wrecks of the fall, which was not the portion of man even before that moral catastrophe.

But I forget the piece of gold; no fellow was found

for it here; but in a ravine, seven miles distant, a little girl this morning picked up what she thought a curious stone, and brought it to her mother, who, on removing the extraneous matter, found it a lump of pure gold, weighing between six and seven pounds. The news of this discovery silenced all the picks here for half an hour, and set as many tongues going in their places. Twenty or thirty started at once to explore the wonders of this new locality. Gold among hunters, like a magnet in the midst of ferruginous bodies, attracts every thing to itself.

Wednesday, Oct. 18. We are camped in the centre of the gold mines, in the heart of the richest deposits which have been found, and where there are many hundred at work. I have taken some pains to ascertain the average per man that is got out; it must be less than half an ounce per day. It might be more were there any stability among the diggers; but half their time is consumed in what they call prospecting; that is, looking up new deposits. An idle rumor, or mere surmise, will carry them off in this direction or that, when perhaps they gathered nothing for their weariness and toil. A locality where an ounce a day can be obtained by patient labor is constantly left for another, which rumor has enriched with more generous deposits. They who decry this instability in others, may hold out for a time, but yield at last to the same phrensied fickleness. I have never met with one who had the strength of purpose to resist these roving temptations. He will not swing a pick for an ounce a day, with the rumor of pounds ringing in his ears. He shoulders his implements to chase this phantom of hope.

THURSDAY, OCT. 19. All the gold-diggers through the entire encampment, were shaken out of their slumbers this morning by a report that a solid pocket of gold had been discovered in a bend of the Stanislaus. In half an hour a motley multitude, covered with crowbars, pickaxes, spades, rifles, and washbowls, went streaming over the hills in the direction of the new deposits. You would have thought some fortress was to be stormed, or some citadel sapped. I had seen too much of these rumored banks of gold to be moved from my propriety, and remained under my old camping-tree. Near this I pecked out from a small crevice of slate rock, a piece weighing about half an ounce. It had evidently travelled some distance, and taken refuge from the propulsive storms of ages in this little hiding-place, as a good man from the persecutions of the world glides down at last to his sainted repose. But I have no compunction for having disturbed this piece of gold; it may yet be shaped into an ear-drop, and kiss the envied cheek of beauty; or it may be studded with diamonds, and swell on a billow that seems to blush at the flash of its ray; or it may be shaped into the marriage-ring, and set its seal on the purest bliss that greets the visits of angels; or it may be stamped into a coin, and as it drops into the hands of the widow or orphan, prove that—

> "The secret pleasure of a generous act
> Is the great mind's great bribe."

But evening is returning, and with it the gold-diggers from their pursuit of the new deposit. Their jokes, as they clatter down the slopes of the ravine, are sufficient evidence that they have been on a wild-goose chase. Disappointment will make a single man sober, but when it falls on a multitude, is often converted into a source of railery and fun. There is something extremely consoling in having the company of others, when we have been duped through our vanity or exaggerated hopes. This comfort was deeply felt by the diggers this evening. All had lost a day, and with it the most enchanting visions of wealth. All had returned hungry as a wolf on a desert; or a recluse listening in his last penance to the sound of his cross-bones, shaken by the wind.

CHAPTER XXII.

VISIT TO THE SONORANIAN CAMP.—FESTIVITIES AND GAMBLING.—THE DOCTOR AND TEAMSTER.—AN ALCALDE TURNED COOK.—THE MINER'S TATTOO.—THE LITTLE DUTCHMAN.—NEW DEPOSITS DISCOVERED.—A WOMAN KEEPING A MONTÉ TABLE.—UP TO THE KNEE AND NINE-PENCE.—THE VOLCANOES AND GOLD.—ARRIVAL OF A BARREL OF RUM.

FRIDAY, OCT. 20. I threw myself into my saddle at an early hour this morning, and started for a cañada, about ten miles distant. The foot-trail which I followed, lay over several sharp ridges to the quick waves of the Stanislaus, and then up a steep mountain spur. I was obliged to dismount, draw myself up by the bushes, and trust to the fidelity of my horse to follow. At last we gained the summit, but it was only to gaze down a wild precipitous descent, where the cliffs hung in toppling terror. A vein of white quartz run along the ridge, like a line of unmelted snow, with here and there spangles of gold glittering in the sun. I had no implement with me but my hunting-knife, and vainly broke the point of that. I tried one of my pistols; the bullet knocked out the gold-drop, but jewel and lead went over the steep verge together. I let myself down by the bushes, blessing every lythe limb and steadfast root, while my horse, more sagacious, fetched a circuit, and reached the plain before me.

Ascending another ridge, the ravine, which had induced this adventure, lay in jagged wildness beneath. It was in uproarious life; an elk had been shot; and the miners were feasting on its fat ribs. The repast was hardly over, when the monté table, with its piles of gold, glimmered in the shade. It was the great camp of the Sonoranians, and hundreds were crowding around to reach the bank, and deposit their treasures on the turn of a card. They seemed to play for the excitement, and often doubled their stakes whether they won or lost. They apparently connect no moral obliquity with the game; one of them, who sleeps near my camping-tree, will kneel by the half hour on the sharp rock in his Ave Marias, while the keen night-wind cuts his scarce clad frame, then rise and stake his last dollar at monté. At the break of day he is on his knees again, and his prayer trembles up with the first trill of the waking birds. It was in this ravine that a few weeks since the largest lump of gold found in California was discovered. It weighs twenty-three pounds, is nearly pure, and cubic in its form. Its discovery shook the whole mines; the shout of the *eureka* swelled on the wind like the cheer of seamen when the pharos breaks through a stormy night. I waved my adieu to the miners, and fetching a bold circuit to the east, reached at night-fall my camping-tree.

Saturday, Oct. 21. Extravagant charges here are often made as offsets. A doctor of my acquaintance, wishing to remove to another cañada a few miles off, tost his machine into an empty wagon, bound in that direction, and on arriving, asked the teamster what he was to pay; the reply was a hundred dollars! which was planked down without a word. Soon after this the teamster had a grip of the cholic, from which he sought relief in two or three of the doctor's pills. The relieved patient now asked what *he* was to pay; the doctor, after a few moment's abstraction, in which he seemed to be rummaging his memory more than his medicines, replied, "The charge is exactly one hundred dollars!" "Ah," said the wagoner, "I knew that cradle would yet rock thunder at me." But he paid the fee, and squared the account.

I have been out for several hours this morning scouring a conical hill crowned with quartz. I took with me the sailor, who knocked his cup of gold out of sight by an accidental glance of his pick. We searched the hill from top to bottom, shivered the quartz on its summit, and rummaged among the fragments of the same, which the storms of ages had swept to its base, but we found no gold. Following one of the slopes which terminated in a glen, overhung with willows, and where a current had flowed, we struck into a confined basin, where we found, among the pebbles, a deposit of gold, and gathered, in the course of the day, about two ounces; with beautiful trophies we returned to camp.

Monday, Oct. 23. It was now near noon, and

my day to cook the dinner; so I hastened back to our camping-tree, and piling up the half-extinguished brands, soon raised a fire. Then taking a tin pan, which served alternately as a gold-washer and a bread-tray, I turned into it a few pounds of flour, a small solution of saleratus, and a few quarts of water, and then went to work in it with my hands, mixing it up and adding flour till I got it to the right consistency; then shaping it into a loaf, raked open the embers, and rolled it in, covering it with the live coals. While this baking was going on, I placed in a stew-pan, after pounding it pretty well between two stones, a string of jerked-beef, with a small quantity of water, and lodged it on the fire. Then taking some coffee, which had been burnt the evening before, I tied it in the end of a napkin, and hammering it to pieces between two stones, turned it into a coffee-pot filled with water, and placed that, too, on the fire. In half an hour or so my bread was baked, my jerk-beef stewed, and my coffee boiled. I settled the latter by turning on it a pint of cold water. The bread was well done; a little burnt on one side, and somewhat puffed up, like the expectations of the gold-digger in the morning, or the vanity of a stump-orator just after a cheer. My companions returned, and seating ourselves on the ground, each with a tin cup of coffee, a junk of bread, and a piece of the stewed jerky, our dinner was soon dispatched, and with a relish which the epicure never yet felt or fancied. The water here is slightly impregnated with iron and sulphur; the one acting as a tonic, the other as an aperient. And then this fine mountain air, some eight hundred feet above the level of the sea, all conduce to health and buoyancy of spirits. Among the hundred gold-diggers around, not one hypochondriac throws on rock or rill the shadow of a long countenance. Even they who hardly get out gold enough to pay their way, laugh at their bad luck, and hope for better success to-morrow. They have yet plenty of tickets in the lottery, and some of them may turn out prizes. At any rate, they are not going to despond while these glens contain an undisturbed bar, or these hills lift their cones of white rock in the sun.

TUESDAY, OCT. 24. The ravine in which we are camped runs nearly north and south, and is walled by lofty ranges of precipitous rock. It is near ten o'clock of the day before the rays of the sun strike its depths; but when they do reach you, it is with a power that drives you at once into the shade. It is twilight in the glen, while the cliffs above still blaze in the radiance of the descending orb. As darkness comes on, the camp-fires of the diggers, kindled along the ravine, throw their light into every recess, where forms are seen, gathered in groups, or glancing about, while every now and then some merry tale or apt joke explodes in a roar of laughter. At eight o'clock every tin pan and brass kettle is put in requisition, and the thumpers beat a tattoo, which is concluded with the simultaneous discharge of several muskets.

The jargon is enough to frighten the wolf out of his cavern; and yet no harmony that ever rolled from theatrical orchestra or cathedral choir, can charm you half as much. It is the music of the heart reeling itself off through tin pans in melodious numbers. But the musicians are now all sound asleep; their camp-fires wane, and there is only heard the dirge of the pines, murmuring in the night-wind. Thousands who lie on beds of down, under canopies of silk, might envy the sleepers on these rocks their quiet repose. The stars gaze on no groups where slumber shakes from its wings such a refreshing dew.

WEDNESDAY, OCT. 25. A little Dutchman came to me this morning, and informed me, in whispers, that he and his companion had, unbeknown to the rest, stolen off to a glen about three miles distant, where they had found a rich deposit, and then invited me to come and share it with them. He took my pan, which had served as a bread-tray, and we wound over the hills to his glen. Here we found his red-haired companion, knee-deep in mud, which he was shovelling out to reach the bed of clay beneath. On this bed lay the gold in grains about the size of wheat-kernels. Every now and then the water, which was as cold as ice, would gather in the hole, and required to be bailed out or drained off. The chill of the water was enough for me; I had tried that once before, and felt no disposition to repeat the experiment. The mud I could stand, for I was already dirty as a pig just rolling out of his *siesta*. So I told my young friends to go to work, and I would poke about the edges. They urged me to jump in; and truly the temptation was strong, and required some share of prudence to resist it, but I contented myself with working where I could keep my feet dry. But they several times called for my pan, and filled it with earth, scraped from the clay bed, which I washed out, and then found at the bottom fifteen or twenty dollars in gold. They obtained, as the result of their joint labors through the day, about a thousand dollars. Night was advancing, and I returned over the hills to our camping-tree.

THURSDAY, OCT. 26. Where is the little Dutchman and the red-haired Paddy? ran in excited inquiry through the ravine this morning, for they had now been missed from the camp twenty-four hours, and no doubt existed on the minds of many that they had found a rich deposit somewhere, and were secretly working it out. I knew well where they were, but no one thought of questioning me on the subject, for I was looked upon as a sort of amateur gold-hunter, very much given to splitting rocks and digging in unproductive places; and, indeed, this was not far from the truth, for my main object was information, and a specimen of wild mountain life.

But to return to the little Dutchman. All knew him to be a shrewd gold-hunter, and determined to find him before he should exhaust his discovery. No child lost in the woods ever awakened half the concern: some started in this direction, others in that, till all the cardinal points in the heaven, and all the glens between, had men travelling towards them. The most curious feature in this business is, that out of a regiment of gold-hunters, where the utmost apparent confusion prevails, the absence of two men should be noticed. But the motions of every man are watched. Even when he gathers up his traps, takes formal leave, and is professedly bound home, he is tracked for leagues. No disguise can avail him; the most successful war-stratagem would fail here.

FRIDAY, OCT. 27. I have just returned from another ravine, five miles distant, where there are eighty or a hundred gold-diggers. They are mostly Sonoranians, and, like all their countrymen, passionately devoted to gambling. They were playing at monté; the keeper of the bank was a woman, and herself a Sonoranian. There was no coin on the table; the bank consisted of a pile of gold, weighing, perhaps, a hundred pounds; and each of the players laid down his ounce or pound, as his means or courage permitted. The woman, on the whole, appeared to be the winner, though one man, in the course of half an hour, took ten pounds from her yellow pile. But such a loss was felt only for the moment, and only had the effect to stimulate others to lose what little they had left. A Sonoranian digs out gold simply and solely that he may have the wherewithal for gambling. This is the rallying thought which wakes with him in the morning, which accompanies him through the day, and which floats through his dreams at night. For this he labors, and cheerfully denies himself every comfort. All this is the result of habit. A Mussulman looks upon gambling as a species of larceny,—as a crime which deserves the bastinado. I saw a Turkish cadi at Smyrna sentence a man to thirty-nine lashes for having, as he termed it, *swindled* another out of fifty dollars at faro. Give me a Turk where there is a rogue to be caught or a crime punished. The flashings of the sword of justice follow the crime as light the shark in a phosphoric sea.

SATURDAY, OCT. 28. A portion of the party that went in quest of the little Dutchman have found him, and helped him to dig out his new deposit—a sort of assistance for which he can feel no very profound obligation. It was much like that rendered by Prince Hal in the division of the spoils secured by the knight of sack at Gad's hill. A successful gold-hunter is like the leader of hounds in the chase —the whole pack comes sweeping after, and are sure to be in at the death. No doubling hill, or covert, or stream throws them upon a false scent. I advise all fox-hunters to come here and train their hounds, and throw away their horns. Even his Grace of Wellington, who is still so hotly keen in the chase, that the snows of eighty winters fall from his locks unperceived, might catch some valuable hints in the gold mines of California.

Monday, Oct. 30. I encountered to-day, in a ravine some three miles distant, among the gold-washers, a woman from San José. She was at work with a large wooden bowl, by the side of a stream. I asked her how long she had been there, and how much gold she averaged a day. She replied, "Three weeks and an ounce." Her reply reminded me of an anecdote of the late Judge B——, who met a girl returning from market, and asked her, "How deep did you find the stream? what did you get for your butter?" "Up to the knee and nine-pence," was the reply. Ah! said the judge to himself; she is the girl for me—no words lost there: turned back, proposed, was accepted, and married the next week; and a more happy couple the conjugal bonds never united: the nuptial lamp never waned; its ray was steady and clear to the last. Ye, who paddle off and on for seven years, and are at last perhaps capsized, take a lesson of the judge. That "up to the knee and nine-pence" is worth all the rose letters and melancholy rhymes ever penned. But I am wandering; I did intend to write this journal without an episode, but they will keep forcing themselves in, like the curiosity of the crowd in a family jar, or remembrances of wrong upon a guilty conscience. I know the interest of a journal depends much on the continuity of its thread; but it is the easiest thing in the world to be continuously stupid, and *that* is my apology for these episodical breaks. If the reader don't like this reason, then let him look up a better; while I plunge into that o'ershadowed glen, and see if it contains any gold.

TUESDAY, OCT. 31. I have collected, since my arrival in the mines, several singular and beautiful specimens of the gold. One of the pieces resembles a pendulous ear-drop, and must have assumed that shape when the metal was in a state of fusion. That all the gold here has once been in that state is sufficiently evident from the forms in which it is found. I have a specimen, weighing several ounces, in which the characteristics of the slate rock are as palpable as if they had been engraved. I have another specimen, in which a clear crystal of quartz is set, with a finish of execution which no jeweller can rival. I have another specimen still, where the gold gleams up, in the shape of buck-shot, from a basis of sand-stone; and another still, where it has taken the form of a paper-folder, and may be used to cut the leaves of a book, which have escaped the knife of the binder. A most interesting cabinet of curiosities might be gathered from the variety of combinations and forms which the gold in these mines has assumed. Nature never indulged in fancies more elegant and whimsical. If these are the works of the volcano, then jewellers, instead of looking to the laboratories of Paris, or Amsterdam, for models, should come and seat themselves by the side of these craters. Here are laboratories, which no human power has constructed, and models, which no human skill can rival.

WEDNESDAY, Nov. 1. There are several persons among the gold-diggers here who rarely use any implement but their wooden bowls. Into these they scrape the dirt left by others, which they stir and whirl till the gold gradually works its way to the bottom. The earth, as these heavier particles descend, is thrown off by the hands, and the gold remains. This process is what they call dry washing: it is resorted to where there is no water in the vicinity, and will answer pretty well where the gold is found in coarse grains; but the finer particles, of course, escape. The Sonoranians obviate this difficulty to some extent by calling their lungs into requisition. They rub the earth into their bowls, through their hands, detaching and throwing away all the pebbles, and then blow off the sand and dust, leaving the gold at the bottom. But on some of the streams, particularly the Yuba, the gold is too fine even for this process. It is amusing to see a group of Sonoranians, seated around a deposit, blowing the earth out of their bowls. But for the dust they raise, you would think they were cooling hasty-pudding. Their cheeks swell out, like the chops of a squirrel, carrying half the beech-nuts on a tree to his hole. A more provident fellow he than his two-legged superior! He lays in his stores against the inclemency of winter; while the Sonoranian squanders his at the gambling-table. There is more practical wisdom in an ant-hill than is often found in a city. But I am digressing again—a propensity which I shall never get over.

THURSDAY, Nov. 2. Quite a sensation was produced among the gold-diggers this morning by the arrival of a wagon from Stockton, freighted with provisions and a barrel of liquor. The former had been getting scarce, and the latter had long since entirely given out. The prices of the first importation were—flour, two dollars a pound; sugar and coffee, four dollars; and the liquor, which was nothing more nor less than New England rum, was twenty dollars the quart. But few had bottles: every species of retainer was resorted to; some took their quart cups, some their coffee-pots, and others their sauce-pans; while one fellow, who had neither, offered ten dollars to let him suck with a straw from the bung. All were soon in every variety of excitement, from prattling exhilaration, to roaring inebriety. Some shouted, some danced, and some wrestled: a son of Erin poured out his soul on the beauties of the Emerald isle; a German sung the songs of his father-land; a Yankee apostrophized the mines, which swelled in the hills around; an Englishman challenged all the bears in the mountain glens to mortal combat; and a Spaniard, posted aloft on a beetling crag, addressed the universe. The multitudinous voices which rang from every chasm and cove of the ravine, rivalled the roar that went up around the tower of Babel. But night has come; the camp-fires burn dim; and the revellers are at rest, save here and there one who strides about in his delirium, commanding silence among the wolves who bark from the hills. What exciting, elevating, and expanding powers there are in a barrel of New England rum! It makes one to-day monarch of peopled realms, and their riches; but leaves him to-morrow in rags, and with only ground enough in which to sink his pauper grave.

"Thou sparkling bowl! thou sparkling bowl!
  Though lips of bards thy brim may press,
And eyes of beauty o'er thee roll,
  And song and dance thy power confess—
I will not touch thee; for there clings
A scorpion to thy side that stings."

PIERPONT.

CHAPTER XXIII.

NATURAL AMPHITHEATRE.—NO SCIENTIFIC CLUE TO THE DEPOSITS OF GOLD.—SOIL OF THE MINES.—LIFE AMONG THE GOLD-DIGGERS.—LOSS OF OUR CABALLADA.—THE OLD MAN AND ROCK.—DEPARTURE FROM THE MINES.—TRAVELLING AMONG GORGES AND PINNACLES.—INSTINCTS OF THE MULE.—A MOUNTAIN CABIN.

FRIDAY, Nov. 3. At the head of the ravine, where our camping-trees wave, stands an amphitheatre reared by nature, and unrivalled in the grandeur of its proportions, and the stateliness and strength of its architecture. It unrolls its wild magnificence on the eye with a more majestic power than even Rome's great wonder. From its ample arena, circling ranges of crags soar one over the other to the lofty sweep of the architrave, where sentinel-trees toss their branches against the sky. Had nature reared this theatre on the banks of the Tiber, the beauty and bravery of Rome would have flashed over the arena's gladiatorial tumult. But it was here in California, where even the Roman eagle, in its earth-embracing circuit, flew not.

A new deposit was discovered this morning near the falls of the Stanislaus, and in the crevices of the rocks over which the river pours its foaming sheet. An Irishman had gone there to bathe, and in throwing off his clothes, had dropped his jack-knife, which slipped into a crevice, where he first discovered the gold. He was soon tracked, and in less than an hour a storm of picks and crowbars were shivering the rocks. The accessible pockets were readily exhausted, but beyond these only the drill and blast of the practical miner can extend. And this is true of all the rock-gold in California; the present harvest glows near the surface; but there are under-crops, which the sunlight has never visited. Deep mining here, as elsewhere, will be attended with uncertain results; but a fount so capacious on its rim, must have its replenishing depths. The largest fish are taken with the longest line.

SATURDAY, Nov. 4. The deposits here baffle all the pretensions of science. The volcanoes did their work by no uniform geological law; they burst out at random, and scattered their gold in wanton caprice. Were not those old Vulcans dead, they would laugh at the blundering vanity exhibited around them. The old landmarks are the quartz; these are general indications, but too vague when applied to alluvial deposits, and frequently serve only to bewilder and betray. We have a young geologist here who can unroll the whole earth, layer by layer, from surface to centre, and tell the properties of each, and how it came to be deposited there, who unsuspectingly walked over a bank of gold, which a poor Indian afterwards stirred out with a stick. I have seen this *savan* camp down and snore soundly through the night, with a half-pound piece of gold within a few inches of his nose; and then rise at peep of day to push his learned theory into some ledge of rocks, where not a particle of the yellow ore ever existed. I have seen a digger take from a bank of decomposed granite, in a space not larger than a man's hat, between three and four pounds of gold, while his only clue to it was a blast on the opposite side of the glen, through which he believed the deil had blown the gold into the bank, where he was at work. What a burlesque on all geological laws as applied to gold deposits! There is only one of these laws, in reference to alluvial deposits, worth a pin, and that is the simple fact that a heavy body will tumble down hill faster than a lighter one, or that a nut shaken from a tree will drop through the fog to the ground.

SUNDAY, Nov. 5. I rose this morning with the intention of proposing to the diggers a religious service. But mid-day came, and only here and there one broke from slumbers doubly deep from the overpowering fatigues of the week In a shaded recess of the hills three of us found a little sanctuary: neither of the two with me was a professor of religion, but each retained in vivid remembrance the religious instructions of his childhood and youth. Time and distance had not effaced these impressions; each lettered trace remained as legible as the footprints of the primeval bird in the fossil rock. Such is the inscription of parental fidelity on the heart of a child: the wave may wear away the mound which it laves, and the marble dissolve under the touch of time, but *that* inscription remains.

MONDAY, Nov. 6. Vein-gold in these rocks is as uncertain and capricious as lightning; it straggles where you least expect it, and leaves only a stain where its quick volume seemed directed. It threads its way in a rock without crevice or crack, and where its continuity becomes at times too subtle for the naked eye, and then suddenly bulges out like a lank snake that has swallowed a terrapin. The great Hebrew proverbialist says there are three things about which there is no certainty,—the way of an eagle in the air, the way of a serpent upon a rock, the way of a ship in the midst of the sea; and he might have added— the way of a thread of gold in a vein of California quartz; but probably California, with its treasures, had not then been discovered, though some of our wiseacres are trying to make out that this *el dorado* was the Ophir of the Old Testament: if so, the men of Joppa must have been pretty good seamen, especially as they had no compass. It may be, but I somewhat doubt it, that the Hottentots or Patagonians are the descendants of some shipwrecked men bound in a wherry from Tarsus to California. The adventurers, even in that case, would have been quite as sober in their calculations as some who put to sea on a gold-hunt in these days.

Degrees of fortune in the California Gold diggings

Tuesday, Nov. 7. The price of provisions here is no criterion of their market value on the seaboard, or even at the embarcadaros nearest the mines. The cost of a hundred pounds of flour at Stockton, only sixty miles distant, is twenty dollars; but here it is two hundred dollars. This vast disparity is owing to the difficulty of transportation and the absence of competition. But few can be persuaded to leave the expectations of the pick for the certainties of the pack—the promises of the cradle for the fulfilments of the freighted wagon. All live on drafts upon the future, and though disappointed a hundred times, still believe the results of to-morrow will more than redeem the broken pledges of to-day. Though all else may end in failure, hope is not bankrupt here.

The soil in the mines is evidently volcanic; it resembles in places the ashes which cover Pompeii. You can walk through it when dry, though every footstep stirs a little cloud; but when saturated with the winter rain you slump to the middle. No horse can force his way forward; every struggle but sinks him the deeper, and the miner himself retires to his cabin, as thoroughly cut off from the peopled districts of the coast, as a sailor wrecked on some rock at sea. Years must elapse before human enterprise can bridge a path to these mines, or render communication practicable in the rainy season; nor at any period can heavy machinery be transported here without an immense outlay of capital. The quartz rock has yet some time to roll back the sunlight before it crumbles under the steam-stamper.

WEDNESDAY, Nov. 8. Some fifty thousand persons are drifting up and down these slopes of the great Sierra, of every hue, language, and clime, tumultuous and confused as a flock of wild geese taking wing at the crack of a gun, or autumnal leaves strown on the atmospheric tides by the breath of the whirlwind. All are in quest of gold; and, with eyes dilated to the circle of the moon, rush this way and that, as some new discovery, or fictitious tale of success may suggest. Some are with tents, and some without; some have provisions, and some are on their last ration; some are carrying crowbars; some pickaxes and spades; some wash-bowls and cradles; some hammers and drills, and powder enough to blow up the rock of Gibraltar—if they can but get under it, as the monkeys do, when they make their transit, through a sort of Thames tunnel, from the golden but barren sands of Africa to the green hills of Europe. Wise fellows they, notwithstanding the length of their tails —they won't stay on the Congo side of the strait, to gather gold, when, by crossing, they can gather grapes. Wisdom is justified of her children.

But I was speaking of the gold-hunters here on the slopes of the Sierra. Such a mixed and motley crowd—such a restless, roving, rummaging, ragged multitude, never before roared in the rookeries of man. As for mutual aid and sympathy—Samson's foxes had as much of it, turned tail to, with firebrands tied between. Each great camping-ground is denoted by the ruins of shovels and shanties, the bleaching bones of the dead, disinhumed by the wolf, and the skeleton of the culprit, still swinging in the wind, from the limb of a tree, overshadowed by the raven. From the deep glen, the caverned cliff, the plaintive rivulet, the croaking raven, and the wind-toned skeleton come voices of reproachful interrogation—

> "Slave of the dark and dirty mine!
> What vanity has brought thee here?"

THURSDAY, Nov. 9. Our baccaro came in this morning, and startled us with the intelligence that last night, while he was on the watch—sound asleep, of course—the wild Indians came, and stole all our horses and mules, save one, little Nina, whom he had tethered close to his post. Rather an awkward predicament for us, in the California mountains, three hundred miles from home, and our horses and mules in the hands of wild Indians, driving them off into some unknown fastness, to be killed for food! But I was on the trail of a small piece of gold, and followed it up with that sort of listless equanimity with which a man will sometimes pick up a curious shell on the rocks where his vessel floats in fragments. If you would acquire those habits which no disaster can disturb, come to California. One year here will do more for your philosophy than a life elsewhere. I have seen a man sit, and quietly smoke his cigar, while his dwelling went heavenward in a column of flame. It seemed as if it were enough for him that his wife and children were safe, and that the green earth, with its bright-eyed flowers and laughing rills, remained; so let the old tenement pass off in smoke to pall some mountain peak, or throw its dusky shadow where—

"The owlet builds his ivy tower."

FRIDAY, Nov. 10. The Sonoranian, who has been one of the most successful diggers in the ravine, besieged me to-day to sell him my pistols. They are an elegant pair, silver mounted and rifle bore, and good for duck or duelist — no matter which — for twenty or thirty paces. He offered me a pound of gold; so I determined to try the non-resistant principle, and let him have them. As he belted them about his waist, and strode off, you would have advised even a California bear to get out of his way. How well prepared for a last extremity is a man with a new weapon at his side, or a new patent pill in his pocket! The only difference is, that with the former he may chance to kill some one else, and with the latter he is pretty sure to kill himself. But I promised to make no more remarks; my apology must be the loss of our horses, the probable necessity of being obliged to pick our way home on foot, and the refuge which even an irrelevant thought affords from such a dismal prospect. Men have betrayed flashes of humor on the block—an evanescent ray on the verge of endless night! Then why should not my poor pill have place in the pedestrian prospect of three hundred miles, and that, too, through a region marked only by the footprints which linger dimly in the trail of the wild Indian?

SATURDAY, Nov. 11. I encountered an old man to-day, sitting listlessly on a rock under the broken shade of a decayed oak. A few gray hairs strayed from under his camping-cap, and his face was deeply wrinkled; but his eye flashed, at intervals, with the fires of an unquenched spirit. He had not, as he told me, obtained an ounce of gold in this ravine, and was about trying some other locality. I advised him to roll over the rock on which he was sitting; he said he would do it to please me; but as for gold, he might as well look for a weasel in a watchman's rattle. The rock was easily rolled from its inclined position; beneath it was found a layer of moss, and beneath this, in the crevices of another rock, a deposit of gold, in the shape of pumpkin-seeds, bright as if fresh from the mint, and weighing over half a pound. The eyes of the old man sparkled: but he was thinking of his home and those left behind

SUNDAY, Nov. 12. Could the parents of the youth in these glens cast a glance at their children, what a tide of affection and concern would rush through their hearts! No treasured ship at sea was ever environed by deeper perils; storms lower in thick darkness above, and breakers thunder below, and no pharos throws its friendly ray from the shrouded cliff. The only light they have to guide them is in their own tempest-tost bark, and the lamp in the binnacle is dim. The merchant who should send his ship to sea without compass or rudder, would not be more frantic and foolish than the parent who sends his son out upon the world without any religion in his soul. These youths in these glens are to shape the destinies of California; under their hands her political, social, and moral institutions are to be reared. Unless religion lie at the foundations, these structures, though columned with gold, will fall. It was frailty and rottenness at the base that has left all the proud fabrics of the Old World a storied mass of ruins.

Monday, Nov. 13. A mounted company of gold-diggers arrived on our camping premises last evening, and we struck in for four horses, which we purchased at their own prices. Mine is an Indian pony from Oregon, full of heart and hardihood; but as for ease of motion, you might as well ride a trip-hammer. But an extremity makes the most indifferent gift of nature a blessed boon.

We reduced our effects to the fewest articles possible, and packing these, with provisions for three or four days, upon little Nina, were ready for a start. Two Oregonian trappers joined us, and before the sun's rays struck the depths of the ravine, we were off, with three hearty cheers from the diggers. An hour brought us to the summit of an elevation, beneath which lay, in panoramic life, the ravines, rivulets, rambling paths, and roving groups of the gold-hunters. I have walked on the roaring verge of Niagara, through the grumbling parks of London, on the laughing boulevards of Paris, among the majestic ruins of Rome, in the torch-lit galleries of Herculaneum, around the flaming crater of Vesuvius, through the wave-reflected palaces of Venice, among the monumental remains of Athens, and beneath the barbaric splendors of Constantinople: but none of these, nor all combined, have left in my memory a page graven with more significant and indellible characters than the gold *diggins* of California.

Our route lay for several miles through a succession of narrow ravines, above which soared the stupendous steeps of a mountain range, through which some convulsion of nature had sunk these shadowy chasms. Here and there some giant bluff had plunged into the winding abyss, as if to shut out the profane intruder from its silent sanctuaries. These granite gates became at last so frequent, that we determined to try the ridge, the table-rock, or less precipitous slope. We wound up the steep sides of the pass one by one, as a weary bird at sea scales the tempest-cloud; and at last emerged upon a lofty range of trap, feathered by the fir and low pine, and where the eagle had made himself a home. A wide sea of chasms and cones lay around us. These were evidently the bleak monuments of volcanoes, which ages since had rested from their labors. The sun threw its level rays along their summits, while the abysses lay in perpetual shadow. No path threw its trail on the eye. Rounding a pinnacle, which stood as a fortress at the abrupt termination of one of the ranges, we discovered a slope which slanted off less steeply than the rest. Here, dismounting, we let ourselves down for several hundred yards by the bushes; Nina, sure of foot as a fox, followed first; my Indian pony next; and then the rest, as the docility or courage of each induced. All our horses had been trained by mountaineers, and well knew, if left behind, what must be their fate. What a strange affection for such an animal springs up at such an hour as this! As he comes down to join you, selecting you out as his rider, snuffing about you, and inviting you to mount again, you involuntarily throw your arms about his neck, and try to make him understand the kindness you feel for him.

We discovered in the last flashes of twilight a gush of waters from the rocks, which beetled over a cañada, where the grass was fresh from the showering spray. We had struck this spot through no sagacity of our own; Nina, snuffing the water long before it flashed upon us, had turned into the ravine, and dashed ahead upon the gallop. Here we camped for the night. The dried willows supplied us with fuel, the cascade with water, and our panniers with a piece of pork, and a few pounds of flour, which the kneading-tray and embers soon converted into bread. The stones were made to grind our coffee, and we were soon seated to a supper from which the epicure might perhaps turn away, but which these rough mountains made a luxury. And then the repose, though on the earth with your saddle for a pillow, yet how refreshing and profound! Nor bark of wolf, nor murmur of cascade, nor rustle of the bear disturbed my dreams that night.

TUESDAY, Nov. 14. We were up, had taken our coffee, and were ready for a start, while as yet only the whispering trees on the higher cliffs had been greeted by the sun. Our course, which was determined by a pocket-compass, now lay among mountain spurs, till we reached the rollers, which ridge the plain of the San Joaquin. In a copse of birch, which shadows one of these, we discovered a spring, where we lunched and rested for an hour, while our animals refreshed themselves on the grass, still green on the marge of the fount. We were now off for a hard ride of several hours. My little Indian hammered into it with a resolution that paid but little heed to the discomfort of his rider. Our object was to reach before nightfall the cabin of an old friend, who had nested himself out here among these wild mountain crags. We dashed around this steep, and over that, like hunters in the chase; while Nina, without rein or rider, led the way. We had no trail to guide us,—only the instinct of our animals, and that sagacity which a mountain life converts into a sort of prophetic knowledge. The day was dying fast, and no gleam of the cabin cheered the eye. The night would render all search hopeless. At last we struck the stream on which we knew the cabin stood, but whether up or down its current, we could not decide; but Nina, after pausing a moment, led quick and resolutely up the stream, and we struck in after. The step of a weasel may turn the balanced rock.

Three miles of fast riding brought us to a grove of oak, now wrapped in the purple twilight. Along this we streamed till reaching a bold bend, which circled up into its shadows, when the fagot flame of the cottage struck the eye. Our horses bounded forward on the gallop, knowing as well as we that the weary day was now over. Here we found my friend, Dr. Isabell and his good lady, who gave us a hearty welcome. True, their cabin had but one room in it; but what of that?—hearts make a home in the wilderness. Our first care was for our animals, which were soon watered and turned into a rich meadow, with a faithful Indian to watch them through the night. Our busy hostess soon announced supper—beefsteak, omelet, hot rolls, and coffee, with sugar and cream! If you want to know how that supper relished, come and live a month in the mines of California. We run over our adventures since leaving Monterey, and they chimed in well with those of our host in his wild-wood home. Kindred and friends far away came sweeping down on the stream of memory, and gathered life-like and warm at our sides. We lived over again all our school-days, our rustic sports, our husking-bees, our youthful loves, and those stolen kisses, which the sterner rules of refinement have interdicted only to give place to Polkas, in which modesty is too much bewildered to blush. Our hospitable friends welcomed us to all the sleeping comforts which their cabin afforded; but we camped under the trees, and were soon afloat in the realm of dreams, amid its visioned forms.

> "Alas! that dreams are only dreams!
> That fancy cannot give
> A lasting beauty to those forms,
> Which scarce a moment live."

CHAPTER XXIV.

A LADY IN THE MOUNTAINS.—TOWN OF STOCKTON.—CROSSING THE VALLEY OF THE SAN JOAQUIN.—THE ROBBED FATHER AND BOY.—RIDE TO SAN JOSÉ.—RUM IN CALIFORNIA.—HIGHWAYMEN.—WOODLAND LIFE.—RACHEL AT THE WELL.—FAREWELL TO MY CAMPING-TREE.

WEDNESDAY, Nov. 15. Another day had dawned fresh and brilliant; we breakfasted with our friends, who ordered up their horses, and started with us for Stockton, twelve miles distant. Our lady hostess and myself led off; she had crossed the Rocky Mountains on horseback into California, and was, of course, at home in the saddle. She was mounted on a spirited animal, and my little Indian almost blew the wind out of him to keep up. My companion, though accomplished in all the refinements of metropolitan life, was yet in love with the wild scenes in which her lot had been cast. The rose of health blushed in her cheek, and the light of a salient soul revelled in her eye. "I would not exchange," she said, "my cabin for any palace in Christendom. I have all that I want here, and what more could I have elsewhere? I have tried luxury without health, and a wild mountain life with it. Give me the latter, with the free air, the dashing streams, the swinging woods, the laughing flowers, and the exulting birds; and

> "Let him who crawls enamored of decay,
> Cling to his couch, and sicken years away.'"

We were now at Stockton, the nucleus of a town at the head waters of a narrow arm of the San Joaquin. The site is well chosen; its central position to the gold mines, the broad fertile plain which spreads around it, and the water communication which connects it with the commerce of the Sacramento and San Francisco, will lift it into a town of the first importance. Charles Weber, a gentleman much esteemed for his liberality and enterprise, is the owner of the land now occupied by the town, and many leagues adjacent. He has given spacious lots to all who would erect buildings. His policy is marked with wisdom; he will find his advantage in the results. His ample store is well filled with provisions, groceries, and ready-made clothing. The amount of business is immense, and the profits would phrensy our Philadelphia merchants.

We found Stockton without a hotel, the private houses unfinished; and, caring but little for either, camped under the trees. We took supper with Mr. Weber, and, at a late hour, wound ourselves in our blankets for repose. The dew fell heavy, but we slept through it without the least harm. A hydropathist might have exchanged his sheet for a twist in one of our wet blankets. But we had no rheumatic joints to be relaxed, and no bone-burrowed mercury to be douched. What an envied lot, that of the pearl-diver! He gets not only his bath, but a pearl besides. And what a happy fellow is a fish! He is always head and tail in the hydropathic process. I wonder if it is not this that gives the shark such an appetite, and lends wings to the flying-fish. Even the bullfrog comes up only to twang his joy, and the whale to blow off his excess of pleasure, while the mermaid, lost in transport, sings in her coral hall till the listening naiads feel

"Their souls dissolve in her melodious breath."

THURSDAY, Nov. 16. Replenishing our panniers with hard bread, and a few pounds of dried venison and coffee, we bade adieu to our Oregonian friends and the hospitable proprietor of Stockton, and were off for our distant home. Our trail for sixteen miles lay through an arid plain, when we brought up on the bold bank of the San Joaquin. Our saddles, bridles, packs, and persons were thrown into a boat, our horses driven into the stream, and over we dashed to the opposite bank, where we paid two dollars each for our ferriage, and mounted for a fresh start. It was near sunset when we reached the line of trees which belt, with their thick umbrage, the great valley which stretches in barrenness beyond. Here we camped for the night, and soon found, to our pleasurable surprise, our friends Lieut. Bonnycastle and Lieut. Morehead, of the army, in a camp not more than an arrow's flight distant. They were on their way to the mines, and if excellent qualities of head and heart can secure success, must return with fortunes. Night deepened apace, and our simple repast finished, we wrapped ourselves in our blankets, and were soon in sound sleep.

FRIDAY, Nov. 17. The day glimmered over the hill-tops: a cup of coffee, a cake of hard bread, and a scrap of dried venison, and we were under way again. Our trail lay for fifteen miles over the prairie of the San Joaquin. Though now in November, yet the heat was oppressive. We encountered groups of disbanded volunteers, on their way to the mines. The soldiers' improvidence had left but very few the means of procuring horses, and they were generally on foot, and crippled with blisters. Going *to* the mines is one thing; returning *from* them is another A dream of victory animates the soldier, and visions of gold stimulate the digger. It is only the result under which the heart droops and the muscles give way.

It was mid-day when we struck the hills which roll their low forests to the verge of the prairie. In a glen, where sparkled a spring and the pine threw its shadows, we encountered an elderly man and his little boy. The parent was silent, downcast, and abstracted, and his boy was evidently trying to cheer him. The father, in reply to our inquiries, informed us that they had been in the mines, where, by great industry and good fortune, they had got out twenty pounds of gold; that on their return they had camped for the night near Stockton; that leaving their camping-tree for a few hours to renew their stock of provisions, they had buried their bag of gold under the tree; but on their return their gold could not be found! that the most diligent search had led to no results; that he had been robbed! that the loss was less for him, but that he had eight motherless children, dependent on him for a support. Who could listen to such a tale as this and not feel his blood tingle at the callous wretch who could thus ruin another? Even the forgiving Uncle Toby would deliver him over to the avenging angel, to be driven down under double-bolted thunder: nothing could rescue him, unless the Universalists catch him in their creed, which saves a man in spite of the Evil One, and in spite of himself, too.

We invited the father and son to join our company; and when on the way, the little boy, who was mounted on a pony at my side, told me a subscription had been started at Stockton for his father, and that Mr. Weber and Dr. Isabell had subscribed a pound of gold each. Blessings on those liberal men! such a charity will throw a circle of light around misfortune, should it ever be *their* lot. The sun was far down his western dip when we reached the hospitable hearth of our friend Mr. Livermore; but finding that he had no grain for our horses, and that the grass around had utterly perished under the summer's drought, we determined to push on; and, crossing a plain of eight miles, reached the mountain rollers, where we struck into a ravine, through which a streamlet murmured, and where a plot of grass still preserved some portion of its freshness. Here we tethered and camped. The brief twilight that remained had passed into night's bosom before we had gathered sufficient wood for our camp-fire: and we needed a large pile; for the air was chill and penetrating. We made our supper on hard bread, dried venison, and coffee; while clouds, the sure precursors of the winter rains, drifted above in sluggish masses. Our camp-fire threw its column of waving flame on the beetling crags; not a sound from cavern or cliff disturbed the silence; we gazed into the fire, lost in pensive musing; and a more melancholy group seldom gathers over that face—

"Where life's last parting pulse has ceased to play,"

when an owl perched near, gave a deep hoot! Each broke into an involuntary laugh. The philosophy of that transition I leave to those whose metaphysical acumen can split the shadow which falls between melancholy and mirth.

SATURDAY, Nov. 18. Another morn full of rosy charms comes blushing over the hills; at the glance of her eye the shadows flee away, and the birds awaken into song. The stir of preparation rustles the leaves under our camping-tree, and while the dew yet gems the grass, we are up and away. What salient freshness and force are in the heart which takes its pulses from the waving wild-wood and the dashing stream! The exhilaration in its fullest tide never ebbs; it bears you on with sympathies and enjoyments still expanding, till all nature, with her intense life and rapture, is yours.

Our path, which lay through a mountain gorge, bent its line to a winding rivulet, laughing and singing through the solitude. Little cared *that* for marble fount or sculptured dolphin; it was happy in its own free life, and the kisses of the enamored pebbles, which danced in its limpid wave. And now the white walls of the old church, where the mission of San José reared its altars, glimmered into vision. Fast and far the separating interval was left behind, when we dashed up to its welcome portal. Here we found an Irish restaurant, and set its culinary functions in motion—

> "Nothing's more sure at moments to take hold
>   Of the best feelings of mankind, which grow
> More tender, as we every day behold,
>   Than that all-softening, overpowering knell,
>   The tocsin of the soul—the dinner-bell!"

SUNDAY, NOV. 19. My companions pushed on last evening to San José—fifteen miles distant. My old Russian friend, who occupies one of the mission buildings, invited me to spend the Sabbath with him; an invitation which I gladly accepted, as it afforded a refuge from the restaurant, with the roar of its revelry and rum. The United States have sent out enough of this fire here to burn up a continent. The conflagration, kindled by the battle-brand or bolt of the electric cloud, may sweep a forest, or lay a city in ashes; but from the smouldering ruins new structures will rise, and a new generation of plants spring; but where the spirit of rum hath spread its flame a desolation follows, which the skill of man and the reviving dews of heaven can never reach. It is barren and verdureless as the sulphurous marl which paves

"The deep track of hell."

MONDAY, NOV. 20. For a moment this morning I regretted having parted with my pistols, and thrown myself on the non-resistant principle. I was alone, and on my way to San José, when two horsemen suddenly broke from the covert of the woods on my left, and swept down upon the line of my path. They were well mounted, and had the dare-devil air of the brigand. It was near this spot, too, that a young friend of mine had been recently murdered. To attempt flight on my Indian pony from the lightning hoof of my pursuers, would have given to consternation itself a hue of the ludicrous. I determined to die decently, if die I must. My supposed assailants dashed close to my side, and then, without uttering a word, spurred back to the forest, from which they had debouched. They were foreigners, disguised as Californians; for a native always salutes you, and would, were his hand on the trigger of his pistol. They went as they came, and the secret of their impetuous visit is in their own keeping. I was quite willing to part with their company, and ascribe their intrusion to a violent curiosity, or any other motive untouched by crime, so that they would let me pass in peace to the Pueblo of San José.

TUESDAY, Nov. 21. Arriving at the Pueblo, I found my companions had hired four horses, accustomed to the harness, attached them to the wagon, which we had left here, on our way to the mines, and were ready to start for Monterey. I threw my saddle, bridle, and blanket into the wagon, and parted with my Indian pony : he had done me good service, and got me out of a bad fix in the mines; he had pounded me some, it is true ; but that was no fault of his ; nature never intended him to tread on flowers without bending their stems. May his new owner treat him kindly; and when age has withered his strength, not turn him out on a public common to die ! Had we as little mercy shown us as we extend to the noblest animal committed to our care, we should never get to heaven.

The sun was far down his western slope when we reached the rancho of Mr. Murphy, and camped for the night under the evergreen oaks, which throw the soft shade of their undying verdure over a streamlet that murmurs near his door. The old gentleman invited us in to share his restricted apartments, but we had so long slept under trees, that we preferred the free air, the maternal earth, and the stars to light us to our slumber. Truly I never slept so soundly on the

"Come, old fellow, you had better knock off, and go home with me."—"No, I'll be ding'd if I do. I'm in for the gold, and will find it, or dig out the other side. I'm told it is only eight thousand miles through! so, here goes!"

garnished couch, and never found in sleep such a renovating refreshment. I can now comprehend why it is the hunter clings to his wild life, and prefers the precarious subsistence of his rifle to teeming stalls. He lives out of himself; his sympathies are with nature; his sensations roll through boundless space. It is for *his* eye the violet blooms, and the early cloud catches the blush of morn; it is for *his* ear the bird sings from its green covert, and the torrent shouts from its cliff; it is to cheer *his* footsteps that the twilight lingers, and the star blazes in the coronet of night: all the changes of the varied year are for *him;* and around his wild-wood home the seasons lead the hours in perpetual dance; and when his being shall resign its trust, the dirge of the deep wood will sing his requiem, and the wings of the wind, filled with the fragrance of flowers, bear his spirit to its bright abode.

WEDNESDAY, Nov. 22. We broke camp at sunrise, took our coffee, harnessed up, and began to lumber ahead. Our driver, who owned the dull steeds which he reined, was a native of New England, and betrayed his origin in the perpetual hum of a low plaintive tune, which spun on for hours in the same unconscious monotony. Even the crack of his whip, which came in frequently, had only the effect to give some note a slight emphasis, while the low dirge still murmured on, true to its unbroken flow as the tick of the death-watch to its admonitory errand. Thus the hours of the day, their tender requiem being sung, stole silently into the past.

But now occurred a wayfaring incident which could not thus be charmed to rest. Our team, about half way up the long hill of San Juan, balked, and the wagon began to roll back to its base. We jumped out and clogged the wheels, for we had no idea of returning again to the mines. Having breathed a moment, we made another attempt, but without success; we now put our shoulders to the wheels, while the lash fell fast on the flanks of our horses. But no pushing, coaxing, or whipping availed; our journey for the day was done, and abruptly too as that of a migratory goose struck by a rifle ball. The shadows of the mountain pines were lengthening fast, and we retired into a glen at a short distance, and camped. It was my duty to procure water for coffee; the spring where the horses drank was too full of impurities; I followed up the unseen vein marked by the green willows, till its flowing wave murmured on the ear from the depths of a shadowy chasm. But the method of reaching it puzzled me as much as the faithful proxy of the Patriarch would have been, but for the pitcher and line of the gentle Rachel. How free of affectation and false alarm that daughter of Israel, as her snow-white arms drew the limpid tide to quench the stranger's thirst! How free of a distrustful spirit, or disdaining pride, when told that one whom her father loved, sued for her bridal hand! The wave which swelled in her milk-white bosom may have trembled a moment, like the leaf stirred in the rosy twilight, and the dream of her pillowed slumber may have flushed through the snow-curl of her cheek, but with the early lark, she was up and away—happy in her own youth and innocence, and in the thought that these were inwoven with the happiness of another. How hollow the pretexts of protracted delay, when touched by the light which glimmers down through ages from the example of this primitive maiden! But where am I?—in the infant world instead of these chasmed rocks, which frown through the wrinkles of its decrepitude and age. How thought annihilates time and space! The flower that first bloomed on the verge of the globe, as it emerged from chaos, and the cinder that will fade last in the embers of its final conflagration, lie side by side in the domain of thought; and the star that hailed its birth, and the planet that will guard its tomb, are twin-born in the eternity of time. But I am off again in a philosophic revery, and must come back to my coffee-pot and chasm! With the aid of a long riata, my bucket was lowered sufficiently to dip the unseen stream; but drawing it up I discovered in its wave, as the surface became tranquil, what might well startle any one whose nerves were not of steel. It was a human face of bronze hue, half covered with tangled locks, and a beard of hermit growth, and so like that bent above, there was a relief in the ripple that destroyed the resemblance. But my camping companions will never, at this rate, get their coffee.

THURSDAY, Nov. 23. We escaped this morning another balk of our animals by a circling road which in the dusk of the last eve we had missed. It was mid-day when we rumbled from the hills of San Juan upon the plain of the Salinas, and near sunset when we reached the river, which rolls its yellow wave fifteen miles from Monterey. We might have pushed through, but why be impatient over a night's delay? I had no one there watching a husband's return, or waiting a father's kiss. These objects of endearment were in other lands, and oceans rolled between. More than three long years had worn away since I waved my adieu, and weary moons must set before my return. I may find the eyes that beamed so kindly, closed forever; the bud of infant being, on which their last light fell, withered.

We were roused in the night by screams from the river; an ox-cart, with three women in it, had tumbled down the opposite bank. The cattle seemed as much frightened as their passengers, and fared better, as they had struck a shallower bottom. We plunged in and reached the cart. Our first impulse was to take the women out and *tote* them ashore, but their great size and weight forbade. We wished to carry the thing through as gallantly as it had been begun; but after casting about—the cold stream all the while lowering the thermometer of our enthusiasm—we concluded to drive the team out, and scramble out ourselves.

Friday, Nov. 24. We broke camp at an early hour, and were off for Monterey. I left my camping-tree as one parts with a tried friend. It was the last of a vernal band, that had thrown over me, at burning noon and through the chilly night, their protecting shade. While our driver hummed his low monotonous stave to his steeds, my neglected reed murmured in the counter—

TO MY CAMPING-TREE.

Farewell to thee, my camping-tree,
   The last to shade this breast,
Where twilight weaves, with tender leaves,
   Her couch of rosy rest.

Thy trembling leaf seemed shook with grief,
   As on it gleamed the dew;
As woke the bird, by night-winds stirred,
   The stars came dancing through.

In lucid dreams I caught the gleams—
   Through chasmed rocks unrolled—
Of gems, where blaze the diamond's rays,
   And massive bars of gold.

I saw a ship her anchor trip,
   All stowed with gold below,
Depart this bay for Joppa's quay,
   Three thousand years ago!

A star-lit dome, of amber foam,
   Loomed in the liquid blue,
Where reigned of old, on thrones of gold,
   The Incas of Peru.

The midnight moans, and phrensied groans,
    Of miners near their last,
In tones that cursed the gold they nursed,
    Came trembling on the blast.

While one apart, with gentler heart,
    His still tears dashed aside,
That he might trace a pictured face,
    At which he gazed, and died.

On steep and vale, in calm and gale,
    Like music on the sea—
Sweet slumber stole, within my soul,
    Beneath the camping-tree.

A low-voiced tone, the wind hath thrown
    Upon my dreaming ear,
Of ONE, whose smiles, and gentle wiles,
    Are still remembered here :—

Of one, whose tears—where each endears
    The more the heart that wept—
From swimming lid in silence slid,
    And on her bosom slept.

A blue-eyed child, with glee half wild,
    In infant beauty's beams,
And lock that rolled, in waving gold,
    Came glancing through my dreams.

Farewell to thee, my camping-tree;
    Till life's last visions gleam,
Thy leaves and limbs, and vesper hymns,
    Shall float in memory's dream.

CHAPTER XXV.

CAUSE OF SICKNESS IN THE MINES.—THE QUICKSILVER MINES.—HEAT AND COLD IN THE MINES.—TRAITS IN THE SPANISH CHARACTER.—HEALTH OF CALIFORNIA LADIES.—A WORD TO MOTHERS.—THE PINGRASS AND BLACKBIRD.—THE REDWOOD-TREE.—BATTLE OF THE EGGS.

SATURDAY, DEC. 2. I found Monterey, on my return from the mines, under the same quiet air in which her green hills had soared since I first beheld their waving shade. Many had predicted my precipitate return, from the hardships and baffled attempt of the tour; but I persevered, taking it rough and tumble from the first, and have returned with improved health. I met with but very few cases of sickness in the mines, and these obviously resulting from excessive imprudence. What but maladies could be expected, where the miner stands by the hour in a cold mountain stream, with a broiling sun overhead, and then, perhaps, drinking every day a pint of New England rum? Why, the rum itself would shatter any constitution not lightning-proof. I wish those who send this fire-curse here were wrapped in its flames till the wave of repentance should baptize them into a better life.

I have missed but two things, since my return, from my goods and chattels—my walking-cane and my Bible; both have been carried off during my absence.

I hope the latter will do the person who has taken it much good: I forgive the burglary for the sake of the benefit. Prometheus was chained to the Caucasian rock for having filched fire from heaven; but no such fearful retribution awaits him who has stolen my Bible, flooded though it be with a higher light than ever dawned on the eyes of the guilty Titan. May its spirit reach the offender's soul, and quicken thoughts that shall wander without rest till they light on the Cross, where hang the hopes of the world.

Tuesday, Dec. 12. The quicksilver mines of California constitute one of the most important elements in her mineral wealth. Only one vein has as yet been fully developed; this lies a few miles from San José, and is owned by Hon. Alexander Forbes, British consul at Typé, in Mexico—a gentleman of vast means and enterprise—and who has a heart as full of generous impulses as his mine is of wealth. Many of our countrymen, in misfortune, have shared his munificent liberality. His mine, in the absence of suitable machinery, has been worked to great disadvantage; and yet, with two whaling-kettles for furnaces, he has driven off a hundred and fifty pounds a day of the pure metal. If this can be done with an apparatus intended only for trying blubber, a ton may be rolled from a capacious retort constructed for the purpose. The title of Mr. Forbes to this mine has excited some inquiry, but it will be found among the soundest in California.

Instead of attempting to shake this title, a more wise and profitable course will be to open a fresh vein. They lie in the contiguous spurs of the same mountain range, and only require a small outlay of labor and capital to develop their untold wealth. The metal need not travel from California to find a market; vast quantities will be required in the gold mines: the cradle and bowl must give place to more complicated machinery; the sands of the river pass through a more delicate process; and the quartz of the steep rock, crumbled under the stamper, surrender its gold to the embrace of quicksilver. This stupendous issue is close at hand; and they who anticipate it, will find the fruits of their sagacity and enterprise in sudden fortunes.

Monday, Dec. 25. The multitudes who are in the mines, suffer in health and constitution from the extreme changes of temperature which follow day and night. In some of the ravines in which we camped, these variations vibrated through thirty and forty degrees. In mid-day we were driven into the shade to keep cool, and in the night into two or three blankets to keep warm. The heat is ascribable in part to the nature of the soil, its naked sandy features, its power of radiation, and the absence of circulation in the glens. But the cold comes with the visits of the night wind from the frosty slopes of the Sierra Nevada.

These extreme variations follow the miner through

the whole region in which his tempting scenes of labor lie, and require a degree of prudence seldom met with in that wild woodland life. The consequence is, a group of maladies under which the strongest constitution at length breaks down. But I am convinced from personal experience, that with proper precaution and suitable food, many, and most of these evils may be obviated. The southern mines are in elevations which exempt them from the maladies incident to the low lands which fringe the streams farther north. There are no stagnant waters, no decomposition of vegetable matter, no miasma drifting about in the fog, to shake and burn you with alternate chill and fever. I never enjoyed better health and spirits; and never encountered in a great moving mass, notwithstanding their irregularities, so few instances of disease traceable to local causes. I have seen more groaners and grunters in one metropolitan household, than in any swarming ravine in the southern mines

SUNDAY, JAN. 7. Lapses from virtue are not unfrequently associated, in the character of the Spanish female, with singular exhibitions of charity and self-denial. She is often at the couch of disease, unshrinkingly exposed to contagion, or in the hovel of destitution, administering to human necessity. She pities where others reproach, and succors where others forsake. The motive which prompts this unwearied charity, is a secret within her own soul. It may be as a poor expiation for conscious error, or the impulse of those kindly sentiments not yet extinct, or gratitude for that humanity which foregoes merited reprehension. Be the cause what it may, it justly retains her within the pale of Christian charity, and entitles her to that sympathy in her own misfortunes which she so largely bestows on the sorrows of others.

Denunciation never yet protected the innocent, confirmed the wavering, or recovered the fallen. That spirit of ferocity which breaks the bruised reed, partakes more of relentless pride than virtuous disapprobation. Many sever themselves from all sympathy with the erring, from the mistaken apprehension that the wider the chasm, the more advantageous the light in which *they* will appear. But that chasm which seems so wide to them, narrows to a faint line in the eye of Omniscience. Forgiveness is our duty; not that forgiveness which scorns and forsakes the object on which it is bestowed, but which seeks to reclaim the erring, and reinstate the fallen in merited confidence and esteem. When repentant guilt trembled and blushed in the presence of Him whose divine example is our guide, no frown darkened His brow, no malediction fell from His lips; His absolving injunction was—*go, and sin no more.* The brightest stars are they which have emerged from a horizon of darkness.

Tuesday, Jan. 16. The climate on the seaboard

is remarkably equable; it varies at Monterey, the year round, but little from sixty. You never lay aside your woollen apparel, and always feel ready for a bear-hunt, or any other field-sport that may tempt your taste or skill. Till the Americans came here there was hardly a house in the town which contained a fireplace; even the cooking was done in a detached apartment, seemingly to avoid the straggling rays of its grate. The children ran about in the winter months without a shoe, and in their little cotton slips, the perfect pictures of health. The girl of seventeen, the mother of forty, and the venerable lady, who had reached her threescore and ten, were never seen hovering around a fire: they were at their household affairs, in apartments where a coal had never been kindled; or in their gardens, where the last rain had revived their drooping plants; or out in the woods at pic-nics, where the very birds sung out in rivalry of their jocund mirth. Health spread its rose in the cheek, and elastic life thrilled in the bounding limb. The birth of a child was only a momentary pause in this scene of pleasurable activity, and more than compensated for its brief encroachment in a new bud of being, to be clustered among the rest—now blooming in fragrant life around the parent tree.

Think of this, ye mothers who cloister your daughters in air-tight parlors, with furnaces blowing in hot steam from below. It is no wonder they wither from their cradles, and that their bridal couch is often ashes. Your mistaken tenderness, vanity, and pride have supplied death with trophies long enough. Look here to California; among all these mothers and daughters, there is not one where the cankerworm of that disease is at work which has spread sorrow and dismay around your hearths. The insidious disguises and sapping advances of the consumption are not known here; I have not yet met with the first instance where this disease, contracted here, has found a victim. It is your in-door habits, hot parlors, prunellas, and twisting corsets, that clothe this generation with weeds, and bequeath to the next constitutions that fall like grass under the scythe of death. If your daughters won't take out-door exercise from persuasion, then drive them forth as the guardian angel of Eden your erring progenitrix. It may have been that the development of her physical forces, as well as retributive justice, induced her expulsion from the luxurious roses, the balmy airs, and lulling streams of her first abode. But your Eves will come back again, and sparkling eyes, and buoyant spirits, and a vigorous pulse will commend your maternal wisdom; and when a man, worthy of your confidence and the affections of your daughters, wants a wife, his choice will not lie in a group of valetudinarians. He carries off a bird that floats a strong wing, and that can sing in concert with him as they build the nest out of which other harmonies are to charm the warbling grove; and then, too, the young fledglings will come back to you, all bright and beautiful, and touched with the spirit of gladness in which their breezy cradle swung. Why, is not this enough to make a mother's soul leap to her laughing eyes!

WEDNESDAY, JAN. 24. Nature never leaves any portion of her troubled domain without a compensation. Here, where the hills and plains, under the long summer's drought, become so parched and dry that the grasshoppers cease to sing, she presents a pingrass, on which the cattle still thrive; and when this fails, it has already dropped a seed even more nutritious than the stem which sustained its bulbous cradle. For this, a California horse will leave the best bin of oats that ever waved in the harvest-moon. The first copious shower, which usually occurs in November, destroys it, but around its ruins another grass springs, to throw its green velvet, inwrought with millions of flowers, on the charmed eye. It is no wonder the birds here sing through the year, and forego those migrations to which they are subjected in other climes. The lay of the robin, the whistle of the quail, and the tender notes of the curlew, are always piping in the grove, or filling with melody the garden-tree.

Were the blackbird to migrate, and never come back, no farmer would regret his absence; for he is a mischievous bird, who has no respect for the rights of property. He squats by millions where he likes, and would rob a wheat-field of its last kernel with a thousand thunders rattling overhead. His legions darken the heaven where they fly, and drown all other harmonies in the jargon of their obstreperous chatter. They are said to be good for a pot-pie; and there are enough of them here to plump a pie around which nations might sit and carve at will: and how much better to be carving a common pie than carving into each other's lands,—to be popping at blackbirds than shooting each other. There is not a blackbird but what laughs under his glossy wing when he sees a man levelling his gun at another, which the sable rogue knows ought to be levelled at him; and when the smoke-clouds loom up from the field of battle, he chatters in very glee, and even the eyes of the sedate raven are filled with unwonted light. Man makes himself a mournful tragedy and ludicrous comedy in the great creation of God.

WEDNESDAY, FEB. 7. There is one tree in California that is worthy of note, which is peculiar to the country, and as deserving a place on her coat-of-arms as her grizzly bear, and much more so, unless her people intend to overawe their neighbors with the terrors of their insignia. This tree is called the redwood, and closely resembles, in its texture, size, and antiseptic qualities, the giant cedars which have pinnacled, through the storms of a thousand years, the steeps of Lebanon. It is found on the table-lands between the coast range and the sea, and grows in distinct forests, like the savage tribes which once slumbered in its shadows. Its shaft rises straight and free of limbs, till high over the wave of other trees it can spread its emerald sails to the wind, compact as the royals of a ship of the line. The wood is of a pale red hue, and easily yields to any shape under the implements of the carpenter, but is not sufficiently firm for the severer tests of cabinet work. It resists decay, whatever may be its exposure, and in the ground or on the roof is true to its trust. The same shingle which shook the rain from your grandsire, wards it from you; and the same board which pannelled his coffin, echoes to the rumbling sounds of yours as you go down to join him. In a grove of these trees, only a short ride from Monterey, stands one measuring sixty feet in circumference! Of its height I am not certain, as I had no means of measuring it—say three hundred feet—or at least as high as the steeple of that church, a warden of which, who had caught the spirit of its elevation, is reported to have said in reply to a proposition for the introduction of lamps and an evening service, "this line goes through by daylight." Let those versed in moral mensuration determine the elevation of that warden's spiritual pride, and they will have the height of my tree exactly.

FRIDAY, FEB. 16. Mr. Larkin has closed the amusements of the carnival with a splendid entertainment, graced with all the beauty and bravery of Monterey. As no egg could be broken after midnight, without trenching on the solemnities of Lent, each went equipped with these weapons, ready for an early contest. Several small volleys opened the engagement between some of the parties; while the fandango engrossed the attention of others. In this oval war the ladies are always the antagonists of the gentlemen, and, generally, through their dexterity, and larger supply of ammunition, bear off the palm. They will sometimes carry two or three dozen rounds each, and as snugly stowed away as cartridges in the box of a new recruit. Still both parties will fight it out—

> "With blow for blow, disputing inch by inch,
> Where one will not retreat, nor t'other flinch."

But there were two shot in the company, in the shape of goose eggs, well filled with cologne, to which an unusual interest attached. One of them had been brought by Gen. M——, the other by Donna J——, and each was only watching an opportunity for a crash on the head of the other. Both were endowed with physical force, dexterity, and firmness, and a heart in which pity relaxed none of these energies. Neither turned an eye but for a moment from the other; but in that moment the donna dashed to the side of the general, and would have crashed her egg on his head, had not the blow been instantly parried. The assailed now became the assailant, and both were in for the last tests of skill—

> "While none who saw them could divine
> To which side conquest would incline."

The donna changed her tactics, stood on the defensive and parried, and in one of these dexterous foils dashed her egg on the head of her antagonist, who, in the same instant, brought his down plump on hers. Both were drenched in cologne; both victors in defeat: a shout followed, which shook the rafters of the old tenement. The engagement now became general; each had his antagonist, and must "do or die;" the battle swayed this way and that—sometimes in single combat, and at others in vollied platoons; and then along the whole blazing line: each recoil was recovered by a more vigorous assault; each retreat in rallied thunder, more than redeemed; while first and foremost, where wavered or withstood the foe—

" The *donna* cheered her band."

But, in this most critical crisis of the field, the fire began to slacken along the line of the men; their ammunition was giving out; only a few rounds here and there remained; the heroines perceived this, and opened with double round and grape on their foes—

" Who form—unite—charge—waver—all is lost!"

The bell tolled the hour of midnight, and Lent came in with her ashes to bury the dead! They may trifle who will with this field; but there was more in it worthy of a good man's remembrance than half the fields fought from Homer's day to this. If this be treason to the bullet and blood chivalry—make the most of it.

CHAPTER XXVI.

THE PUBLIC DOMAIN.—SCENERY AROUND MONTEREY.—VINEYARDS OF LOS ANGELS.—BEAUTY OF SAN DIEGO.—THE CULPRIT HALL.—THE RUSH FOR GOLD.—LAND TITLES.—THE INDIAN DOCTRESS.—TUFTED PARTRIDGE.—DEATH OF COM. BIDDLE.

SATURDAY, FEB. 24. All the land grants in California are blindly defined; a mountain bluff, lagoon, river, or ravine serve as boundaries; and these not unfrequently comprehend double the leagues or acres contemplated in the instrument. No accurate surveys have been made; and the only legal restrictions falling within these vague limits, is in the shape of a provision that the excess shall revert to the public domain. This provision, which is inserted in most of the grants, will throw into the market, under an accurate survey, some of the best tracts in California. These will be seized upon by capitalists and speculators, and held at prices beyond the means of emigrants, unless some legislative provision shall extend peculiar privileges to actual settlers.

The lands which lie through the gold region are uninvaded by any private grants, except one on the Maraposa, owned by Col. Fremont; one on the Cosumes, owned by W. E. P. Hartnell, and the limited claims of Johnson on Bear river, and Capt. Sutter on the Americano. All the other lands stretching from Feather river on the north, to the river Reys on the south, covering five hundred miles along the slopes of the Sierra Nevada, belonging to the public domain, and should never become private property so long as it is for the interests of the United States to encourage mining in California. Any system of private proprietorship will result in monopoly and bloodshed. Let companies lease their sections, and private individuals pay their license; and let every regulation look more to the encouragement it extends, than the revenue it exacts.

TUESDAY, FEB. 27. At an early hour this morning a huge floating mass, with her steep sides dark as night, was seen winding into the bay without sail, wind, or tide. Such a wizard phenomenon was never seen before on this coast, and might well alarm the natives, especially when the great guns of the fort rolled their thunder at her: and still she neared! heaving the still waters into cataracts at her side, and sending up her steep column of smoke, as if a young Etna were at work within. They who had witnessed such things in other parts of the world, shouted "The steamer! the steamer!" and instantly the echo came back with redoubled force from a hundred crowded balconies. The whole community was thrown into excitement, wonder, and gratulation; cheers and shouts of welcome rent the air; all liquors were free to brim the bumpers; and basket after basket of champagne went gratuitously into the streets, till their flying corks rose like musket-shot in a general feu de joie. The last distrust of good faith in the government vanished; and all saw the dawn of a higher destiny breaking over California. The enterprise of a Howland and Aspinwall blazed in this new aurora, and filled the whole horizon with light. The golden promise which had floated in doubt and earnest hope had been redeemed and the union of California with the glorious confederacy achieved. What now were oceans and an isthmus!—only a few waves and a narrow line of earth, unfelt under the conquering powers of steam. Such was the tumult of transport which hailed the first steamer; such her welcome to the *el dorado* of the West. No gold mine sprung in the Sierra ever roused half the wonder, hope, and general joy.

MONDAY, MARCH 5. The scenery around Monterey and the *locale* of the town, arrest the first glance of the stranger. The wild waving background of forest-feathered cliffs, the green slopes, and the glimmering walls of the white dwellings, and the dash of the billows on the sparkling sands of the bay, fix and charm the eye. Nor does the enchantment fade by being familiarly approached; avenues of almost endless variety lead off through the circling steeps, and winding through long shadowy ravines, lose themselves in the vine-clad recesses of the distant hills. It is no wonder that California centred her taste, pride, and wealth here, till the Vandal irruption of gold-hunters broke into her peaceful domain. Now all eyes are turned to San Francisco, with her mud bottoms, her sand hills, and her chill winds, which cut the stranger like hail driven through the summer solstice. Avarice may erect its shanty there, but contentment, and a love of the wild and beautiful, will construct its tabernacle among the flowers, the waving shades, and fragrant airs of Monterey. And even they who now drive the spade and drill in the mines, when their yellow pile shall fill the measure of their purposes, will come here to sprinkle these hills with the mansions and cottages of ease and refinement. Among these soaring crags the step of youth will still spring, and beauty garland her tresses with wild-flowers in the mirror of the mountain stream. Alas! that eyes so bright should be closed so soon, and that a step so light and free should lead but to that narrow house which holds no communion with the pulses which will still roll through nature's great heart!

WEDNESDAY, MARCH 7. Emigrants, when the phrensy of the mines has passed, will be strongly attracted to los Angeles, the capital of the southern department. It stands inland from San Pedro about eight leagues, in the bosom of a broad fertile plain, and has a population of two thousand souls. The San Gabriel pours its sparkling tide through its green borders. The most delicious fruits of the tropical zone may flourish here. As yet, only the grape and fig have secured the attention of the cultivator; but the capacities of the soil and aptitudes of the climate are attested in the twenty thousand vines, which reel in one orchard, and which send through California a wine that need not blush in the presence of any rival from the hills of France or the sunny slopes of Italy. To these plains the more quiet emigrants will ere long gather, and convert their drills into pruning-hooks, and we shall have wines, figs, dates, almonds, olives, and raisins from California. The gold may give out, but these are secure while nature remains.

San Diego is another spot to which the tide of immigration must turn. It stands on the border line of Alta California, and opens on a land-locked bay of surpassing beauty. The climate is soft and mild the year round; the sky brilliant, and the atmosphere free of those mists which the cold currents throw on the northern sections of the coast. The sea-breeze cools the heat of summer, and the great ocean herself modulates into the same temperature the rough airs of winter. The seasons roll round, varied only by the fresh fruits and flowers that follow in their train. I would rather have a willow-wove hut at San Diego, with ground enough for a garden, than the whole peninsula of San Francisco, if I must live there. The one is a Vallambrosa, where only the zephyr stirs her light wing; the other a tempest-swept cave of Æolus, where the demons of storm shake their shivering victims. The lust of gold will people the one, but all that is lovely in the human heart spread its charm over the other. Before the eyes that fall on these pages are under death's shadow, San Diego will have become the queen of the south in California, encircled with vineyards and fields of golden grain, and gathering into her bosom the flowing commerce of the Colorado and Gila.

THURSDAY, MARCH 8. The town-hall, on which I have been at work for more than a year, is at last finished. It is built of a white stone, quarried from a neighboring hill, and which easily takes the shape you desire. The lower apartments are for schools; the hall over them—seventy feet by thirty—is for public assemblies. The front is ornamented with a portico, which you enter from the hall. It is not an edifice that would attract any attention among public buildings in the United States; but in California it is without a rival. It has been erected out of the slender proceeds of town lots, the labor of the convicts, taxes on liquor shops, and fines on gamblers. The scheme was regarded with incredulity by many; but the building is finished, and the citizens have assembled in it, and christened it after my name, which will now go down to posterity with the odor of gamblers, convicts, and tipplers. I leave it as an humble evidence of what may be accomplished by rigidly adhering to one purpose, and shrinking from no personal efforts necessary to its achievement. A prison has also been built, and mainly through the labor of the convicts. Many a joke the rogues have cracked while constructing their own cage; but they have worked so diligently I shall feel constrained to pardon out the less incorrigible. It is difficult here to discriminate between offences which flow from moral hardihood, and those which result, in a measure, from untoward circumstances. There is a wide difference in the turpitude of the two; and an alcalde under the Mexican law, has a large scope in which to exercise his sense of moral justice. Better to err a furlong with mercy than a fathom with cruelty. Unmerited punishment never yet reformed its subject; to suppose it, is a libel on the human soul.

FRIDAY, MARCH 9. There is one event in the recent history of California, which has carried with it decisive moral results. Till the intelligence of peace reached here, a bewildering expectation had been entertained by many, that Mexico would never consent to part with this portion of her domain. This idea, vague and groundless as it was, interfered with all permanent plans of action affecting individual capital and enterprise. To this state of uncertainty the news of peace, which reached here in August, gave an effectual quietus. The event was announced to the community by order of Gen. Mason, through a national salute from the fort; and hardly had the echoes died away among the hills, when its certainty sunk deep and firm into the convictions of all. The result was a revulsion of feeling towards Mexico, which no repentant action on her part could ever overcome. The native people felt that they had been *sold*, and expressed in no measured terms their indignation. They had no objections to the transfer of allegiance; but they scorned the *barter*, and denounced the treachery, as they termed it, which had put a *price* upon their heads. The old Spanish blood was up, and flaming, like the lake which rolls its tide of fire in the breast of Vesuvius. From that day to this, I have never heard one native citizen express for Mexico even that poor sentiment of regard with which pity sometimes softens an indignant contempt. The only regret was, that the American arms were withdrawn from that country, and that her national existence was not extinct. This feeling remains, and will still be felt in the various relations of society, when the native mass has been swallowed up in the emigrant tide, as a rivulet in the majesty of the mountain stream.

SUNDAY, MARCH 11. What crowds are rushing out here for gold! what multitudes are leaving their distant homes for this glittering treasure! Can gold warrant the hazards of the enterprise? Can it compensate the toils and suffering which it imposes? Can it repair a shattered constitution, or bring back the exhilarating pulse and play of youth? Let the wrecks of those who have perished speak; let the broken hearts and hopes of thousands utter their admonition: their voices come surging over these pines, breaking from these cliffs, sighing in the winds, and knelling from the clouds. Your treasures you must resign at the dark portal of the grave: there the glittering heap, and the strong arms which wrenched it from the mine, lie down together; the spirit walketh alone through that troubled night; but a ray twinkles through its long aisle of darkness: follow that in meekness and faith, and it will lead you to the spirit-land. There dwell your kindred who adorned virtue with a spirit of contentment,—there the parent whose latest prayer was for you,—there the sister, who, in the hush of voices around, heard the sweet strains of an unseen harp, and was charmed away from the delusive dreams of earth, ere a hope of the heart had been broken, or sorrow had saddened a smile. What is wealth to such an inheritance? what the society of kings to such companionship? Plume your wing for heaven ere it droops in the death-dew of its dissolving strength.

TUESDAY, MARCH 20. The land-titles in California ought to receive the most indulgent construction. But few of them have *all* the forms prescribed by legislative enactments, but they have official insignia sufficient to certify the intentions of the government. To disturb these grants would be alike impolitic and unjust; it would be to convert the lands which they cover to the public domain, and ultimately turn them over to speculators and foreign capitalists. Better let them remain as they are: they are now in good hands; they are held mostly by Californians,—a class of persons who part with them on reasonable terms. No Californian grinds the face of the poor, or refuses an emigrant a participation in his lands. I have seen them dispose of miles for a consideration less than would be required by Americans for as many acres. You are shut up to the shrewdness and sharpness of the Yankee on the one hand, and the liberality of the Californian on the other. Your choice lies between the two, and I have no hesitation in saying, give me the Californian. If he has a farm, and I have none, he will divide with me; but who ever heard of a Yankee splitting up his farm to accommodate emigrants? Why, he will not divide with his own sons till death has divided him from both. Yankees are good when mountains are to be levelled, lakes drained, and lightning converted into a vegetable manure; but as a landholder, deliver me from his map and maw. He wants not only all on this side of creation's verge, but a *leetle* that laps over the other.

WEDNESDAY, MARCH 28. A young friend of mine had been several months in Monterey, confined to his room, and nearly helpless, from an ugly sore on one of his limbs. The skill of the whole medical profession here, in the army and navy, and out of them, had been exerted in this case, and baffled. At last, the discouraged patient sent for an old Indian woman, who has some reputation among the natives for medical sagacity in roots and herbs. She examined the sore, and the next day brought to the patient a poultice and pot of tea. The application was made and the beverage drank as directed. These were renewed two or three times, and the young man is now running about the streets, or hunting his game, sound as a nut.

This same Indian woman is the only physician I had when attacked with the disease which carried off Lieut. Miner and several others attached to the public service. In a half-delirious state, which followed close upon the attack, I looked up and saw bending over me the kind Mrs. Hartnell—one of the noblest among the native ladies of California—and at her side stood this Indian woman feeling my pulse. Mrs. H. remained, while her medical attendant went away, but returned soon with the Indian medicaments which were to arrest, or remedy this rapid and critical disease. I resigned myself to all her drinks and baths; she did with me just what she pleased. She broke the fever without breaking me; restored my strength, and in a week I was in my office, attending to my duties. What she gave me I know not, but I believe her roots and herbs saved my life, as well as the leg of my friend.

SATURDAY, APRIL 7. The quail, or tufted partridge, abounds in California, and is a delicious bird. A walk of ten minutes in any direction from Monterey, will bring you into their favorite haunts. But they are extremely shy; it is no easy matter to strike them on the wing; they are out of one bush and into another before you can level your piece, unless, like the

Irishman hitting his weasel, you fire first and take aim afterwards. I must attribute my success frequently to hits of this kind; for a deliberate aim was sure to come too late,—just like an old bachelor's proposal of marriage, which, as his vanity whispers him, might have been accepted had it been made a *little* sooner, but now the dulcinia has changed her mind, and the fat is all in the fire. What a pity that such a pelican should be left alone in this world's wilderness, and the community be deprived of all the little pelicans that might have been! But I was speaking of quail, and not of pelicans, and of the difficulty of hitting them. Gen. Mason is the best shot here; a quail, to fly his fire, must be as quick on the wing as a message, in its sightless career, over one of Morse's magnetic wires. To me one of the most enticing features in California life is presented in her game. It comes in every variety of form, from the elk and buck that rove her forests and prairies, to the rabbit that undermines the garden-hedge; and from the wild goose and duck, which sweep in clouds her ruffled waters, to the little beca that feeds on her figs. A good sportsman might live the year round, amid these meadows and mounds, on the trophies of his fowling-piece and rifle, and as independent of civilized life as any savage that ever bent the bow or steadied his bark canoe over the rushing verge of the cascade.

Tuesday, April 17. That spirit of prophecy which sometimes trembles in an adieu, occurred forcibly to me on receiving the intelligence of the death of Com. Biddle. His last words were omens, if such a thing may be. He had ordered the Columbus to be ready for sea the next morning, and had come ashore for a walk in the woods which skirt Monterey. We had ascended the summit of a hill which commands a wide range of waving woods, gleaming meadows, and ocean's blue expanse. The great orb of day was on the horizon, and the eye of the commodore was fastened upon it as it sunk in solemn majesty from sight. He had not spoken for several minutes; when, turning to me, he said—"This is my last walk among these hills, and something whispers me that all my walks end here." This was said with that look and manner in which the undertone of a man's thoughts will sometimes find words without his will. It was utterly at variance with the cool, philosophical habits which were eminently characteristic of the commodore, and which he seldom relinquished, except in some sally of humor and wit. This remark woke like a slumber of the shroud, on the sudden intelligence of his death. It may be a superstition, but I shall never resign, to a skeptical philosophy, the omen and its seeming fulfilment. The future is often prefigured in an incident or sentiment of the present

> " An undefined and sudden thrill,
> That makes the heart a moment still—
> Then beat with quicker pulse, ashamed
> Of that strange sense itself had framed."

The hill-top and the waving forest remain, but the commodore—where is he? Gone, like a star from its darkened watch-tower on high! But the night which quenched the beam is still fringed with light. To this surviving ray we turn in bereavement and grief. His genius lighted the objects of thought on which it touched, and glanced, with an intuitive force, through the subtle problems of the mind. His mental horizon was broad, and yet every object within its wide circle was distinctly seen, and seen in its true position and relative importance. The trifling never rose into the great, and the majestic never became tame. Each stood, in his clear vision, as truth and reason had stamped it. He was cool and collected without being stoical, and immovably firm without being arbitrary. He had that courage which could never be shaken by surprise, made giddy with success, or quelled by disaster. Whatever subject he assayed, he mastered. He has left but few behind him, out of the legal profession, more thoroughly versed in questions of international law and maritime jurisprudence. Had not his early impulses taken him to the deck, he might have been eminent at the bar, in the cabinet, or hall of legislation. He had all the clearness and comprehensiveness of a great statesman. Gratitude twines this leaf of remembrance and respect into that chaplet which the bereavement of the service has woven on his grave.

CHAPTER XXVII.

THE GOLD REGION.—ITS LOCALITY, NATURE, AND EXTENT.—FOREIGNERS IN THE MINES.—THE INDIANS' DISCOVERY OF GOLD.—AGRICULTURAL CAPABILITIES OF CALIFORNIA.—SERVICES OF UNITED STATES OFFICERS.—FIRST DECISIVE MOVEMENT FOR THE ORGANIZATION OF A CIVIL GOVERNMENT.—INTELLIGENCE OF THE DEATH OF GEN. KEARNY.

THURSDAY, APRIL 26. The gold region, which contains deposits of sufficient richness to reward the labor of working them, is strongly defined by nature. It lies along the foot hills of the Sierra Nevada—a mountain range running nearly parallel with the coast—and extends on these hills about five hundred miles north and south, by thirty or forty east and west. From the slopes of the Sierra, a large number of streams issue, which cut their channels through these hills, and roll with greater or less volume to the Sacramento and San Joaquin rivers. The Sacramento rises in the north, and flowing south two hundred and fifty miles, empties itself into the Suisun, or upper bay of San Francisco. The San Joaquin rises in the south, and flowing north two hundred miles, discharges itself into the same bay. The source of the San Joaquin is a narrow lake lying still further south, and extending in that direction about eighty miles. The streams which break into these rivers from the Sierra Nevada, are from ten to thirty miles distant from each other. They commence with Feather river on the north, and end with the river Reys on the south. They all have numerous tributaries; are rapid and wild on the mountain slopes, and become more tranquil and tame as they debouch upon the plain. Still their serpentine waters, flashing up among the trees which shadow their channels, give a picturesque feature to the landscape, and relieve it of that monotony which would otherwise fatigue the eye. But very few of these rivers have sufficient depth and regularity to render them navigable. Their sudden bends, falls, and shallows would puzzle even an Indian canoe, and strand any boat of sufficient draft to warrant the agency of steam.

The alluvial deposits of gold are confined mainly to the banks and bars of these mountain streams, and the channels of the gorges, which intersect them, and through which the streams are forced when swollen by the winter rains. In the hills and tablelands, which occupy the intervals between these currents and gorges, no alluvial deposits have been found. Here and there a few detached pieces have been discovered, forming an exception to some general law by which the uplands have been deprived of their surface treasures. The conclusion at which I have arrived, after days and weeks of patient research, and a thousand inquiries made of others, is, that the alluvial deposits of gold in California are mainly confined to the banks and bars of her streams, and the ravines which intersect them. The only material exception to this general law is found in those intervening deposits, from which the streams have been diverted by some local cause, or some convulsion of nature. Aside from these, no surface gold to any extent has been found on the table-lands or plains. Even the banks of the Sacramento and San Joaquin, stretching a distance of five hundred miles through their valleys, have not yielded an ounce. The mountain streams, long before they discharge themselves into these rivers, deposit their precious treasures. They contribute their waters, but not their gold. Like cunning misers they have stowed this away, and no enchantments can make them whisper of its whereabouts. If you would find it, you must hunt for it as for hid treasures.

MONDAY, MAY 14. Much has been said of the amounts of gold taken from the mines by Sonoranians, Chilians, and Peruvians, and carried out of the country. As a general fact, this apprehension and alarm is without any sound basis. Not one pound of gold in ten, gathered by these foreigners, is shipped off to their credit : it is spent in the country for provisions, clothing, and in the hazards of the gaming-table. It falls into the hands of those who command the avenues of commerce, and ultimately reaches our own mints. I have been in a camp of five hundred Sonoranians, who had not gold enough to buy a month's provisions—all had gone, through their improvident habits, to the capacious pockets of the Americans. To drive them out of California, or interdict their operations, is to abstract that amount of labor from the mines, and curtail proportionably the proceeds. If gold, slumbering in the river banks and mountains of California, be more valuable to us than when stamped into eagles and incorporated into our national currency, then drive out the Sonoranians: but if you would have it *here* and not *there*, let those diggers alone. When gold shall begin to fail, or require capital and machinery, you will want these hardy men to quarry the rocks and feed your stampers; and when you shall plunge into the Cinnebar mountains, you will want them to sink your shafts and kindle fires under your great quicksilver retorts. They will become the hewers of wood and drawers of water to American capital and enterprise. But if you want to perform this drudgery yourself, drive out the Sonoranians, and upset that cherished system of political economy founded in a spirit of wisdom and national justice.

Tuesday, May 22. I was in possession of a fact which left no doubt of the existence of gold in the Stanislaus more than a year prior to its discovery on the American Fork. A wild Indian had straggled into Monterey with a specimen, which he had hammered into a clasp for his bow. It fell into the hands of my secretary, W. R. Garner, who communicated the secret to me. The Indian described the locality in which it was found with so much accuracy that Mr. G., on his recent excursion to the mines, readily identified the spot. It is now known as "Carson's diggings." No one who has been there can ever forget its wild majestic scenery, or confound its soaring cliffs or sunless chasms with the images projected from other objects. It was the full intention of Mr. G. to trail this Indian at the first opportunity, and he was prevented from doing it only by the imperative duties of the office. His keeping the discovery a secret, proceeded less from any sinister motive than an eccentricity of character. He had another mineral secret which has not yet transpired—the existence of a tin mine, near San Louis Obispo. The extent is not known, but certainly the specimen shown me was very rich. Mr. Garner is now dead: it was his melancholy fate to fall with five others by the wild Indians on the river Reys. To that party I should have been attached had I remained in California another month. How narrow those escapes which run their mystic thread between two worlds! On the grave of my friend, gratitude for important services, and a remembrance of many sterling virtues, might well erect a memorial.

THURSDAY, MAY 24. The capabilities of the soil of California for agricultural purposes involve a question of profound interest, and one which is not easily answered. There are no experimental facts of sufficient scope to warrant a general conclusion. Where the soil itself leaves no doubt of its richness, its productive forces may be baffled by local circumstances or atmospheric phenomena. Some of the largest crops that have ever rewarded the toil of the husbandman, have been gathered in California; and yet those very localities, owing to a slender fall of the winter rains, have next season disappointed the hopes of the cultivator. The farmer can never be certain of an abundant harvest till he is able to supply this deficiency of rain by a process of irrigation. This can be done, in some places, by the diversion of streams, and must be accomplished in others through artesian wells. It will be some years before either will be brought into effective force in the agricultural districts.

The lands on which cultivation has been attempted occupy a narrow space between the coast ranges and the sea; it seldom exceeds in width thirty miles, and is often reduced to ten by the obtrusion of some mountain spur. East of this range no plough has ever travelled; no furrow has ever been turned in the long valley of the San Joaquin; and if the other sections of this valley correspond to those over which I passed, there can be very little encouragement for the introduction of husbandry. The soil is light and gravelly; the grass meagre and sparse; even the wild horses and elk seek its margin, as if afraid to trust themselves to the Sahara of its bosom. Still, in some of its bays, the evidences of fertility exist, but as a district it will never add much to the agricultural wealth of California.

The valley of the Sacramento has many localities of great fertility; but few of them, as yet, have been subjected to the plough and harrow; their adaptation to agriculture is inferred from their vigorous vegetation. The same evidences of productive force cover several tracts north of San Francisco, on the Russian river, and in the vicinity of Sonoma. But the most fertile lands in California, as yet developed, lie around the missions of Santa Clara and Santa Cruz, through the long narrow valleys of San José and San Juan, along the margin of the Salinas, through the dells of San Louis Obispo, and in the vicinity of los Angeles. These, and other insular spots, may be made perfect gardens; but take California as a whole, she is not the country which agriculturists would select. Her whole mining region is barren; nature rested there with what she put *beneath* the soil. You can hardly travel through it in midsummer without loading your mule down with provender to keep him alive. The productive forces of such a state as New York, Ohio, or Pennsylvania, sweep immeasurably beyond the utmost capabilities of California. It is the *golden* coronet that gives this land her pre-eminence, and puts into her hand a magic wand, that will shake for ages the exchanges of the civilized world.

TUESDAY, JUNE 12. At the return of Gen. Kearny,

the command of the military posts of the country, the suppression of popular disturbancies, the protection of property from the incursion of the Indians, and the collection of the custom-house revenues have devolved on Gen. Mason. To these complicated duties he has surrendered his energies with an unwearied fidelity and force. No one great interest confided to his indomitable activity has languished. He has derived indispensable aid from the intelligent services of Col. Stevenson, Maj. Folsom, Capt. Halleck, and Lieut. Sherman, of the army, and Lieut. Lanman, of the navy. These officers, and others that might be named, without any increased compensation, and subjected to heavy expenses, have cheerfully discharged the onerous duties devolved upon them by the condition of the country.

The regiment of volunteers under Col. Stevenson arrived too late for any active participation in the war. The insurrection had been suppressed, and the country was in the peaceful occupation of the Americans. Still they were with great propriety retained in the service, and their presence at different points tended to discourage any attempts at revolutionary movements. They were, many of them, youth who nad not been reared under the most auspicious circumstances, and the adventures of a camp life were but little calculated to supply the defects of education. They gave the colonel and his officers some trouble, and the communities where they were stationed some solicitude. But they are now in a condition, where every one is thrown upon his own resources, where every thing good in a man may be developed. They have been sowing their wild oats, and will now go to planting corn.

SATURDAY, JUNE 16. The primary movements in California for the organization of a civil government had no connection with any instructions from Washington. The first great meeting on the subject was held in Monterey in January, 1849. At this meeting I was called upon to draft a preamble and resolutions, setting forth the condition of the country, the necessity of a civil organization, and providing for the election of proper delegates to a convention, to be held at San José on the 27th of February, in which all the districts of the Territory were to be represented, and where a suitable constitution was to be framed. These resolutions were sent to all the principal towns, and adopted. But upon more mature reflection, it was deemed expedient, in order to prevent any collision with the possible action of Congress, to postpone the assembling of the convention to the first of May, that the proceedings of that body might be known. This is the true history of those primary and decisive measures which have resulted in that noble constitution which now throws its sacred ægis over California. The friends of the last and present administration, instead of contending for the honor of an active participation in the origin and progress of this instrument, deftly box back and forth the responsibility of its provisions. But their political timidity is without any just grounds; for neither afforded any countenance or aid till the rubicon had been passed: so that all this shuttlecock business between the last and present administration, is a superfluous exhibition of dexterity and skill. Much good may it do the players, only let not California suffer too much while the sport is going on.

WEDNESDAY, JUNE 20. The causes which exclude slavery from California lie within a nut-shell. All here are diggers, and free white diggers wont dig with slaves. They know they must dig themselves: they have come out here for that purpose, and they wont degrade their calling by associating it with slave-labor: self-preservation is the first law of nature. They have nothing to do with slavery in the abstract, or as it exists in other communities; not one in ten cares a button for its abolition, nor the Wilmot proviso either: all they look at is their own position; they must themselves swing the pick, and they wont swing it by the side of negro slaves. That is their feeling, their determination, and the upshot of the whole business. An army of half a million, backed by the resources of the United States, could not shake their purpose. Of all men with whom I have ever met, the most firm, resolute, and indomitable, are the emigrants into California. They feel that they have got into a new world, where they have a right to shape and settle things in their own way. No mandate, unless it comes like a thunder-bolt straight out of heaven, is regarded. They may offer to come into the Union, but they consider it an act of condescension, like that of Queen Victoria in her nuptials with Prince Albert. They walk over hills treasured with the precious ores; they dwell by streams paved with gold; while every mountain around soars into the heaven, circled with a diadem richer than that which threw its halo on the seven hills of Rome. All these belong to them; they walk in their midst; they feel their presence and power, and partake of their grandeur. Think you that such men will consent to swing the pick by the side of slaves? Never! while the stream owns its source, or the mountain its base. You may call it pride, or what you will, but *there* it is—deep as the foundations of our nature, and unchangeable as the laws of its divine Author.

TUESDAY, JUNE 26. The intelligence of the death of Gen. Kearny has been received here with many expressions of affectionate remembrance. During his brief sojourn in California, his considerate disposition, his amiable deportment and generous policy, had endeared him to the citizens. They saw in him nothing of the ruthless invader, but an intelligent, humane general, largely endowed with a spirit of forbearance and fraternal regard. The conflict which arrested his progress at Pasquel, and the disaster in which so many of his brave men sunk overpowered, were contemplated, by the more considerate of the inhabitants, rather with a sentiment of regret than an air of triumph. They seemed to regard these events as a waste of life—as a reckless resistance on their part, which, if successful for a time, could only have the effect to continue, for a brief period, the sway of leaders in whose prudence and patriotism they had no confidence. They took leave of him with regret, and have received the tidings of his death with sympathy and sorrow. It is not for me to write his eulogy; it is graven on the hearts of all who knew him. His star set without a cloud; but its light lingers still: when all the watch-fires of the tented field have gone out, a faithful ray will still light the shrine which affection and bereavement have reared to his worth.

> "Still o'er the past warm memory wakes,
>   And fondly broods with miser-care;
> Time but the impression deeper makes,
>   As streams their channels deeper wear."

Jacob R. Snyder

CHAPTER XXVIII.

RIDE OF COL. FREMONT FROM LOS ANGELES TO MONTEREY AND BACK.—THE PARTY.—THE RELAYS.—CHARACTER OF THE COUNTRY.—THE RINCON.—SKELETONS OF DEAD HORSES.—A STAMPEDE.—GRAY BEARS.—RECEPTION AT MONTEREY.—THE RETURN.—THE TWO HORSES RODE BY COL. FREMONT, —AN EXPERIMENT.—THE RESULT.—CHARACTERISTICS OF THE CALIFORNIA HORSE.—FOSSIL REMAINS.—THE TWO CLASSES OF EMIGRANTS.—LIFE IN CALIFORNIA.—HEADS AGAINST TAILS.

The ride of Col. Fremont in March, 1847, from the ciudad de los Angeles to Monterey in Alta California—a distance of four hundred and twenty miles—and back, exhibits in a strong light the iron nerve of the rider, and the capacities of the California horse. The party on this occasion, consisted of the colonel, his friend Don Jesúse Pico, and his servant Jacob Dodson. Each had three horses, nine in all, to take their turn under the saddle, and relieve each other every twenty miles; while the six loose horses galloped ahead, requiring constant vigilance and action to keep them on the path. The relays were brought under the saddle by the lasso, thrown by Don Jesúse or Jacob, who, though born and raised in Washington, in his long expeditions with Col. Fremont, had become expert as a Mexican with the lasso, sure as a mountaineer with the rifle, equal to either on horse or foot, and always a lad of courage and fidelity.

The party left los Angeles on the morning of the 22d, at daybreak, though the call which took the colonel to Monterey, had reached him only the evening before. Their path lay through the wild mountains of San Fernando, where the steep ridge and precipitous glen follow each other like the deep hollows and crested waves of ocean, under the driving force of the storm. It was a relief when a rough ravine opened its winding gallery on the line of their path. They reached at length the maritime defile of El Rincon, or Punto Gordo, where a mountain bluff shoulders its way boldly to the sea, leaving for fifteen miles only a narrow line of broken coast, lashed at high tide, and in the gale, by the foaming surf. The sun was on the wave of the Pacific, when they issued from the Rincon; and twilight still lingered when they reached the hospitable rancho of Don Thomas Robbins—one hundred and twenty-five miles from los Angeles. The only limb in the company which seemed to complain of fatigue was the right arm of Jacob, incessantly exercised in lashing the loose horses to the track, and lassoing the relays. None of the horses were shod—an iron contrivance unknown here, except among a few Americans. The gait through the day had been a hand-gallop, relieved at short intervals by a light trot. Here the party rested for the night, while the horses gathered their food from the young grass which spread its tender verdure on the field.

Another morning had thrown its splendors on the

forest when the party waved their adieu to their hospitable host, and were under way. Their path lay over the spurs of the Santa Barbara mountains; and close to that steep ridge, where the California battalion, under Col. Fremont, encountered on the 25th Dec., 1846, a blinding storm, which still throws its sleet and hail through the dreams of those hardy men. Such was its overpowering force, that more than a hundred of their horses dropped down under their saddles. Their bleaching bones still glimmering in the gorges, and hanging on the cliffs, are the ghastly memorials of its terrific violence. None but they, who were of their number, can tell what that battalion suffered. The object of that campaign accomplished, and the conquest of California secured, the colonel, with his friend and servant, was now on his brief return. Their path continued over the flukes and around the bluffs of the coast mountains, relieved at intervals by the less rugged slopes and more level lines of the cañada. The hand-gallop and light trot of their spirited animals brought them, at set of sun, to the rancho of their friend, Capt. Dana, where they supped, and then proceeding on to San Luis Obispo, reached the house of Don Jesúse, the colonel's companion, at nine o'clock in the evening—one hundred and thirty-five miles from the place where they broke camp in the morning!

The arrival of Col. Fremont having got wind, the rancheros of San Luis were on an early stir, determined to detain him. All crowded to his quarters with their gratulations, and the tender of a splendid entertainment, but his time was too pressing: still escape was impossible, till a sumptuous breakfast had been served, and popular enthusiasm had expressed its warm regard. This gratitude and esteem were the result of that humane construction of military law, which had spared the forfeited lives of the leaders in the recent insurrectionary war. It was eleven o'clock in the morning before the colonel and his attendants were in the saddle. Their tired horses had been left, and eight fresh ones taken in their places, while their party had been increased by the addition of a California boy, in the capacity of vaquero. Their path still lay through a wild broken country, where primeval forests frowned, and the mountain torrent dashed the tide of its strength. At eight in the evening they reached the gloomy base of the steep range which guards the head waters of the Salinas or Benaventura, seventy miles from San Luis. Here Don Jesúse, who had been up the greater part of the night previous, with his family and friends, proposed a few hours rest. As the place was the favorite haunt of marauding Indians, the party for safety during their repose, turned off the track, which ran nearer the coast than the usual rout, and issuing through a cañada into a thick wood, rolled down in their serapes, with their saddles for their pillows, while their horses were put to grass at a short distance, with the Spanish boy in the saddle to keep watch. Sleep once commenced, was too sweet to be easily given up; midnight had passed when the party were roused from their slumbers by an *estampedo* among their horses, and the loud calls of the watch boy. The cause of the alarm proved not to be Indians, but gray bears, which infest this wild pass. It was here that Col. Fremont with thirty-five of his men, in the summer preceding, fell in with several large bands of these ferocious fellows, who appeared to have posted themselves here to dispute the path. An attack was ordered, and thirteen of their grim file were left dead on the field. Such is their acknowledged strength and towering rage, when assaulted, the bravest hunters, when outnumbered, generally give them a wide berth. When it was discovered that they had occasioned this midnight stampede, the first impulse was to attack them; but Don Jesúse, who understood their habits and weak points, discouraged the idea, stating that "people *gente* can scare bears," and with that gave a succession of loud halloos, at which the bears commenced their retreat. The horses by good fortune were recovered, a fire kindled, and by break of day, the party had finished their breakfast, and were again in the saddle. Their path, issuing from the gloomy forests of the Soledad, skirted the coast range, and crossed the plain of the Salinas to Monterey, where they arrived three hours to set of sun, and ninety miles from their last camping-tree.

The principal citizens of Monterey, as soon as the arrival of Col. Fremont was announced, assembled at the office of the alcalde, and passed resolutions inviting him to a public dinner; but the urgency of his immediate return obliged him to forego the proffered honor. At four o'clock in the afternoon of the day succeeding that of their arrival, the party were ready to start on their return. The two horses rode by the colonel from San Luis Obispo, were a present to him from Don Jesúse, who now desired him to make an experiment with the abilities of one of them. They were brothers, one a year younger than the other, both the same color—cinnamon—and hence called *el canelo*, or *los canelos*. The elder was taken for the trial, and lead off gallantly as the party struck the plain which stretches towards the Salinas. A more graceful horse, and one more deftly mounted, I have never seen. The eyes of the gathered crowd followed them till they disappeared in the shadows of the distant hills. Forty miles on the hand-gallop, and they camped for the night. Another day dawned, and the elder canelo was again under the saddle of Col. Fremont, and for ninety miles carried him without change, and without apparent fatigue. It was still thirty miles to San Luis, where they were to pass the night, and Don Jesúse insisted that canelo could easily perform it, and so said the horse in his spirited look and action. But the colonel would not put him to the trial; and shifting the saddle to the younger brother, the elder was turned loose to run the remaining thirty miles without a rider. He immediately took the lead, and kept it the whole distance, entering

San Luis on a sweeping gallop, and neighing with exultation on his return to his native pastures. His younger brother, with equal spirit, kept the lead of the horses under the saddle, bearing on his bit, and requiring the constant check of his rider. The whole eight horses made their one hundred and twenty miles each in this day's ride, after having performed forty the evening before. The elder cinnamon, who had taken his rider through the forty, carried him ninety miles further to-day, and would undoubtedly have taken him through the remaining thirty miles had Col. Fremont continued him under the saddle.

After a detention of half a day at San Luis Obispo by a rain-storm, the party resumed the horses they had left there, and which took them back to los Angeles in the same time they had brought them up. Thus making their five hundred miles each in four days, with the interval of repose occupied in the ride from San Luis to Monterey and back. In this whole journey from los Angeles to Monterey and back—making eight hundred and forty miles—the party had actually but one relay of fresh horses: the time on the road was about seventy-six hours. The path through the entire route lies through a wild broken country, over ridges, down gorges, around bluffs, and through gloomy defiles, where a traveller, unused to these mountains, would often deem even the slow trot impracticable. The only food which the horses had, except a few quarts of barley at Monterey, was the grass on the road: though the trained and domesticated horses, like the canelos, will eat or drink almost every thing which their master uses. They will take from his caressing hand bread, fruits, sugar, coffee; and, like the Persian horse, will not refuse a bumper of wine. They obey with gentlest docility his slightest intimation; a swing of his hand, or a tap of his whip on the saddle, will spring them into instant action, while the check of a thread-rein on the Spanish bit will bring them to a dead stand; and yet in these sudden stops, when rushing at the top of their speed, they manage not to jostle their rider, or throw him forward. They go where their master directs, whether it be a leap on the foe, up a flight of stairs, or over a chasm. But this is true only of the conduct and behavior of those horses trained like the canelos, who vindicate, in the mountain glens of California, their Arabian origin. They are all grace, fleetness, muscle, and fire; gentle as the lamb, lively as the antelope, and fearless as the lion.

MARINE REMAINS.

The hills around Monterey are full of marine shells. You can turn them out wherever you drive your spade into the ground. The Indians dig and burn them for lime, which is used in whitewashing the adobe walls of houses, and which makes them glimmer in the sun like banks of freshly-driven snow. It has not sufficient strength for the mason, but no other was in use when we landed at Monterey. The first regular lime-kiln was burnt by me for the town-hall.

I found the stone about ten miles from Monterey, and the lime it produced of a superior quality. When the lime, hair, lath, and sand were brought together, no little curiosity was awakened by the heterogeneous mass, and the admiration was equally apparent when each took its place and performed its part in the plaster and hard finish of the wall and ceiling. Thousands came to see the work ; it was the lion of the day. But the curiosity of the geologist would turn from this to the fossil oyster-shells in the hills; and when he has exhausted those on the coast, let him turn inland, and he will find on the mountains, two hundred miles from the sea, and on elevations of a thousand feet, the same marine productions; and not only these, but the skeleton of a whale almost entire. How came that monster up there, high and dry, glimmering like the pale skeleton of a huge cloud between us and the moon ? Did the central fire which threw up the mountain ridge, throw him up on its crest ? How astonished he must have been to find himself up there, blowing off steam among volcanoes and comets ! Now let our *savans* quit their cockle-shells and petrified herring, and tell us about that whale. They will find him near the rancho of Robert Livermore, on a mountain which overlooks the great valley of the San Joaquin. There he reposes in grim majesty, while the winds of ages pour through his bleaching bones their hollow dirge.

THE TWO CLASSES OF EMIGRANTS.

The emigrants to California are composed of two classes—those who come to live by their wits, and those who come to accumulate by their work. The wit capitalists will find dupes for a time—small fish in shallow waters—but a huge roller will soon heave them all high and dry! This is the last country to which a man should come, who is above or beneath the exercise of his muscles. Every object he meets addresses him in the admonitory language which gleams in the motto of the Arkansas bowie-knife—"root, hog, or die." But then he has this encouragement: he can root almost anywhere, but *root* he must. They who come relying on their physical forces, and who are largely endowed with the organs of perseverance, will succeed. But if they stay too long in San Francisco, their enthusiasm will have an ague-fit, and their golden dream turn to sleet and hail. They should hasten through and dash at once into their scene of labor; nor should they expect success without corresponding efforts; if fortune favors them to-day, she will disappoint them to-morrow; her favors and frowns fall with marvellous caprice; the digger must be above the one and independent of the other; he must rely upon his own resources; and upon his fidelity to one unchanged and unchangeable purpose. He comes here to get gold, not in pounds or ounces, but in grains; his most instructive lesson will be by the side of the ant-hill. There he sees a little industrious fellow, foregoing the pastimes of other insects, and bringing another grain to his heap; working on with right good heart through the day, and sometimes taking advantage of the moon, and plying his task through the luminous night. Let him watch that ant, and go and do likewise, if he would return from California with a fortune. I don't recommend him to come here and convert himself into a pismire for gold; but if he *will* come, the more he has of the habits of that little groundling the better.

CALIFORNIA ON CHARACTER.

Life in California impresses new features on old characters, as a fresh mintage on antiquated coins. The man whose prudence in the States never forsakes him, and whose practical maxim is, " a bird in the hand is worth two in the bush," will *here* throw all his birds into the bushes, seemingly for the mere excitement of catching them again. He finds himself in an atmosphere so strongly stirred and stirring, that he must whirl with it, and soon enjoys the strong eddy almost as much as the still pool. He may hang perhaps a moment on the verge of a cataract, but if it spreads below to a tranquil lake, down he goes, and emerges from the boiling gulf calm and confident as if lord of the glittering trident. Or he may have been, while in the States, remarked for his parsimony, pinching every cent as it dropped into the contribution-box as if there was a spasm between his avarice and alms. But in California that cent so awfully pinched soon takes the shape of a doubloon, and slides from his hand too easily to leave even the odor of its value behind. I have known five men, who never contributed a dollar in the States for the support of a clergyman, subscribe here five hundred dollars each per annum, merely to encourage, as they termed it, "a good sort of a thing in the community." I have seen a miser, who would have sold a hob-nail from his heel for old iron, in bartering off his saddle throw in the horse; and then exchange a lump of perfectly pure gold for one half quartz, merely because it struck his fancy! Such are some of the anomalies in character which a life in California produces. If you doubt it, make the experiment, and you will soon find your own heart, though gnarled as a knot, cracking open, and turning inside out like a kernel of parched corn.

HEADS AND TAILS.

My friend William Blackburn, alcalde of Santa Cruz, often hits upon a method of punishing a transgressor, which has some claims to originality as well as justice. A young man was brought before him, charged with having sheared, close to the stump, the sweeping tail of another's horse. The evidence of the nefarious act, and of the prisoner's guilt, was conclusive. The alcalde sent for a barber, ordered the offender to be seated, and directed the tonsor to shear and shave him clean of his dark flowing locks and curling moustache, in which his pride and vanity lay.

This was hardly done, when Mr. B, counsel for the prisoner entered, and moved an arrest of judgment. "Oh, yes," said the alcalde, "as the shears and razor have done their work, judgment may now rest." "And under what law," inquired the learned counsel, "has this penalty been inflicted?" "Under the Mosaic," replied the alcalde: "that good old rule—eye for eye, tooth for tooth, hair for hair." "But," said the biblical jurist, "*that* was the law of the Old Testament, which has been abrogated in the New." "But we are still living," returned the alcalde, "under the old dispensation, and must continue there till Congress shall sanction a new order of things." "Well, well," continued the counsel, "old dispensation or new, the penalty was too severe—a man's head against a horse's tail!" "That is not the question," rejoined the alcalde: "it is the hair on the one against the hair on the other; now as there are forty fiddles to one wig in California, the inference is just, that horsehair of the two is in most demand, and that the greatest sufferer in this case is still the owner of the steed." "But, then," murmured the ingenious counsel, "you should consider the young man's pride." "Yes, yes," responded the alcalde, "I considered all that, and considered too the stump of that horse's tail, and the just pride of his owner. Your client will recover his crop much sooner than the other, and will manage, I hope, to keep it free of the barber's department in this court;" and with this, client and counsel were dismissed.

SPANISH COURTESIES.

The courtesies characteristic of the Spanish linger in California, and seem, as you encounter them amid the less observant habits of the emigration, like golden-tinted leaves of Autumn, still trembling on their stems in the rushing verdure of Spring. They exhibit themselves in every phase of society and every walk of life. You encounter them in the church, in the fandango, at the bridal altar, and the hearse: they adorn youth, and take from age its chilling severity. They are trifles in themselves, but they refine social intercourse, and soften its alienations. They may seem to verge upon extremes, but even then they carry some sentiment with them, some sign of deference to humanity. I received a cluster of wildflowers from a lady, with a note in pure Castilian, and bearing in the subscription the initials of the words, which rudely translated mean, " I kiss your hand." One might have felt tempted to write her back—

> Thou need'st not, lady, stoop so low
> To print the gentle kiss:
> Can hands return what lips bestow,
> Or blush to show their bliss?

CHAPTER XXIX.

THE TRAGEDY AT SAN MIGUEL.—COURT AND CULPRITS.—AGE AND CIRCUMSTANCES OF THOSE WHO SHOULD COME TO CALIFORNIA.—CONDITION OF THE PROFESSIONS.—THE WRONGS OF CALIFORNIA.—CLAIMS ON THE CHRISTIAN COMMUNITY.—JOURNALISTS.

RETRIBUTION follows fast on the heels of crime in California. Two persons, a Hessian and Irishman, whom I had met in the Stanislaus, left the mines for the seaboard. On their way to Stockton, they fell in with two miners asleep under a tree, whom they murdered and robbed of their gold; with this booty they hastened across the valley of the San Joaquin, and skirting the mountains to avoid all frequented paths, held their course south to La Solidad. Here they fell in with three deserters from the Pacific squadron, who joined them, and the whole party proceeded south to San Miguel, where they quartered themselves for the night on the hospitality of Mr. Reade, an English ranchero of respectability and wealth. In the morning they took their departure, but had proceeded only a short distance, when it was agreed they should return and rob their host. During the ensuing night they rose on the household, consisting of Mr. Reade, his wife, and three children, a nswoman with four children, and two Indian domestics, and murdered the whole! Having rifled the money-chest of a large amount of gold dust, the bloodstained party renewed their flight south, and had reached a secluded cove in a bend of the sea, below Santa Barbara, where they were overtaken by a band of citizens, who had tracked them from the neighborhood of San Miguel. The fugitives were armed, and avowed their determination to shoot down any person who should attempt to apprehend them. The citizens, though few, and badly provided with weapons, were resolute and determined. A desperate conflict ensued, in which one of the felons was shot dead; another, having discharged the last barrel of his revolver, jumped into the sea and was drowned; the remaining three were at length disarmed and secured. Of the citizens several were wounded, and one—the father of a beloved family—lay a corpse! The next morning, as there was no alcalde in the vicinity, the three prisoners were brought before a temporary court organized for the purpose, wherein twelve good and lawful men took oath to render judgment according to conscience. Each person when brought to the bar told his own story, inextricably involving his associates in the guilt of deliberate murder, and who, in their turn, wove the same terrible web about him. Of their guilt, though convicted without the testimony of an impartial witness, no doubt remained to disturb the convictions of the court. They were sentenced to death, and before the sun went down were in their graves! The whole five were buried among the stern rocks which frown on the sea, and which seem as if there to stay the tide of crime, as well as the storms of ocean. What a tragedy of depravity and despair! Thirteen innocent persons—men, women, and children—swept in an unsuspecting moment from life; and the five perpetrators of the crime, crushed into a hurried grave, under the avenging arm of justice! There is a spirit in California that will rightly dispose of the murderer; it may at times be hasty, and too little observant of the forms of law, but it reaches its object; it leaves the guilty no escape through the defects of an indictment, the ingenuity of counsel, or the clemency of the executive. It plants itself on the ground that the first duty society owes itself, is to protect its members; and to secure this object, it throws around the sanctity of life, the defenses found in the terrors of death. The grave is the prison which God has sunk in the path of the murderer. Let not man attempt to bridge it.

WHO SHOULD STAY AND WHO COME.

The indiscretion with which so many thousands are rushing to California will be a source of regret to them, and of sorrow to their friends. Not one in twenty will bring back a fortune, and not more than one in ten secure the means of defraying the expenses of his return. I speak now of those whose plans and efforts are confined to the mines, and who rely on the proceeds of their manual labor: when they have defrayed the expenses incident to their position, liquidated all demands for food, clothing, and implements for the year, their yellow heap will dwindle to a point. This might serve as the nucleus of operations which are to extend through a series of years; but as the result of the enterprise, involving privation and hardship, is a failure, no man should come to California under the impression that he can in a few months pick a fortune out of its mines. He may here and there light on a more productive deposit, but the chances are a hundred to one that his gains will be slenderly and laboriously acquired. He is made giddy with the reports of sudden wealth; these are the rare *prizes*, while the silence of the grave hangs over the multitudinous *blanks*.

A young man endowed with a vigorous constitution, and who possesses sterling habits of sobriety and application, and who has no dependencies at home, can do well in California. But he should come with the resolute purpose of remaining here eight or ten years, and with a spirit that can throw its unrelaxed energies into any enterprise which the progress of the country may develop. He must identify himself for the time being with all the great interests which absorb attention, and quicken labor. If he has not the enterprise and force of purpose which this requires, he should remain at home. There is another class of persons whom domestic obligations and motives of prudence should dissuade from a California adventure. It is blind folly in a man, who has a family dependent on him for a support, to exhaust the little means, which previous industry and frugality have left, in defraying the expenses of a passage here, with the vague hope that in a year or two he can return with an ample competence. I respect his feelings and motives, but honorable intentions cannot save him from disappointment. When the expenses which the most rigid economy could not avoid have been paid, and the obligations connected with the support of his family at home have been discharged, the results of his enterprise will leave him poor. He may never tell you of broken hopes and a shattered constitution, but his hearth-stone is strewn with their pale, admonitory fragments. Let me persuade those whom God has blessed with a faithful wife and interesting family, not to abandon these objects of affection for the gold mines of California. Do not come out here under the delusive belief that you can in a few months, or a brief year, on the proceeds of the mattock and bowl, accumulate a fortune. This has rarely if ever been done, even where the deposits were first disturbed by the more fortunate adventurer. If it could not be done in the green tree, what are you to expect in the dry? If when the *placers* were fresh, many gathered but little more than sufficient to meet their current wants, what can you anticipate when they are measurably exhausted? They who inflame your imagination with tales of inexhaustible deposits which only wait your spade and wash-bowl, abuse your credulity, and dishonor their own claims to truth.

THE PROFESSIONS AND PURSUITS.

All the secular professions and more privileged or prescribed pursuits in California are crowded to overflowing. Physicians are without patients; lawyers without clients; surveyors without lands; hydrographers without harbors; actors without audiences; painters without pupils; financiers without funds; minters without metals; printers without presses; hunters without hounds, and fiddlers without fools. And all these must take to the plough, the pickaxe, and spade. Even California, with all her treasured hills and streams, fell under that primal malediction which threw its death-shade on the infant world. It is as true here as among the granite rocks of New England—in the sweat of thy face shalt thou eat bread. Let none think to escape this labor-destiny here; it environs the globe, and binds every nation and tribe in its inexorable folds.

The merchant, whose shrewdness avails him everywhere else, will often be wrecked here. The markets of a single month have all the phases of its fickle moon. The slender crescent waxes into the circle; and the full orb passes under a total eclipse. The man that figured on its front is gone, and with him the hopes of the millionaire. The bullfrog in his croaking pond, and the owl in his hooting tree, remain; but the speculator, like a ghost at the glimmer of day, hath fled. You can only dimly remember the phantom's shape and where he walked, and half doubt the dream in which he denizened and dissolved from sight. But still the gulf of vision swarms with realities—with beings where the play of life and death, joy and grief, wealth and want, are the portion of the living and the legacy of the dead. California is a continent swelling between the hopes of the future and the wrecks of the past; but like all other continents, will be visited with the alternation of day and night. The cloud will travel where the sunbeam hath been.

WRONGS OF CALIFORNIA.

The neglect and wrongs of California will yet find a tongue. From the day the United States flag was raised in this country, she has been the victim of the most unrelenting oppression. Her farmers were robbed of their stock to meet the exigences of war; and her emigrants forced into the field to maintain the conquest. Through the exactions of the customhouse the comforts and necessaries of life were oppressively taxed. No article of food or raiment could escape this forced contribution; it reached the plough of the farmer, the anvil of the smith; the blanket that protected your person, the salt that seasoned your food, the shingle that roofed your cabin, and the nail that bound your coffin. Even the light of heaven paid its contribution in its windowed tariff. And who were the persons on whom these extortions fell? Citizens whom the government had promised to relieve of taxation, and emigrants who had exhausted their last means in reaching their new abode! There was treachery and tyranny combined in the treatment which they received. A less provocation sunk the dutied tea in the harbor of Boston, and severed the indignant colonies from the British crown.

Nor does this gross injustice stop here : this oppressive tax was enforced at a time when there was but little specie in the country; the whole circulating medium was absorbed in its unrighteous demands. Nor was the case materially relieved by the discovery of gold ; this precious ore was extorted at ten dollars the ounce, and forfeited at that arbitrary valuation if not redeemed within a given time. There was no specie by which it could be redeemed, and it went to the clutches of the government at ten dollars, when its real value at our mints is eighteen dollars. If this be not robbery, will some one define what that word means? It was worse than robbery—it was swindling under the color of law. All this has been carried on against a community without a representation in our national legislature, and without any civil benefits in return. Not even a light-house rose to relieve its onerous injustice. Hundreds of thousands, not to say millions thus extorted, are now locked up in the sub-treasury chest at San Francisco. Every doubloon, dollar, and dime that reaches the country is forced under that inexorable key. In this absorption of the circulating medium, commercial loans can be effected only on ruinous rates of interest, and the civil government itself is bankrupt.

Every dollar of these ill-gotten gains should be placed forthwith at the disposal of the state of California. It belongs to her; it never was the property of the United States under any law of Congress. It has been exacted under executive circulars, under the naked dictates of arbitrary power. I blame not the revenue functionaries of the general government in California; they were bound by the orders and instructions which they received; the responsibility rests nearer home: it rests with those who have usurped and exercised powers not conferred by the Constitution, or the consent of the American people. Nor do these aggressions and wrongs stop here. Who has authorized a captain of U. S. dragoons to drive, at the point of his flashing glaive, peaceful citizens from their gardens and dwellings on the bay of San Francisco, under the pretext of a government reservation, and then to farm out those grounds under a ten years' lease? Who has conferred this impudent stretch of authority, and this private monopoly of the public domain? Let the citizens thus trampled upon maintain their right, even with their rifles, till they can be made the proper subjects of judicial investigation or legislative action.

CLAIMS ON THE CHRISTIAN.

With the Christian community California has higher claims than those which glitter in her mines. The moral elements which now drift over her streams and treasured rocks will ere long settle down into abiding forms. The impalpable will become the real, and the unsubstantial assume a local habitation and a name. Shall these permanent shapes, into which society is to be cast, take their plastic features from the impress of blind accident and skeptical apathy, or the moulding hand of religion? These primal forms must remain and wear for ages the traces of their deformity or beauty, their guilty insignificance or moral grandeur. Through them circulates your own life-blood; in them is bound up the hopes of an empire. Not only the destiny of California is suspended on the issue, but the fate of all the republics which cheer the shores of the Pacific. The same treason to religion which wrecks the institutions of this country, will sap the foundations of a thousand other glorified shrines. It is for you, Christian brethren, to prevent such a disaster; it is for you to pour into California an unremitted tide of holy light. The Bible must throw its sacred radiance around every hearth, over every stream, through every mountain glen. The voice of the heralds of heavenly love must be echoed from every cliff and chasm and forest sanctuary. On you devolves this mission of Christian fidelity. It is for your faith and philanthropy to say what California shall be when her swelling population shall burst the bounds of her domain. You can write her hopes in ashes, or stars that shall never set. Every school-book and Bible you throw among her hills will be a source of penetrating and pervading light. when the torch of the caverned miner has gone out

The images which you impress on her gold, age will efface; but the insignia of truth, stamped into her ardent heart, will survive the touch of time, and gleam bright in the night of the grave.

PROPHETIC SHADOWS AND JOURNALISTS.

Coming events cast their shadows before. When Com. Jones, several years since, captured Monterey, no political seer discovered in the event the precursor of an actual, permanent possession. No flag waved on the horoscope save the Mexican; no thunder broke on the ear of the augur, except what disturbed the wrong quarter of the heaven; and even the birds, which carried the fate of nations in their sounding beaks, flew in a wrong direction. But the first occupation, though it came and went as a shadow, was an omen, which has now become a reality—a great eventful *fact* in the history of the age. The commodore, who struck this first uncertain blow, is now here entrusted with the defence of the new acquisition. His spirit of intelligence and enterprise is making itself felt in every department, that justly falls within the prerogatives of a commander-in-chief.

There are a multitude of topics connected with the wild life and new condition of affairs in California, which must escape the pen of any one journalist. Some of them are touched with vivid force in the graphic pictures of "El Dorado," others are sketched with lively effect in the pages of "Los Gringos," while California as she was, before gold had cankered her barbaric bliss, is thrown wildly on our vision, by the author of "Two Years Before the Mast." Her geography, the habits of her citizens, and her resources, when little known beyond the furtive glances of the coaster, are faithfully delineated in the pioneer pages of Col. Fremont, Capt. Wilkes, and Mr. Robinson. Every traveller can find in California some new untouched feature for a sketch. They unroll themselves on the eye at every glance. With the reader they are rather sources of wonder and amusement, than solid advantage. Our globe was invested with no claims to utility till it had emerged from chaos; then verdure clothed its hills and vales; then flowing streams made vocal the forest aisles; then rolled the anthem of the morning star.

CHAPTER XXX.

THE GOLD-BEARING QUARTZ.—THEIR LOCALITY.—RICHNESS AND EXTENT.—SPECIMENS AND DOUBTFUL CONCLUSIONS.—THE SUITABLE MACHINERY TO BE USED IN THE MOUNTAINS.—THE COURT OF ADMIRALTY AT MONTEREY.—ITS ORGANIZATION AND JURISDICTION.—THE CASES DETERMINED.—SALE OF THE PRIZES.—CONVENTION AND CONSTITUTION OF CALIFORNIA.—DIFFICULTIES AND COMPROMISES.—SPIRIT OF THE INSTRUMENT.

THE surface gold in California will in a few years be measurably exhausted; the occasional discovery of new deposits cannot long postpone such a result; nor will it be delayed for any great number of years, by any more scientific and thorough method of securing the treasure. California will prove no exception in these respects to other sections of the globe where surface gold has been found. The great question is, will her mountains be exhausted with her streams and valleys? Will her rock gold give out with her alluvial deposits? The gold-bearing quartz is the sheet-anchor at which the whole argosy rides; if this parts, your golden craft goes to fragments.

When an old Sonoranian told me in the mines that the quartz *swetted* out the gold, all the young savans around laughed at the old man's stupidity; and I must say the *perspiration* part of the business rather staggered my credulity, which has some compass, where there are no laws to guide one. But the old digger was nearer the truth than many who have more felicitous terms in which to express their theories. Though the gold may not ooze from the quartz as water drips from a rock, yet it is *there*, and often beads from the surface like a tear that has lost its way among the dimples of a lady's cheek. In other instances it shows itself only in fine veins; and in others still, is wholly concealed from the naked eye, and even eludes the optical instrument; but when reduced to powder with the quartz, flies to the embrace of quicksilver, and takes a virgin shape, massive and rich. The specimens of quartz which have been subjected to experiment, have yielded from one to three dollars the pound. These specimens were gathered at different points, in the foot range of the Sierra Nevada, and are deemed only a fair average of the yield that may be derived from the quartz.

The gold rocks of Georgia and Virginia yield, on an average, less than half a cent to the pound, and yet the profits are sufficient to justify deep mining. What then must be the profits of working a rock which lies near the surface, and which yields over a dollar to the pound! The result staggers credulity; and we seek a refuge from the weakness of faith in the more reasonable persuasion, that the specimens tested are richer than the average of the veins and quarries which remain. And yet the poorest specimen, which the casual blow of the sledge has knocked from the sunlit peak, has seemingly more gold in its shadow, than the rock unhouseled from its mine in Virginia beneath forty fathoms of darkness. The only real defence for our incredulity lies in the presumption, that the gold-bearing quartz, like the surface deposits, has its confined localities. And yet Mr. Wright, our member of Congress from California, who has traversed the slopes of the Sierra, collected more specimens, and made more experiments than any other individual, is sanguine in the opinion that the gold-bearing quartz occupies a broad continuous vein through the entire extent of the foot range: and in this opinion the Hon. T. Butler King, in his lucid report, coincides. Still such a wide departure in nature from all her known laws, or capricious impulses, in the distribution of gold, leaps beyond my belief. In no other part of her wide domain has she deposited in the quartz rock a proportion of gold more than sufficient barely to compensate the hardy miner: and it is difficult to believe, that with all her affection for California, she has been so prodigal of her gifts. It surpasses the rainbow-inwoven coat bestowed by the partial love of the patriarch on his favorite child.

When a simple swain saw a necromancer break a cocoanut shell and let fly half a dozen canary birds, he remarked, there was no doubt the young birds were hatched in the cocoanut; but what puzzled him was, to know how the old bird could get in to lay the eggs. But a deeper puzzle with me is, that each and every cocoanut on this California tree, should have a nest of canaries in it. And yet, with all these dogged doubts and dismal dissuasives, were I going to invest in California speculations, my inklings would turn strongly to quartz and stampers.

But I would send out no machinery which should have a piece in it weighing over seventy or eighty pounds : no other can be taken through the gorges, and over the acclivities to the lofty steeps where the quartz exists. The machinery which can be readily taken to the mines in Virginia, would cost a fortune in its transportation to the proper localities in California. The heaviest capitalist would find himself swamped before he got to work. Every piece must be taken over elevations where a man can hardly draw himself up, and where his life is often suspended on the strength of the fibres which twine the bush to the fissures of the rock. It should be so light as to render its removal to any new and more productive locality practicable, without involving a ruinous expense. A machine wielding the force of one man, and stamping on the spot, will be more productive than a forty-horse power working at a distance. All the transportation must be done by hand, for no animal can subsist among the steeps where the quartz prevail. Watch the eagle as he soars to his high cliff with a writhing snake in his beak, and then seize your light machinery and pursue his track. But, chained to a heavy engine, you would make about as much progress as that mountain bird with his talons driven into the back of a mastodon or whale.

COURT OF ADMIRALTY.

There were seven prize cases introduced into the court of admiralty at Monterey, on which condemnation and sale of the property libelled ensued. They were all clearly cases of legal capture, and came under the well-established rule of international law, that the hostile character attaches to the commerce of the neutral domiciled in the enemy's country. This rule is enforced by every consideration of sound policy and national justice. If the flag of the neutral can protect the property over which it waves, the entire commerce of the belligerent might assume this neutral garb, and be as safe in time of war as peace. To prevent such an abuse, the comity of nations has conceded the general principle, that all commerce flowing to or emanating from a mercantile house, established in the enemy's country, shall be deemed hostile, and be held liable to seizure.

A much more difficult question arose connected with the competency of the court. Its organization arose out of the exigences of war; the alternative lay between a recognition of its jurisdiction, and the extreme right of the belligerent to burn and sink his captures. Congress, in a declaration of war, virtually invests the executive with authority to prosecute it, and secure the ends for which it has been waged. He is necessarily entrusted with extraordinary discretion and corresponding powers; when, in the due prosecution of these measures, he finds himself borne beyond their statutory provisions, and surrounded by exigences, lying at the time perhaps beyond the purview of legislative enactment, he must either forego the objects which animated the acts of the national legislature, or temporarily assume the responsibility which the crisis demands. He must authorize the maintenance of civil government in territories acquired by our arms, and judicial proceedings in cases of capture on the high seas, which cannot be brought within the jurisdiction of our established courts.

Nor is there any thing in such judicial proceedings which trenches upon the laws of nations; these laws never assume the right to define the powers vested in the executive of a realm. They claim no authority to bring into court the constitutional prerogatives of a prince or of the president of a republic; these are questions which appertain to the forms of government where the acts originate, where the power is exercised, and which must be disposed of as the wisdom of the nation may deem proper. It is enough that national law allows the captor at his peril to burn or sink his prize. Any executive measure to prevent such a precipitate result, and to subject the legality of the capture to the forms of a judicial investigation, is in accordance with every dictate of moral justice, and that strong sense of right which binds every civilized nation in a period of war as well as peace. Nor can the captor, from a want of jurisdiction in the court that determines his case, lose his prize. All the claimant can do is to require him to appear before a court of competent authority, where the case must be examined and decided *de novo* on its merits. This great principle in maritime jurisprudence has been recognized and confirmed in the decision of the High Court of Admiralty in England. Half a century has rolled over that decision, but its authoritative force remains firm and unshaken as the base of the sea-girt isle.

It devolved on the court at Monterey not only to determine the prize cases submitted, but to assume an onerous responsibility in the disposal of the property libelled and condemned. The cargo of one of these prizes consisted of a large amount of cotton, paper, and iron, destined to a Mexican market, and for which there was no adequate demand in California. The highest cash bid that could be procured at a sale duly notified, was $34,000. To this bid the property must be knocked down, or surrendered to a credit bid of $60,000, involving conditions for the benefit of the purchaser wholly inadmissible in law. In this perplexity I bid the ship and cargo in; placed a faithful, competent agent and crew on board, and sent the whole to Mazatlan, which had become a port of entry. The result was, that after discharging all claims existing against the property, I paid over to the Secretary of the Navy, as the net proceeds of the sales, the sum of $68,000, and stand credited with that amount on the books of the department. But this is rather a matter of personal service than a topic of public interest; it is, however, connected with official duty, and exhibits one of the many forms in which private responsibility may be tasked in saving from sacrifice property confided to its care. A failure in such cases often brings ruin ; and even success may be obliged to seek its meagre remuneration through the slow forms of legislative relief.

CONSTITUTION OF CALIFORNIA.

The desires of the people of California for a civil government, suited to their new condition, at length found utterance at the ballot-box. The best informed and most sedate of her citizens were elected in their several districts, and commissioned to proceed to Monterey, for the purpose of drafting in concert the provisions of a constitution. Never were interests, habits, and associations more diverse than those represented in this body. Unanimity could be reached only through the largest concessions. It was the conquerors and the conquered, the conservatives and the progressives ; they who owned the lands, and they who worked the mines, assembling to frame organic laws which should equally secure and bind the interests of all. No cloud ever cast its shadow on equal incongruities grouped in cliffs and chasms, pinnacles and precipices, without having it broken into a thousand fragments. But the honest and patriotic purpose which animated the convention, raised that body above all national prejudice and local interests, and poured its spirit in blending power over its measures.

They had been commissioned to plan and perfect a constitution for California, and they were true to their trust. Day after day they labored at that eventful instrument; no passion, no prejudice disturbed their counsels: where opinions clashed, they were softened; where interests jarred, they were harmonized; where local feeling sought assertion, it was surrendered. Till at last, through this spirit of deference, compromise, and public concern, the instrument was finished. And now let us glance at its prominent features.

This constitution is thoroughly democratic; no prescriptive privileges, or invidious distinctions are recognized; the interests of the great mass fill every provision. Political and social equality are its bases, while the rights of private judgment and individual conscience flow untrammelled through its spirit. It is the embodiment of the American mind, throwing its convictions, impulses, and aspirations into a tangible, permanent shape. It is the creed of the thousands who wield the plough, the plane, the hammer, the trowel, and spade. It is the palladium of freedom, rolled in from the seaboard, and down from the mountains, and which has caught its echoes from every river, steep, and valley. It is the fraternal oath of a great people, uttered in the presence of God and the hearing of nations. Millions will turn their eyes to the fulfilment of its promises, when time and disaster have engulfed the monuments of their own splendor and strength.

The 13th of October, 1849, will never fade from the annals of California. It was not the sun, circling up into a broad and brilliant heaven, that gave this morn its brightness: it was not the thunder of the Pacific on the sea-beaten strand, that gave the day its impressive force: it was not the long heavy roll of the artillery that most signalized the hour; nor the harmony of the winds rolling their anthems from the steep forests that stirred most strongly the human heart. It was the silent signatures of the members of the convention to the constitution, which had been confided to their wisdom and patriotic fidelity. It was this last crowning act in an eventful moral enterprise, having its source in the exigences of a great community. I wonder not the old pioneer of the Sacramento pronounced it the greatest day of his life; I wonder not that the veteran "Hero of Contreras" forgot the laurels gathered on that field of fame, in the higher and nobler honors showered upon him in this day's achievements. It was his steady purpose and fearless responsibility that threw into organized forms and practical results, the plans and purposes of the people of California. He will find his reward in the happiness and prosperity of a great state, over which the flag of the Union shall never cease to wave. The tide of Anglo-Saxon blood stops not here; it is to circulate on other shores, continents, and isles; its progress is blent with the steady triumphs of commerce, art, civilization, and religion. It will yet flow the globe round, and beat in every

DECLARATION OF RIGHTS IN THE CONSTITUTION OF CAJIFORNIA, AND THE SIGNATURES OF THE MEMBERS OF THE CONVENTION.

The 1,346 of October, 1849, will be memorable in the annals of California. On that day the members of the Convention elected to draft a Constitution, set their signatures to that noble instrument. The President of this body was Robert Semple, a native of Kentucky; the Secretary, Wm. G. Marcy, of New York. The following is the declaration of rights which form the Constitution, followed by the fac-similes of the members of the Convention.

Sec. 1. All men are by nature free and independent and have certain inalienable rights, among which are those of enjoying and defending life and liberty; acquiring, possessing and protecting property; and pursuing and obtaining safety and happiness.

Sec. 2. All political power is inherent in the people. Government is instituted for the protection, security and benefit of the people; and they have the right to alter or reform the same, whenever the public good may require it.

Sec. 3. The right of trial by jury shall be secured to all, and remain inviolate forever; but a jury trial may be waived, by the parties, in all cases, in the manner to be prescribed by law.

Sec. 4. The free exercise and enjoyment of religious profession and worship, without discrimination or preference, shall for ever be allowed in this State; and no person shall be rendered incompetent to be a witness on account of his opinions on matters of religious belief; but the liberty of conscience hereby secured shall not be so construed as to excuse acts of licentiousness, or justify practices inconsistent with the peace or safety of this State.

Sec. 5. The privilege of the writ of Habeas Corpus shall not be suspended, unless when, in cases of rebellion or invasion, the public safety may require its suspension.

Sec. 6. Excessive bail shall not be required, nor excessive fines imposed, nor cruel or unusual punishments inflicted, nor shall witnesses be unreasonably detained.

Sec. 7. All persons shall be bailable, by sufficient sureties, unless for capital offences, when the proof is evident, or the presumption great.

Sec. 8. No person shall be held to answer for a capital or otherwise infamous crime, (except in cases of impeachment, and in cases of militia when in actual service, and the land and naval forces in time of war, or which this State may keep, with the consent of Congress in time of peace,) unless on presentment or indictment of a grand jury; and in any trial in any court whatever, the party accused shall be allowed to appear and defend in person and with counsel, as in civil actions. No person shall be subject to be twice put in jeopardy for the same offence; nor shall be compelled, in any criminal case, to be a witness against himself, nor be deprived of life, liberty, or property, without due process of law.

Sec. 9. Every citizen may freely speak, write, and publish his sentiments on all subjects, being responsible for the abuse of that right; and no law shall be passed to restrain or abridge the liberty of speech or of the press. In all criminal prosecutions on indictments for libels, the truth may be given in evidence to the jury; and if it shall appear to the jury that the matter charged as libellous is true, and was published with good motives and for justifiable ends, the party shall be acquitted; and the jury shall have the right to determine the law and the fact.

Sec. 10. The people shall have the right freely to assemble together, to consult for the common good, to instruct their representatives, and to petition the Legislature for redress of grievances.

Sec. 11. All laws of a general nature shall have a uniform operation.

Sec. 12. The military shall be subordinate to the civil power. No standing army shall be kept up by this State in time of peace; and in time of war no appropriation for a standing army shall be for a longer time than two years.

Sec. 13. No soldier shall, in time of peace, be quartered in any house, without the consent of the owner; nor in time of war, except in the manner to be prescribed by law.

Sec. 14. Representation shall be apportioned according to population.

Sec. 15. No person shall be imprisoned for debt, in any civil action on mesne or final process, unless in cases of fraud; and no person shall be imprisoned for a militia fine in time of peace.

Sec. 16. No bill of attainder, ex post facto law, or law impairing the obligation of contracts, shall ever be passed.

Sec. 17. Foreigners who are, or who may hereafter become bona fide residents of this State, shall enjoy the same rights in respect to the possession, enjoyment and inheritance of property, as native-born citizens.

Sec. 18. Neither slavery, nor involuntary servitude, unless for the punishment of crimes, shall ever be tolerated in this State.

Sec. 19. The right of the people to be secure in their persons, houses, papers, and effects, against unreasonable seizures and searches, shall not be violated; and no warrant shall issue but on probable cause, supported by oath or affirmation, particularly describing the place to be searched, and the persons and things to be seized.

Sec. 20. Treason against the State shall consist only in levying war against it, adhering to its enemies, or giving them aid and comfort. No person shall be convicted of treason, unless on the evidence of two witnesses to the same overt act, or confession in open court.

Sec. 21. Every citizen of the United States, and every white male citizen of Mexico, who shall have elected to become a citizen of the United States, under the treaty of peace exchanged and ratified at Queretaro, on the 30th day of May, 1848, of the age of twenty-one years, who shall have been a resident of the State six months next preceding the election, and the county or district in which he claims his vote thirty days, shall be entitled to vote at all elections which are now or hereafter may be authorized by law: Provided, that nothing herein contained shall be construed to prevent the Legislature, by a two-thirds concurrent vote, from admitting to the right of suffrage, Indians, or the descendants of Indians, in such special cases as such a proportion of the legislative body may deem just and proper.

Sec. 22. Electors shall, in all cases, except treason, felony, or breach of the peace, be privileged from arrest on the days of the election, during their attendance at such election, going to and returning therefrom.

Sec. 23. No elector shall be obliged to perform militia duty on the day of election, except in time of war or public danger.

Sec. 24. For the purpose of voting, no person shall be deemed to have gained or lost a residence by reason of his presence or absence while employed in the service of the United States; nor while engaged in the navigation of the waters of this State, or of the United States, or of the high seas; nor while a student of any seminary of learning; nor while kept at any alms-house, or other asylum, at public expense; nor while confined in any public prison.

Sec. 25. No idiot or insane person, or person convicted of any infamous crime, shall be entitled to the privileges of an elector.

Sec. 26. All elections by the people shall be by ballot.

Sec. 27. This enumeration of rights shall not be construed to impair or deny others retained by the people.

Joseph Aram
Ch. T. Botts
Chas. Hoppe
Pablo Noriega
Elam Brown
Elisha O. Crosby
Julian Hanks
John Hollister
José M. Covarrubias
H.W. Halleck
L.W. Hastings
Chas. T. Snyder
José Ant. Carrillo
Pablo de la Guerra
Wm. M. Gwin
Francis J. Lippitt
Thomas O. Larkin
Wnfield S. Sherwood
J. M. Jones
Hon. Dimmick
B. S. Lippincott
H. A. Tefft
K.H. Dimmick
A. P. Crittenden
M. M. McCarver
P. M.
G. W. Wright
Thos. L. Vermeule
R. Semple
Henry Hill
Edw. Gilbert
Miguel de Pedrorena
W. E. Shannon
K. F. Teft
Stephen C. Foster
Abel Stearns
Myron Norton
Benjn. S. Lippincott
Robert M. Price
O. M. Wozencraft
C. M. Wozencraft
Antonio M. Pico

nation's pulse; morn will not blush, or twilight fade where its swelling wave is not; its guiding-star is above the disasters in which the purposes of man are sphered.

I regret my limits will not permit me to follow the Pacific squadron, under the command of Com. Shubrick, to the Mexican coast. The capture and occupation of Mazatlan has hardly stirred a whisper in the trump of fame, which has poured out such strains on the other side of the continent. And yet this achievement of the commodore had in it a spirit of wisdom, resolution, and firmness that might emblazon a much loftier page than mine. When the history of the Mexican war shall be written, and the services of those who shared in its hardships and perils be duly recognized, Com. Shubrick, with the gallant officers and brave men attached to his command, will receive a lasting meed of merited renown. It is now silently written in that international compact which terminated the apprehensions of one republic and sealed the triumphs of another. It was the waving of the stars and stripes on the strand of the Pacific which left a forlorn hope without a refuge, and coerced the terms of an honorable peace; and long may that peace remain unbroken by the monster of discord and war.

CHAPTER XXXI.

GLANCES AT TOWNS SPRUNG AND SPRINGING.—SAN FRANCISCO.—BENICIA.—SACRAMENTO CITY.—SUTTER.—VERNON.—BOSTON.—STOCKTON.—NEW YORK.—ALVEZO.—STANISLAUS.—SONORA.—CRESCENT CITY.—TRINIDAD.

THE growth of towns in California is so rapid, that before you can sketch the last, a new one has sprung into existence. You go to work on this, and dash down a few features, when another glimmers on your vision, till at last you become like the English surgeon at the battle of Waterloo; who began by bandaging individuals, but found the wounded brought in so fast he declared he must splinter by the regiment.

SAN FRANCISCO.—This town has thrice been laid in ashes; but the young phœnix has risen on ampler wings than those which steadied the consumed form of its parent. It must be the great commercial emporium of California in spite of competition, wind, and flame. Its direct connection with the sea, its magnificent bay and internal communications, have settled the question of its ultimate grandeur. It may be afflicted with grog-shops and gamblers, and the mania of speculation, but these are temporary evils which time, a higher moral tone, and the more steady pursuits of man will remedy. Three years ago only a dozen shanties sprinkled its sand-hills; now, even with its heart burnt out, it looks like the skeleton of a huge city. That heart will be reconstructed, and send the life-blood leaping through the system.

BENICIA.—This town on the straits of Carquenas has the advantages of a bold shore, a quiet anchorage, and depth of water for ships of any size. Even without being a port of entry, it must become in time a large commercial depot. The small craft which float the waters of the Suisun, Sacramento, and San Joaquin, and which are ill suited to the rough bay below, will here deposit their cargoes. It has been selected as the most feasible site for a navy-yard, and the army stores are already housed on its quay. It was first selected as the site of a city by Robert Semple, president of the Constitution Convention, and rose rapidly into importance under his fostering care, and the energetic measures of Thomas O. Larkin.

SACRAMENTO CITY.—The site of this town on the eastern bank of the Sacramento, at its junction with the Rio Americano, presents many picturesque features. It is a town in the woods, with the native trees still waving over its roofs. The sails of the shipping are inwoven with the masses of shade, which serve as awnings. Roads diverge from it to the mines on the North, Middle, and South Forks, Bear, Juba, and Feather rivers. The town has been swept by one inundation from the overflow of the Americano. It came upon the inhabitants like a thief in the night; they had only time to jump from their beds; the roaring flood was at their heels: some reached the shipping, and some sprung into the tops of the trees. But a levee is now going up which will shut out the flood; while brick and slate will ward off the flame. This place is destined to figure among the largest towns of California.

SUTTER.—This town, which bears the name of the old pioneer on whose lands it stands, is beautifully located on the Sacramento, at the head waters of navigation. From it issue the roads leading to all the northern mines; the site is not subject to overflow, and the country around possesses great fertility. It has a large commercial business: its central position must secure its prosperity. Its proprietors are Capt. Sutter and John McDugal, lieutenant-governor of the state—gentlemen who pursue the most liberal policy, and reap their reward in the growth of their town.

VERNON.—This is the only town on Feather river, and stands at the confluence of that stream with the Sacramento. It is above the reach of any inundation, and commands a country of wildly varied aspect. Its location, rather than buildings or business, invest it with interest. Its importance is prospective; but the future is fast becoming the present. Its projectors are Franklin Bates, E. O. Crosby, and Samuel Norris.

BOSTON.—This town is located on the American Fork at its junction with the Sacramento. The plot of the town is beautiful—its situation agreeable. Direct roads issue from it to the placers of the Yuba, Feather river, the North, Middle, and South forks of the Americano. Like Sacramento City, it is located within the grant of Capt. Sutter, whose title to the enterprising proprietors will undoubtedly be found valid. Several buildings have been erected, which give an air of stability to the flapping tents which shadow its avenues.

STOCKTON.—This flourishing town is located at the head of an arm of the Suisun bay, and is accessible to small steamers. It stands in the centre of a vast fertile plain, and on a position sufficiently elevated to exempt it from inundation. It is the commercial depot for the southern mines; the miners on the Mokelumne, Stanislaus, Tuolumne, Mariposa, Mercedes, and King's river, are supplied with provisions and clothing from its heavy storehouses. It will yet loom largely in the map of California.

NEW YORK.—This town is located on the triangle formed by the junction of the San Joaquin river and Suisun bay, with its base resting on a broad plain, covered with clusters of live-oak. The banks of the river and bay are bold, and above the reach of tide and freshet. The bay is represented on the surveys which have been made as having sufficient depth for merchantmen of the largest class. The communication with the sea lies through the broad strait of the Carquinas. The town will naturally command the commerce of the San Joaquin and its numerous tributaries. The projectors of the town are Col. Stevenson and Dr. Parker.

ALVEZO.—This town is situated at the head of the great bay of San Francisco, on the Gaudalupe, which flows through it. It is the natural depot of the commerce which will roll in a broad exhaustless tide, through the fertile valleys of Santa Clara and San José. It lies directly in the route to the gold and quicksilver mines, with a climate not surpassed by that of any locality in the northern sections of California. The fertility of the surrounding country must ere long make itself felt in the growth and prosperity of this town. San Francisco is dependant on the products of its horticulture. Fortunes might be made by any persons who would go there and devote themselves exclusively to gardening. But it is not in man to raise cabbages in a soil that contains gold. The proprietors of the town are J. D. Hoppe, Peter H. Burnett, and Charles B. Marvin.

STANISLAUS.—This town, situated at the junction of the Stanislaus and San Joaquin, is fast rising into consideration. It is the highest point to which the lightest steamer can ascend, and is in the immediate vicinity of the richest mines in California. From its storehouses supplies are destined to flow through the whole southern mines. The placers on the Stanislaus, Tuolumne, Mercedes, and King's river must contribute to its growing wealth. It is in the direct route from Monterey to the mines—a route which has been surveyed in reference to a great public road, and through which a portion of the commerce of the Pacific will one day roll. This town was projected by Samuel Brannan, the sagacious leader of the Mormon battalion in California.

SONORA and CRESCENT CITY.—These towns, perched up among the gold mines which overlook the San Joaquin, derive their importance from no river or bay; their resources are in the rocks and sands of the mountain freshet. They are the miner's home—his winter quarters—his metropolis, to which he goes for society, recreation, repose, frolic, and fun. Through the livelong night the rafters ring with resounding mirth, while the storm unheeded raves without. Of all the sites for a hamlet which I have met with in the mining region, I should prefer the one at the head of a ravine near the sources of the Stanislaus. It is a natural amphitheatre, throwing on the eye its sweeping wall of wild cliffs and waving shade. From the green bosom of its arena swells a slight elevation, covered with beautiful evergreen trees. A little rivulet leaps from a rock, and sings in its sparkling flow the year round; while the leaves, as if in love with the spot, whisper in the soft night-wind.

Many a night have I stood there in silent revery, watching the bright stars, the trembling shadows of the trees, and listening to the silver lay of the streamlet. The Coliseum, with its melancholy night-bird and solemn grandeur, can never rival this temple of nature.

THE ONE MOON TOWN.

The recent discovery of Trinidad bay, which lies about two hundred miles north of San Francisco, will have a material effect on the local interests of the country. It will open a new channel of commerce into the northern mines, and render accessible the finest forests in California. This bay, as represented, has sufficient depth and capacity to shelter a large marine. A town has already been laid out on the curve of its bold shore; streets, squares, and edifices have ceased to figure on the map, and become a reality. Where but one moon since the shark and seal plunged and played at will, freighted ships are riding at anchor; while the indignant bear has only had time to gather up her cubs and seek a new jungle.

Before this sheet can get to press, there will be a daily on Trinidad bay, with the price-current of New York and London figuring in its columns, and an opera of Rossini singing its prelude between the reeling anthems of the church-going bell. Why, man! you talk of the slumbers of Rip Van Winkle, and the visions of the seven sleepers of Ephesus! Know you not the whole world is asleep, save what wakes and works on Trinidad bay? It takes an age in other lands to rear a city; but here, one phase of the fickle moon, and up she comes, like Venus from the wave, or the peak of Pico at the call of the morning star. Clear the coast with your old dormitory hulks of slumbering ages, and let this new Trinidad launch her keeled thunder! Her pennant unrolls itself in flame on the wind, and her trident is tipt with the keen lightning. The great whale of the Pacific turns here his startled gaze—plunges, and blows next half way to Japan.

>   Hurra for Trinidad! Let nations sleep,
>   And empires moulder in their misty shroud;
>   She shakes her trident on her golden steep,
>   O'er waving woods, in solemn reverence bowed;
>   Her bright aurora throws its flashing ray
>   Where primal worlds in sunless darkness stray!
>
>   A shout from those touched orbs comes rolling back,
>   As rose the anthem of this earth, when first
>   Around the night that sphered her rayless track,
>   The breaking morn in golden splendors burst—
>   The king of chaos sees the new-born light,
>   And, howling, plunges down the gulf of night.

OLD AND WELL-TRIED FRIENDS.

I must not forget in my reveries over the map marvels of the new towns, the fireside friends of good old Monterey. Among *them* my three years circled their varied rounds, now stored with memories that can never die. I must introduce them to the reader before we part, and pay them the tribute of a farewell word. They have no splendor of outward circumstance to stir your wonder, but hearts as true as ever throbbed in the human breast. Here is David Spence, from the hills of Scotland, a man of unblemished integrity and sterling sense, married to a daughter of the late Don José Estrada, a resident of twenty-five years in Monterey, my predecessor in the office of alcalde, and recently prefect of the department. Here is W. P. Hartnell, from England, married into the Noriega family, the best linguist in the country, and the government translator, with the claims of a twenty-seven years' residence, and a circle of children, in which yours, my gentle reader, would only appear as a few more added to a sweeping flock.

Here is Don Manuel Dias, a native of Mexico, married to a sister of Mrs. Spence, a gentleman whose urbanity and intelligence honors his origin. Here is James McKinley, a gentleman of liberality and wealth from the Grampian Hills, married to a daughter of a Spanish Don from the Bay of Biscay. Here is Don Manuel Jimeno, once secretary of state, married into the Noriega family, to a lady of sparkling wit and gentle benevolence. Here is Milton Little, a man of mind and means, who broke into California many years ago from the west, and whom I joined in wedlock to a fair daughter of the empire state. Here is Don José Abrigo, blest with wealth, enterprise, and a fine family of boys. Here is J. P.

Lease, from Missouri, long resident in California, with ample fortune and generous heart, and whose amiable wife is the sister of Gen. Vallejo. Here is James Watson, born on the Thames; came to Monterey twenty-five years since, married a lady of the country, is now a heavy capitalist, with a charity open as day. Here is Charles Walter, of German origin, a resident of many years, married into the Estrada family, and possessed of wealth. Here is Gov. Pulacio, from Lower California—a gentleman of the old school—with a wife and daughter imbued with the same spirit of refinement. Here is J. F. Dye, from our own shores, long identified with the interests of the country, and married to one of its daughters. Here are Messrs. Toomes & Thoms, bosom friends, partners in business, and men of enterprise and substance. Here is James Stokes, from England, for twenty-five years a citizen of Monterey, a merchant, farmer, and doctor, married to a lady of the country, in whom the afflicted always find a friend.

Here is Señor Soveranez, whose saloon is lit by eyes bright as nuptial tapers, and where the Castilian flows soft as if warbled by a bird. Here is Padre Ramirez, an intelligent, liberal, and warm-hearted canon of the Catholic church; and also the Rev. S. H. Willey, of the Protestant persuasion, who is organizing a society, and who has the zeal and energy to carry the enterprise through. Monterey lost one of its most cherished ladies, when Mrs. Larkin took her departure. Here for eighteen years she had lent a charm to its society. She was the first lady from the United States that settled in California. Long will the good old town lament the departure of T. H. Green. His enterprise and integrity as a merchant, and his benevolence as a citizen, were everywhere felt. The widow and the orphan ever found in him a generous friend. Nor must I forget the young and gentle Saladonia, who has often hovered like a ministering angel in the family of the poor emigrant. Nor must I pass unheeded the grave of my revered friend Don Juan Malerine, beloved in life, and who died

> "Like one who wraps the drapery of his couch
> About him, and lies down to pleasant dreams."

CHAPTER XXXII.

BRIEF NOTICES OF PERSONS WHOSE PORTRAITS EMBELLISH THIS VOLUME, AND WHO ARE PROMINENTLY CONNECTED WITH CALIFORNIA AFFAIRS.

JOHN CHARLES FREMONT

Is a native of South Carolina—was born in 1813—received his education at Charleston College, and first evinced the vigor of his mathematical genius in the efficient aid rendered the accomplished Nicollet in his survey of the basin of the upper Mississippi. The importance of this service was acknowledged by the government in his appointment as a lieutenant in the corps of Topographical Engineers. In 1841 the war department confided to him the interests and objects of an expedition to the Rocky Mountains, in which he discovered and mapped the South Pass. The scientific results of this adventure awakened in the public mind an intense enthusiasm for a more extended exploration. In the following year he left the frontier settlements at the head of a small party, crossed the Rocky Mountains, discovered and surveyed the great valley of the Salt Lake, and extended his researches into Oregon and California. These explorations, which occupied the greater portion of two years, were not confined to topographical questions; they embraced all the departments of natural history, with extended meteorological observations. They fill a volume, in which the trophies of science are blended with the incidents of the wildest adventure.

In 1844, the explorer left the United States again for the western slopes of the Sierra Nevada, and had descended into California, when the declaration of war suspended his scientific pursuits, and summoned him to the field. He had been honored successively with the rank of captain, major, and colonel. A battalion of riflemen enrolled themselves under his command. Their campaign, in the winter of 1846, impressed its intrepid spirit and heroic action on the fate of the war. Constrained by the orders of a superior, Col. Fremont was again in the United States; where, having declined a return of his commission, which he had adorned with eminent service, he threw himself, with unrepressed spirit, on his own energies, and started again for California. This was his seventh adventure across the continent; and owing to the lateness of the season, was attended with hardships and privations, in which many of his brave mountaineers perished. But his force of purpose triumphed over the elements, and carried him through. The new territory, in the vast accessions of a rushing emigration, had suddenly risen to the dignity of a commonwealth. A United States senator was to be chosen: it was the highest·office within the gift of the people, and they conferred it, without distinction of party, on Col. Fremont. The decree of a military tribunal, bound to those rigid rules of discipline which never bend to the force of circumstance, may dispose of the parchment honors of a commission, but the public services and private worth of the individual must remain; the substantial benefits conferred on mankind must remain; the path opened to the golden gates of the west must remain; the flag of the country still fly along its fortified line, and the great tide of emigration roll through its avenue for ages. If Humboldt be the Nestor of scientific travellers, and Audubon the interpreter of nature, Col. Fremont is the Pathfinder of empire.

WILLIAM M. GWIN

Was born in Sumner county, Tennessee, in 1805. His father, the Rev. James Gwin, was a distinguished divine in the Methodist Episcopal church, and one of its founders in the West. He was for fifty years the intimate and confidential friend of Gen. Jackson, and chaplain to his army during the late war with England. Dr. Gwin was graduated at Transylvania University, in Kentucky, and practised his profession, with eminent success for several years, in his native state and Mississippi. He relinquished his profession in 1833, and was appointed, by Gen. Jackson, Marshal of Mississippi,—an office which he filled until after the election of Gen. Harrison to the presidency, when he became a candidate for congress, and was elected by a large majority.

He was remarked, during the session, as a ready,

forcible debater, and was renominated by his district with great unanimity, but declined running, owing to pecuniary embarrassments incurred while he held the office of marshal, and brought about by the paper money system, which involved Mississippi in bankruptcy, and especially the public officers, who, like Dr. Gwin, had been induced, under the decisions of the courts, to take this irresponsible paper in payment of executions. In 1846, Dr. Gwin removed to New Orleans, and was soon after appointed commissioner to superintend the erection of the custom-house in that city, destined to be one of the largest public edifices in the country. From this position he retired on the election of Gen. Taylor to the presidency, and emigrated to California, where he engaged actively in organizing a state government. He was elected a member of the convention from San Francisco, and bore a prominent, influential part in its debates and proceedings, which resulted in the present noble constitution. The importance of these services were duly recognized by the people of California, and they testified their regard and confidence in conferring on him the dignity of a United States senator. He will have it in his power to do much for the new state, and we feel assured she will find in him a resolute champion of her rights.

THOMAS OLIVER LARKIN,

Born in Charleston, Mass., 1803, and emigrated to California eighteen years since. The same spirit of adventure which took him to this country, characterized his subsequent career. He came here without capital, and with no sources of reliance save in his own enterprise and activity. There was then no gold out of which a fortune could be suddenly piled, and no established channels of business through which a man could become regularly and safely rich. But this unsettled state of affairs was suited to the enterprising spirit of Mr. Larkin. He often projected enterprises and achieved them, seemingly through the boldness of the design; but there was ever behind this a restless energy that pushed them to a successful result. Many and most of the public improvements were planned and executed by him; the only wharf and custom-house on the coast were erected through his activity.

Through all the revolutions which convulsed the country, he held the post of United States consul, and vigilantly protected our commercial interests and the rights of our citizens. He was deeply concerned in all the measures which at length severed California from Mexico, and loaned his funds and credit to a large amount in raising means to meet the sudden exigences of the war. The Californians, to cut off these supplies, managed at last, very adroitly, to capture him, and held him as a hostage in any important contingency. But the work had already been measurably accomplished, and a restoration of prisoners soon followed. Mr. Larkin early engaged in the organization of a civil government—was a delegate from Monterey to the convention for drafting a constitution, and impressed his practical genius on many of its provisions. He has never been a candidate for any office, and resigned that of Navy Agent, with which he had been honored, as soon as the condition of public affairs would allow. His commercial enterprise and sagacity work best where they have the most scope; they have secured to him an ample fortune. His house has always been the home of the stranger; his hospitalities are ever on a scale with his ample means.

GEORGE W. WRIGHT.

Among the successful adventurers into California, Mr. Wright holds a prominent place. He was born in Massachusetts in 1816, where he received a business education, and commenced life with no capital beyond his own enterprise and sagacity. Through these he won his way to a partnership in a large commercial house, extensively engaged in the whaling service and its correlative branches of trade. Without disturbing these relations, he determined to push his adventures into California, where he arrived soon after the discovery of the *placers*, and engaged in the commerce of the country. Success and a rapid accumulation of capital attended his efforts. A large banking-house at San Francisco was proposed, and he became the leading partner. This house has withstood all the shocks which have carried ruin to many others, and maintained its credit unshaken. At the adoption of the constitution, two members of Congress were to be chosen, and Mr. Wright was elected to this honorable position. This token of confidence and regard was the more to be appreciated, as it resulted from no constrained party organization, but the decided preference of the citizens, expressed at the ballot-box.

Mr. Wright was the first to collect specimens of the gold-bearing quartz. He traversed the foot hills of the Sierra Nevada for this purpose, and underwent many hardships and perils. He was often for days on the very shortest allowance, and obliged to share even this with his famished mule. The quartz frequently seam the loftiest ridges, and can be reached only through the most exhausting fatigue. None but those of iron muscles can scale the soaring steep, or dislodge, with steady hand and head, the treasured vein in the giddy verge. Against these obstacles Mr. Wright persevered, and gathered a great variety of specimens, curious in themselves and often rich, but valued mainly as indications of the wealth of the quartz, and as leading-clues to their localities. They will serve to stimulate the exertions and guide the footsteps of the subsequent miner. They are not stowed away as secrets for the exclusive benefit of the discoverer: the information they impart is free to all. The only danger lies in conclusions too glowing for the reality, and those hasty adventures in which anticipation overleaps the laborious process. The specimens are genuine, and have been pronounced at the mint the richest that have been tested. The *extent* to which the gold-bearing quartz prevails can be thoroughly known only in the results of mining operations. It has been found in different localities between Feather river and the Mariposa; and if it approaches in value the most ordinary specimens gathered by Mr. Wright and myself, will munificently reward the labors of the miner, and will upset all geological deductions connected with gold-bearing quartz in other countries.

JACOB R. SNYDER.

Born in Philadelphia, 1813, emigrated to the west in 1834, and has been for the last five years a citizen of California. At the commencement of hostilities in that country, Com. Stockton, then in command of the land and naval forces, confided to him the organization of an artillery corps, and subsequently conferred on him the appointment of quarter-master to the battalion of mounted riflemen under Col. Fremont, which office he continued to fill during the war. At the restoration of peace, Mr. Snyder was appointed by Governor Mason surveyor for the middle department of California, where his activity and science were called into play in the settlement of many questions of disputed boundary in land titles. In the organization of a civil government, he was elected delegate from Sacramento district to the convention, and was one of the committee for drafting the constitution. His remarks in the convention are characterized for their pertinency, brevity, and sound sense. He is a good specimen of that versatility which belongs to the "universal nation." Fond of adventure, and with resources in himself to meet all its exigencies,—partial to new positions, new duties, and responsibilities, and yet perfectly at home in each—ever with some beckoning object ahead, which, when attained, is to be relinquished for one of still greater magnitude,—and all this with a sound judgment, inflexible integrity, and unostentatious generosity. He was one of the original projectors of Sacramento City, and is still largely concerned in its prosperity. His liberal policy, sustained by that of his enterprising, intelligent partner, Major Reading, is exhibited in the ample reservations which have been made for churches, school-houses, and public squares.

CAPT. JOHN A. SUTTER.

The leading features of interest in the adventurous life of Capt. Sutter are connected with California affairs. He was born in Switzerland near the close of the last century, and early relinquished its glaciers and lakes for the sunny fields of France. His love of adventure turned his attention to the camp, where his gallant conduct soon secured him an honorable commission. But the wars of the continent being over, he emigrated to the United States, and having resided several years in Missouri, turned his roving eye to the shores of the Pacific.

Through a series of adventures, which seem more

like fictions than realities, he at length reached the valley of the Sacramento, where he procured from the government the grant of a large tract of land. The country around was in the possession of wild Indians, some of whom he conciliated, and through their labors constructed a fort to protect himself from the rest. His influence over these children of the forest was such that in a few years he had over a thousand of their number at work on his farm. He was upright in all his dealings with them, and paid each as punctually as if he had been a king. His place, to which he gave the name of New Helvetia, was for years the emigrant's goal,—the land of promise, which glimmered in warm light through his cold mountain dream. *There* he was sure of a cordial welcome, and a hospitality that knew no bounds; no matter from what clime he came, or what were his credentials; it was enough for his generous host to know that he was an adventurer, poor in all things save a manly purpose. But often the bounty of Capt. Sutter has gone forth to meet the emigrant; it was his sympathy and active benevolence that mainly rescued the emigrants of forty-six from starvation in the California mountains. When his relief reached them, their last animals had been killed and consumed for food, their last pound of provisions, and their last means of subsistence had given out; they were embayed in depths of snow which baffled their exhausted strength, and hunger hung in horror over the dead.

It was on the lands of Capt. Sutter that gold was first discovered; the cut of a mill-race revealed the entrancing treasure; but all were welcome to the results; no spirit of monopoly obstructed the digger, or enriched the proprietor; fortunes went freely to the pockets of those who drove the spade and turned the bowl. When a civil organization was proposed, the generous captain was deputed by the electors in his district to represent them in the convention. He there favored all measures calculated to secure the interests of the emigrants, and develop the resources of the country. When he put his own signature to the constitution, he dropped the pen in very gladness; the light of other days encircled his spirit, he was a child again; all felt the tears which filled the eyes of the old pioneer, and wept in joyous sympathy with their source. The work was done, and California was henceforth to revolve among the glorious orbs of the republic!

DON MARIANO GUADALUPE VALLEJO.

This distinguished Californian was born in Monterey, 1817; his father held a military command under the crown of Spain, and subsequently under the Mexican republic; he lived to the advanced age of 95, and saw his children allied in marriage to the most influential families in the province. Don Mariano entered the service of the government as a cadet; rose rapidly to a post of commanding influence, but always evinced a repugnance to Mexican rule. In 1837, assisted by his nephew, Alverado, he succeeded in driving the satellites of that ill-starred republic out of the country, and in the organization of the new government, was honored with the post of commandante-general.

When the United States flag was raised, Gen. Vallejo saw in it the opportunity of securing the permanent tranquillity and prosperity of California: a thousand of his noble horses went under the saddles of our mounted riflemen. The war over, he was first and foremost in measures for a civil organization, and represented the district of Sonoma in the convention for drafting a constitution. His liberal views and sound policy pervade every provision of the instrument. He was subsequently elected a senator to the state legislature, and might have been a successful candidate for any office within the gift of the people. He is a large landed proprietor; his cattle are on a hundred hills, and his horses in as many vales; while a thousand Indians, whom he has won from savage life, cultivate his fields, and garner his grains. His munificent liberality and profound interest in the cause of education, and the claims of humanity, may be gathered from the following statement contained in the report of the committee of the California legislature on public buildings and grounds, in relation to the permanent location of the seat of government. This committee say:

Gen. Vallejo, a native of California, and now a member of the legislature, offers a site lying upon the Straits of Carquinas and Napa river, where he proposes to lay out the capital to be called Eureka, or such other name as the legislature may suggest. He proposes—

1st. That said permanent seat of government may be laid out in such form as five Commissioners may direct, three of whom shall be appointed by the legislature, and two by himself.

2d. That he proposes to grant to the state, for the following purposes, free of cost:

	Acres.
Capitol and grounds	20
Governor's house and grounds	10
Offices of Treasurer, Comptroller, Secretary of State, &c.	5
State Library and Translator's office	1
Orphan's Asylum	20
Male Charity Hospital	10
Female Charity Hospital	10
Asylum for the Blind	4
Deaf and Dumb Asylum	4
Lunatic Asylum	20
Four Common Schools	8
State University	20
State Botanical Garden	4
State Penitentiary	20

Also, your memorialist proposes to donate and pay over to the state, within two years after the acceptance of his propositions, the following sums of money, for the faithful payment of which he proposes to give to the state ample security.

For building State Capitol	$125,000
Furnishing the same	10,000
Building Governor's House	10,000
Furnishing the same	5,000
State Library and Translator's Office	5,000
State Library	5,000
For the building of the Offices of Secretary of State, Comptroller, Attorney-General, Surveyor-General, and Treasurer, should the Commissioners deem it proper to separate them from the State House	20,000
Building Orphan's Asylum	20,000
Building Female Charity Hospital	20,000
Building Male Charity Hospital	20,000
Building Asylum for Blind	20,000
Building Deaf and Dumb Asylum	20,000
Building State University	20,000
For University Library	10,000
Scientific Apparatus therefor	5,000
Chemical Laboratory therefor	3,000
Mineral Cabinet therefor	3,000
Four Common School Edifices	10,000
Purchasing Books for same	5,000

For the Building of a Lunatic Asylum............................ $20,000
For a State Penitentiary 20,000
For a State Botanical Collection................................... 3,000

In accordance with another proposition of Gen. Vallejo, the committee further report in favor of submitting this offer to the acceptance of the people, at the next general election. The report adds:

"Your committee cannot dwell with too much warmth upon the magnificent propositions contained in the memorial of Gen. Vallejo. They breathe throughout the spirit of an enlarged mind, and a sincere public benefactor, for which he deserves the thanks of this body, and the gratitude of California. Such a proposition looks more like the legacy of a prince to his people, than the free donation of a private planter to a great state."

CHAPTER XXXIII.

THE MISSION ESTABLISHMENTS IN CALIFORNIA.—THEIR ORIGIN, OBJECTS, LOCALITIES, LANDS, REVENUES, OVERTHROW.

THE missions of California are the most prominent features in her history. They were established to propagate the Roman faith, and extend the domain of the Spanish crown. They contemplated the conversion of the untutored natives, and a permanent possession of the soil. They were an extension of the same system which, half a century previous, had achieved such signal triumphs on the peninsula and through the northern provinces of Mexico. The founders were men of unwearied zeal and heroic action; their enterprise, fortitude, and unshaken purpose might rouse all the slumbering strings of the religious minstrel.

In Alta California these missions formed a religious cordon the entire extent of the coast. They were reared at intervals of twelve or fourteen leagues in all the great fertile valleys opening on the sea. The first was founded in 1769; others followed fast, and before the close of the century the whole twenty were in effective operation. Each establishment contained within itself the elements of its strength, the sources of its aggrandizement. It embraced a massive church, garnished with costly plate; dwellings, storehouses, and workshops, suited to the wants of a growing colony; broad lands, encircling meadows, forests, streams, orchards, and cultured fields, with cattle, sheep, and horses, grazing on a "thousand hills," and game in every glade; and above all, a faith that could scoop up whole tribes of savages, dazzling them with the symbols of religion, and impressing them with the conviction that submission to the padres was obedience to God.

These vast establishments absorbed the lands, capital, and business of the country; shut out emigration, suppressed enterprise, and moulded every interest into an implement of ecclesiastical sway. In 1833, the supreme government of Mexico issued a decree which converted them into civil institutions, subject to the control of the state. The consequence was, the padres lost their power, and with that departed the enterprise and wealth of their establishments. The civil administrators plundered them of their stock, the governors granted to favorites sections of their lands, till, with few exceptions, only the huge buildings remain. Their localities will serve as important guides to emigrants in quest of lands adapted to pasturage and agriculture, and their statistics will show, to some extent, the productive forces of the soil. These have been gathered, with some pains, from the archives of each mission, and are grouped for the first time in these pages. They are like the missions themselves—skeletons. California, though seemingly young, is piled with the wrecks of the past; around the stately ruin flits the shade of the padre; his warm welcome to streaming guests still lingers in the hall; and the loud mirth of the festive crowds still echoes in the darkened arches. But all these good olden times are passed—their glorious realities are gone—like the sound and sun-lit splendors of the wave dashed and broken on the remorseless rock.

MISSION OF DOLLORES.

This mission is situated on the south side of the bay of San Francisco, two miles from the town. Its lands were forty leagues in circumference. Its stock, in 1825, consisted of 76,000 head of cattle, 950 tame horses, 2000 breeding-mares, 84 stud of choice breed, 820 mules, 79,000 sheep, 2000 hogs, 456 yoke of working-oxen, 18,000 bushels of wheat and barley, $35,000 in merchandize, and $25,000 in specie. It was secularized in 1834 by order of Gen. Figueroa, and soon became a wreck. The walls of the huge church only remain. Little did the good padre who reared them dream of the great town that was to rise in their shadows!

MISSION OF SANTA CLARA.

This mission is situated in the bosom of the great valley that bears its name, six miles from the embarcadara which strands the upper bend of the great bay of San Francisco. Around it lie the richest lands in California—once its own domain. In 1823 it branded, as the increase of one year, 22,400 calves. It owned 74,280 head of full-grown cattle, 407 yoke of working-oxen, 82,540 sheep, 1890 trained horses, 4235 mares, 725 mules, 1000 hogs, and $120,000 in goods. The church is a gigantic pile, and was once adorned with ornaments of massive silver. The property was secularized in 1834 by order of Gen. Figueroa, when the frolicking citizens of the Pueblo de San José began to revel on its ruins. It has still a fine vineyard, where the grape reels and the pear mellows

MISSION OF SAN JOSÉ.

This mission was founded in 1797, fifteen miles from the town which bears its name, and at the terminus of a valley unrivalled in fertility. It supplied the Russian Company with grain, who sent yearly several large ships for stores for their northern settlements. It is stated, in the archives of this mission, that the mayordomo gathered 8,600 bushels of wheat from 80 bushels sown; and the following year, from the grain which fell at the time of the first harvest, 5200 bushels! The priest told me that Julius Cæsar deposited in the temple of Ceres 362 kernels of wheat, as the largest yield of any one kernel in the Roman empire; and that he had gathered and counted, from one kernel sown at this mission, 365—beating Rome in three kernels! This mission had, in 1825, 3000 Indians, 62,000 head of cattle, 840 tame horses, 1500 mares, 420 mules, 310 yoke of oxen, and 62,000 sheep.

It has still a vineyard, in which large quantities of luscious grapes and pears are raised. It was secularized in 1834; and the old church bell, as if indignant at the change, has plunged from its chiming tower.

MISSION OF SAN JUAN BOUTISTA.

This mission looms over a rich valley, ten leagues from Monterey—founded 1794. Its lands swept the broad interval and adjacent hills. In 1820 it owned 43,870 head of cattle, 1360 tame horses, 4870 mares, colts, and fillies. It had seven sheep-farms, containing 69,530 sheep; while the Indians attached to the mission drove 321 yoke of working-oxen. Its storehouse contained $75,000 in goods and $20,000 in specie. This mission was secularized in 1834; its cattle slaughtered for their hides and tallow, its sheep left to the wolves, its horses taken by the dandies, its Indians left to hunt acorns, while the wind sighs over the grave of its last padre.

MISSION OF SAN CARLOS.

This mission, founded 1770, stands in the Carmel valley, three miles from Monterey. Through its ample lands flows a beautiful stream of water, which every governor of the country, for the last thirty years, has purposed conducting to the metropolis. Its gardens supply the vegetable market of Monterey. Its pears are extremely rich in flavor. In its soil were raised, in 1826, the first potatoes cultivated in California. So little did the presiding padre think of this strange vegetable, he allowed the Indians to raise and sell them to the whalers that visited Monterey, without disturbing their profits. He was satisfied if the Indians would give him one salmon in ten out of the hundreds they speared in the stream which swept past his door. This mission, in 1825, branded 2300 calves; had 87,600 head of cattle, 1800 horses and mares, 365 yoke of oxen, nine sheep-farms, with an average of about 6,000 sheep on each, a large assortment of merchandise, and $40,000 in specie, which was buried on the report of a piratical cruiser on the coast. It was secularized in 1835. The church remains; but the only being I found in it was a large white owl, who seemed to mourn its fall.

MISSION OF SANTA CRUZ.

This mission stands near the coast on the northern side of the bay of Monterey, in a tract of land remarkable for its agricultural capacities, which it developed in the richest harvests. In 1830 this mission owned all the lands now cultivated or claimed by the farmers of Santa Cruz. It had 42,800 head of cattle, 3200 horses and mares, 72,500 sheep, 200 mules, large herds of swine, a spacious church, garnished with $25,000 worth of silver plate. It was secularized in 1834 by order of Gen. Figueroa, and shared the fate of its Carmel sister. Only one padre lingers on the premises, and he seems the last of a perished race.

MISSION OF SOLEDAD.

This mission is situated fifteen leagues southwest of Monterey, in a fertile plain, known by the name of the "llano del rey." The priest was an indefatigable agriculturist. To obviate the summer drought, he constructed, through the labor of his Indians, an aqueduct extending fifteen miles, by which he could water twenty thousand acres of land. In 1826 this mission owned about 36,000 head of cattle, and a greater number of horses and mares than any other mission in the country. So great was the reproduction of these animals, they were given away to preserve the pasturage for cattle and sheep. It had about 70,000 sheep, and 300 yoke of tame oxen. In 1819 the mayordomo of this mission gathered 3400 bushels of wheat from 38 bushels sown. It has still standing about a thousand fruit-trees, which still bear their mellow harvests; but its secularization has been followed by decay and ruin.

MISSION OF SAN ANTONIO.

This mission is situated twelve leagues south of Soledad, on the border of an inland stream, upon which it has conferred its name. The buildings were inclosed in a square, twelve hundred feet on each side, and walled with adobes. Its lands were forty-eight leagues in circumference, including seven farms, with a convenient house and chapel attached to each. The stream was conducted in paved trenches twenty miles for purposes of irrigation: large crops rewarded the husbandry of the padres. In 1822 this mission owned 52,800 head of cattle, 1800 tame horses, 3000 mares, 500 yoke of working-oxen, 600 mules, 48,000 sheep, and 1000 swine. The climate here is cold in winter, and intensely hot in summer. This mission, on its secularization, fell into the hands of an administrator, who neglected its farms, drove off its cattle, and left its poor Indians to starve.

MISSION OF SAN MIGUEL.

This inland mission is situated sixteen leagues south of San Antonio, on a barren elevation; but the lands attached to it sweep a circuit of sixty leagues, and embrace some of the finest tracts for agriculture. Of the sethe Estella tract is one; its fertility is enough to make a New England plough jump out of its rocks; and a hundred emigrants will yet squat in its green bosom, and set the wild Indians and their warwhoop at defiance. In 1822 this mission owned 91,000 head of cattle, 1100 tame horses, 3000 mares, 2000 mules, 170 yoke of working oxen, and 47,000 sheep. The mules were used in packing the products of the mission to Monterey, and bringing back drygoods, groceries, and the implements of husbandry. But now the Indian neophytes are gone, the padres have departed, and the old church only remains to interpret the past.

MISSION OF SAN LUIS OBISPO.

This mission stands fourteen leagues southeast of San Miguel, and within three of the coast. It has always been considered one of the richest missions in California. The presiding priest, Luis Martinez, was a man of comprehensive purpose and indomitable force. His mission grant covered an immense tract of the richest lands on the seaboard. Every mountain stream was made to subserve the purposes of irrigation. He planted the cotton-tree, the lime, and a grove of olives, which still shower their abundant harvests on the tables of the Californians. He built a launch that run to Santa Barbara, trained his Indians to kill the otter, and often received thirty and forty skins a week from his children of the bow. His storehouse at Santa Margarita, with its high adobe walls, was one hundred and ninety feet long, and well stowed with grain. His table was loaded with the choicest game and richest wines; his apartments for guests might have served the hospitable intentions of a prince. He had 87,000 head of grown cattle, 2000 tame horses, 3500 mares, 3700 mules, eight sheep-farms, averaging 9000 sheep to each farm, and the broad Tulare valley, in which his Indians could capture any number of wild horses. The mayordomo of this mission in 1827, scattered on the ground, without having first ploughed it, 120 bushels of wheat, and then scratched it in with things called harrows, and harvested from the same over 7000 bushels. This was a lazy experiment, but shows what the land may yield when activity shall take the place of indolence. Father Martinez returned to Spain, taking with him $100,000 as the fruits of his mission enterprise. On the secularization of the mission in 1834, the property fell a prey to state exigency, and private rapacity. A gloomy wreck of grandeur only remains.

MISSION OF LA PURISIMA.

This mission is located eighteen leagues south of San Luis, at the base of a mountain spur, in the coast range; its lands covered about thirteen hundred square miles, and were at one time so filled with wild cattle, the presiding priest granted permits to any person who desired to kill them for their hides and tallow, the meat being thrown away. Thousands in this shape fell under the lasso and knife, and still the mission numbered in 1830 over 40,000 head of cattle sufficiently domesticated to be coralled, 300 yoke of working-oxen, 2600 tame horses, 4000 mares, 30,000 sheep, and 5000 swine, which were raised for their lard—no one eating the meat. The horses on this mission were celebrated for their beauty and speed; they performed feats under the saddle worthy of the most brilliant page in the register of the turf. But now the steed and his rider are gone, and the willow sighs over the mouldering ruin.

MISSION OF SANTA INEZ.

This mission is seven leagues to the southward of

La Purisima, and thirteen north of Santa Barbara. Its lands were more circumscribed than those of other missions; still it had vast herds of cattle and sheep, and its horses vied in beauty and strength with those of its sister missions. Its property, in 1823, was valued at $800,000. A portion of its lands remain unalienated, and must be held for the benefit of its Indian neophytes, or accrue to the public domain. The last government decree left the whole in the hands of an administrator, who thought more of his own revenues than the claims of the poor Indians whom law had betrayed.

MISSION OF SANTA BARBARA.

This mission is twelve leagues south of Santa Inez. Between the two a steep mountain range shoulders its way to the sea. No wheeled vehicle has ever been driven over it, except that which transported the field-piece attached to Col. Fremont's battalion. The mission being near the beautiful town of Santa Barbara, its profuse hospitality contributed largely to the social pleasures of the citizens. Its vintage never failed, and its friendly fires ever burnt bright; many a gay merrianda has kindled the eye of beauty in its soft shade. The main building is elaborately finished for California. The lands of the mission embraced many leagues. In 1828 it had 40,000 head of cattle, 1000 horses, 2000 mares, 80 yoke of oxen, 600 mules, and 20,000 sheep. It is now under a civil administrator, and a portion of its lands still remain vested in their original object. Around this mission emigrants will ere long settle in great numbers, and devote themselves to agriculture and the cultivation of grapes, olives, figs, for which the climate is peculiarly adapted.

MISSION OF SAN BUENAVENTURA.

This mission is situated about nine leagues south of Santa Barbara, near the seaboard. Its lands covered an area of fifteen hundred square miles, of which two hundred are arable land. In 1825 it owned 37,000 head of cattle, 600 riding horses, 1300 mares, 200 yoke of working-oxen, 500 mules, 30,000 sheep, 200 goats, 2000 swine, a thrifty orchard, two rich vineyards, $35,000 in foreign goods, $27,000 in specie, with church ornaments and clothing valued at $61,000. It was secularized in 1835, and has since been under a civil administrator, but all its wealth soon became a wreck. A small portion of its lands remain, and will tempt the horticultural emigrant to its fertile bosom.

MISSION OF SAN FERNANDO.

This mission, founded 1797, is situated about sixteen leagues south of San Buenaventura, in the midst of a beautiful plain, and has always been celebrated for the superior quality of the brandy distilled from its grapes. In 1826 it owned 56,000 head of cattle, 1500 horses and mares, 200 mules, 400 yoke of working-oxen, 64,000 sheep, and 2000 swine. It had in its stores about $50,000 in merchandise, $90,000 in specie; its vineyards yielded annually about 2000 gallons of brandy and as many of wine. Its secularization was followed by the dispersion of its Indians and ruin of its property. The hills, at the foot of which this mission stands, have, within the last ten years, produced considerable quantities of gold. One house exported about $30,000 of it. This was the first gold discovered in California, and the discovery was made three or four years previous to that on the American Fork. The marvel is the search for it did not extend further.

MISSION OF SAN GABRIEL.

This mission, located a little below los Angeles, was founded in 1771, and for several years led the others in enterprise and wealth. Its lands cover one of the most charming intervals in California; the soil and climate are both well adapted to fruit. In its gardens bloomed oranges, citrons, limes, apples, pears, peaches, pomegranates, figs, and grapes in great abundance. From the latter were made annually from four to six hundred barrels of wine, and two hundred of brandy, the sale of which produced an income of more than $12,000. In 1829 it had 70,000 head of cattle, 1200 horses, 3000 mares, 400 mules, 120 yoke of working-oxen, and 54,000 sheep. The charming rancho of Santa Anita belongs to this mission; it is situated on a gentle acclivity, where fruit trees and flowers scatter their perfume; while a clear lake lies calmly in front, to which the leaping rivulets rush in glee. Here the emigrant will find more charms in the landscape than he has left behind, and a more balmy air than he ever yet inhaled.

MISSION OF SAN JUAN CAPISTRANO.

This mission, situated eighteen leagues south of San Gabriel, was founded in 1776, and was for many years one of the most opulent in the country. Its lands extended fifteen leagues along the seaboard, and back to the mountains, where they swept over many ravines of fertile soil and sequestering shade. Through these roamed vast herds of cattle, sheep, and horses; while the sickle, pruning-knife, and shuttle gleamed in the dexterous hand of the domestic Indian. The earthquake of 1812 threw down the heavy stone church, as if in omen of the disasters which have since befallen the mission. The cattle have gone to the shambles, the Indians are in exile, the mass is over, and the shuttle at rest.

MISSION OF SAN LUIS REY.

This mission, located near the sea, and twelve leagues south of San Juan, was founded in 1798 by padre Peyri, who had devoted himself for years to the improvement of the Indians. The buildings occupy a large square, in the centre of which a fountain still plays; along the front runs a corridor, supported by thirty-two arches, ornamented with latticed railings; while the interior is divided into apartments suited to the domestic economy of a large establishment. Here the wool of the sheep which grazed on the hills around, was woven into blankets, and coarse apparel for the Indians, while the furrowed field waved for miles under the golden grain. The reeling grape, the blushing peach, the yellow orange, the mellow pear, and luscious melon filled the garden, and loaded the wings of the zephyr with perfume. In 1826 it had three thousand Indians, 70,000 head of cattle, 2000 horses, 140 yoke of tame oxen, 300 mules, 68,000 sheep, and a tract of land, around half of which you could not gallop between sun and sun. Its massive stone church still remains, and the remnants of its greatness are now in the hands of an administrator who little heeds the object which animated its founder.

MISSION OF SAN DIEGO.

This mission, situated fourteen leagues south of San Luis Rey, and near the town that bears its name, was founded in 1769 by padre Junipero Lerra, and was the first established in Alta California. Its possessions covered the whole tract of land which circles for leagues around the beautiful bay upon which its green hills look. Here the first cattle were coralled, the first sheep sheared, the first field furrowed, the first vineyard planted, and the first church bell rung. The Indian heard in this strange sound the invoking voice of his God, and knelt reverently to the earth. The success of this mission paved the way for the establishment of others, till the whole coast was sprinkled with their churches, and every green glade filled with their wild converts and lowing herds. But the padres and their neophytes are gone, and all the memorials that remain are a cumbrous ruin. Gigantic skeletons of things that were!

THE RAILROAD TO CALIFORNIA.

The facilities of social and commercial intercourse between our Atlantic and Pacific borders, yet to be created, present a problem of great practical importance. The present route, *via* Chagres and Panama, may be regarded as a necessity to be superseded as soon as practicable, by a railroad directly across the continent, within our own jurisdiction. Besides the formidable political objections to being dependent on foreign powers for a connection between our remotest and most important commercial points, the distance, *via* Chagres and Panama, or by any railroad or canal across the Isthmus yet to be made, in connection with the effects of a hot climate on animal and vegetable products, as subjects of trade between our Atlantic and Pacific coasts, present most insuperable obstacles to a permanent reliance on that route. It is now ascertained, that instead of thirty days between New York and San Francisco, or forty days to the mouth of the Columbia river by steam, or three to six months by sailing craft, either of these points may be reached in seven to eight days by railroad direct, avoiding altogether the deleterious effects of climate on articles of trade, as well as on health and life. These two considerations, so potent and overruling in commercial intercourse, will undoubtedly prove paramount to all antagonistic interests, and the railroad, directly across, may be regarded as already decided by the demands of trade between these remote parts of our present extended domain.

But what shall be the plan, Mr. Whitney's or a government enterprise? If the government undertake it, the chances are a thousand to one, that, like the Cumberland road, it will be broken down by party strifes. Neither of the two great parties of the country would, in any probability, risk the responsibility of taking it on its shoulders as a government work. Shall it, then, be done by a corporate company, with an adequate loan of public credit, as has been proposed? Besides other insuperable objections to a plan of this kind, of a party political character, it must be seen, that all transport on a road built on this plan, must pay a toll to satisfy the interest of the capital invested; whereas, on the Whitney plan, no toll will be exacted, except to keep the road and its machinery in repair. This difference, in its operation on trade and commerce, will be immense, sufficient, as any one may see, to decide the question at once and forever between the two plans. The company proposed will have to *borrow* its capital, the interest of which must be provided for by tolls. This tax on trade and intercourse will necessarily prevent that grand movement of commercial exchanges between the Atlantic and Pacific states, between the United States and Asia, and between Europe and Asia, which is the great object of the enterprise. But the Whitney plan does not borrow, but *creates*, by its own progress, out of the increased value of the lands through which it passes, the capital required to build the road; and thus dispensing with all tolls to pay for the use of capital, it will invite and secure the passage on this line of the great bulk of commerce around the entire globe, and between the great masses of the industrial and producing portions of the human family, which, as will be seen, lie on one great belt of the earth, demanding precisely the direct and cheap channel of intercommunication here proposed, instead of the circuitous, long, and expensive routes of commerce heretofore used.

Moreover, on the company plan, the increased value of the lands on the route, will all go to the corporation; whereas, on the Whitney plan, it will go to the people of the United States, whose property it is, and to the benefit of that trade and commerce which it sets in motion.

The Whitney plan, once executed, will merge in one the interests of our population on the Pacific slope of this continent and those of our population on the Atlantic slope, and by that means they will remain one forever. But the failure of this enterprise, by the neglect of Congress to authorize it, would make the interests of these two vast regions forever independent of and opposed to each other. Such a dereliction of duty, so apparent, would ere long, as a natural if not necessary consequence, create an independent nation on the Pacific.

THE END.

THE CHICANO HERITAGE

An Arno Press Collection

Adams, Emma H. **To and Fro in Southern California.** 1887

Anderson, Henry P. **The Bracero Program in California.** 1961

Aviña, Rose Hollenbaugh. **Spanish and Mexican Land Grants in California.** 1976

Barker, Ruth Laughlin. **Caballeros.** 1932

Bell, Horace. **On the Old West Coast.** 1930

Biberman, Herbert. **Salt of the Earth.** 1965

Casteñeda, Carlos E., trans. **The Mexican Side of the Texas Revolution (1836).** 1928

Casteñeda, Carlos E. **Our Catholic Heritage in Texas, 1519-1936.** Seven volumes. 1936-1958

Colton, Walter. **Three Years in California.** 1850

Cooke, Philip St. George. **The Conquest of New Mexico and California.** 1878

Cue Canovas, Agustin. **Los Estados Unidos Y El Mexico Olvidado.** 1970

Curtin, L. S. M. **Healing Herbs of the Upper Rio Grande.** 1947

Fergusson, Harvey. **The Blood of the Conquerors.** 1921

Fernandez, Jose. **Cuarenta Años de Legislador:** Biografia del Senador Casimiro Barela. 1911

Francis, Jessie Davies. **An Economic and Social History of Mexican California** (1822-1846). Volume I: Chiefly Economic. Two vols. in one. 1976

Getty, Harry T. **Interethnic Relationships in the Community of Tucson.** 1976

Guzman, Ralph C. **The Political Socialization of the Mexican American People.** 1976

Harding, George L. **Don Agustin V. Zamorano.** 1934

Hayes, Benjamin. **Pioneer Notes from the Diaries of Judge Benjamin Hayes, 1849-1875.** 1929

Herrick, Robert. **Waste.** 1924

Jamieson, Stuart. **Labor Unionism in American Agriculture.** 1945

Landolt, Robert Garland. **The Mexican-American Workers of San Antonio, Texas.** 1976

Lane, Jr., John Hart. **Voluntary Associations Among Mexican Americans in San Antonio, Texas.** 1976

Livermore, Abiel Abbot. **The War with Mexico Reviewed.** 1850

Loyola, Mary. **The American Occupation of New Mexico, 1821-1852.** 1939

Macklin, Barbara June. **Structural Stability and Culture Change in a Mexican-American Community.** 1976

McWilliams, Carey. **Ill Fares the Land:** Migrants and Migratory Labor in the United States. 1942

Murray, Winifred. **A Socio-Cultural Study of 118 Mexican Families Living in a Low-Rent Public Housing Project in San Antonio, Texas.** 1954

Niggli, Josephina. **Mexican Folk Plays.** 1938

Parigi, Sam Frank. **A Case Study of Latin American Unionization in Austin, Texas.** 1976

Poldervaart, Arie W. **Black-Robed Justice.** 1948

Rayburn, John C. and Virginia Kemp Rayburn, eds. **Century of Conflict, 1821-1913.** Incidents in the Lives of William Neale and William A. Neale, Early Settlers in South Texas. 1966

Read, Benjamin. **Illustrated History of New Mexico.** 1912

Rodriguez, Jr., Eugene. **Henry B. Gonzalez.** 1976

Sanchez, Nellie Van de Grift. **Spanish and Indian Place Names of California.** 1930

Sanchez, Nellie Van de Grift. **Spanish Arcadia.** 1929

Shulman, Irving. **The Square Trap.** 1953

Tireman, L. S. **Teaching Spanish-Speaking Children.** 1948

Tireman, L. S. and Mary Watson. **A Community School in a Spanish-Speaking Village.** 1948

Twitchell, Ralph Emerson. **The History of the Military Occupation of the Territory of New Mexico.** 1909

Twitchell, Ralph Emerson. **The Spanish Archives of New Mexico.** Two vols. 1914

U. S. House of Representatives. **California and New Mexico:** Message from the President of the United States, January 21, 1850. 1850

Valdes y Tapia, Daniel. **Hispanos and American Politics.** 1976

West, Stanley A. **The Mexican Aztec Society.** 1976

Woods, Frances Jerome. **Mexican Ethnic Leadership in San Antonio, Texas.** 1949

Aspects of the Mexican American Experience. 1976
Mexicans in California After the U. S. Conquest. 1976
Hispanic Folklore Studies of Arthur L. Campa. 1976
Hispano Culture of New Mexico. 1976
Mexican California. 1976
The Mexican Experience in Arizona. 1976
The Mexican Experience in Texas. 1976
Mexican Migration to the United States. 1976
The United States Conquest of California. 1976
Northern Mexico On the Eve of the United States Invasion:
Rare Imprints Concerning California, Arizona, New Mexico, and Texas, 1821-1846. Edited by David J. Weber. 1976